Gordon

Anctins

Silly

Governance Series

Governance is the process of effective coordination whereby an organization or a system guides itself when resources, power, and information are widely distributed. Studying governance means probing the pattern of rights and obligations that underpins organizations and social systems; understanding how they coordinate their parallel activities and maintain their coherence; exploring the sources of dysfunction; and suggesting ways to redesign organizations whose governance is in need of repair.

The Series welcomes a range of contributions – from conceptual and theoretical reflections, ethnographic and case studies, and proceedings of conferences and symposia, to works of a very practical nature – that deal with problems or issues on the governance front. The Series publishes works both in French and in English.

The Governance Series is part of the publications division of the Centre on Governance and of the Graduate School of Public and International Affairs at the University of Ottawa. This volume is the 17th volume published within this Series. The Centre on Governance and the Graduate School of Public and International Affairs also publish a quarterly electronic journal www.optimumonline.ca

Editorial Committee

Caroline Andrew
Linda Cardinal
Monica Gattinger
Luc Juillet
Daniel Lane
Gilles Paquet (Director)

The published titles in the Series are listed at the end of this book.

Deep Cultural Diversity

....

LIBRARY AND ARCHIVES CANADA CATALOGUING IN PUBLICATION

Paquet, Gilles, 1936-
    Deep cultural diversity : a governance challenge / Gilles Paquet.

(Governance series, ISSN 1487-3052)
Includes bibliographical references and index.
ISBN 978-0-7766-0673-6

    1. Multiculturalism--Canada. I. Title. II. Series: Governance series
    (Ottawa, Ont.)

FC105.M8P28 2008   305.800971   C2008-901559-2

....

Published by the University of Ottawa Press, 2008
542 King Edward Avenue
Ottawa, Ontario K1N 6N5
www.uopress.uottawa.ca

The University of Ottawa Press acknowledges with gratitude the support extended
to its publishing list by Heritage Canada through its Book Publishing Industry
Development Program, by the Canada Council for the Arts, by the Canadian
Federation for the Humanities and Social Sciences through its Aid to Scholarly
Publications Program, by the Social Sciences and Humanities Research Council, and
by the University of Ottawa.

DEEP CULTURAL DIVERSITY: A GOVERNANCE CHALLENGE

GILLES PAQUET

*"Some circumstantial evidence is very strong,
as when you find a trout in the milk"—Henry David Thoreau*

Table of Contents

List of Figures

Foreword

the Other is a mirror into which you peer, or in which you are observed, a mirror that unmasks and denudes, which we would prefer to avoid—Ryszard Kapuscinski

Deep cultural diversity is not a new phenomenon. From time immemorial significantly different groups have been forced to face one another, and to decide how they would handle their conflicts and differences. In prehistoric times, archaeologists tell us, small family-tribes numbering thirty to fifty suddenly came across other family-tribes rather different from them in looks, traits, and mores. This encounter with the Other was an important event. They had three choices: they could choose war, apartheid (building a wall around themselves) or dialogue (Kapuscinski 2005).

Chance meetings were at first the way in which deep diversity was revealed. In Canada, for instance, the "discovery" of the country by Europeans in the fifteenth century led to populations with deeply different cultures, Europeans and First Nations, being confronted with each other. Governing such relationships posed daunting challenges.

The matter was most often resolved in a rather simple and brutal way: the "discoverers" simply decided that the populations they had "discovered" were not of their own species. They were declared to be of an "other sort", not quite human, savages, animals of some sort, and brutal terms of engagement were simply imposed on them. Since the Others were not like "Us" they could be dealt with as if they were of another, non-human species, like animals.

For quite some time this has been a standard strategy for governing the interaction of deeply diverse groups. Aboriginals, heretics, blacks, Jews, and others have been so categorized through the ages. This allowed the governance of deep cultural diversity to be resolved by a primitive governing principle: the partitioning of the world into two species, "human" and "other." In this scheme the humans are narrowly defined as members of certain select cultures, while the others are assigned to the category of chattels, along with the rest of the living world, on the assumption that they are meant to be used instrumentally by humans. This particular form of governance of diversity has proved extremely destructive, yet it has continued to re-emerge as a canonical pattern into very recent times, as with blacks in some parts of the United States, the Jews throughout Nazi-controlled Europe or "infidels" in Afghanistan under the Taliban (Gray 2002).

However, over the past fifty years, as transportation costs have plummeted, migrations across national borders have generated an increase in deep cultural diversity in a large number of countries. Coping with diversity has meant that different societies have had to develop philosophies of cultural encounters, idiosyncratic ways to deal with the Other. This has given rise to a large number of experiments, inquiries, and studies, but to even more mythologies. Some have been satisfied to observe the new phenomenon, but most have constructed narratives in support of the desirability or otherwise of deep cultural diversity, based much more on ideology than on facts. This has led to a whole range of points of view, institutions to support them, and discourses to justify them. While the range of possibilities in defining such philosophies has been quite wide, there has been considerable polarization at the two ends of the spectrum: cultural diversity as a goal to be pursued, and cultural diversity as a plague to be avoided.

The Introduction provides some basic scaffolding for the taxonomy of approaches developed to deal with this challenge. It also underlines the important way in which the human rights ideology and its formal legalistic thrust have thrown a wrench into the world of intercultural relations, and significantly distorted their evolution. Then, using the example of Canada to illustrate the complexity of the underpinnings of such approaches, it reveals the full extent to which "the Canadian way" is built on many unverifiable assumptions and resounding proclamations. With the passage of time these have constructed a sort of unchallengeable canon defended by phalanxes of interested parties and academic groups that have displayed much ingenuity in mounting a protective belt for this particular politically correct and "progressive" diversity-enhancing strategy called "multiculturalism." Finally, some reference is made to the precautionary principle having to be invoked

DEEP CULTURAL DIVERSITY

in the event that it is discovered that particular approaches elected by specific countries appear to generate perplexing results and undesirable, unintended consequences. This is not the reaction in good currency in most countries.

Part I focuses on analyzing diversity. Chapter 1 provides a basic lexicon and sketches a framework for the analysis. Such a limited lexicon cannot be expected to encompass all the concepts that will be used throughout the book, but is intended to clarify at least some of the most important and loaded words ("pluralism," "liberalism," "freedom," "culture"), and to provide a provisional introduction to the central notions of moral contract and citizenship, two types of ligatures that are discussed more extensively later in the book. Chapter 1 also proposes a loose problematique to map out this issue domain, to remind the reader of the various foundational dimensions of the diversity question, and to guide the analysis and strategizing to come later. Chapter 2 provides an interpretative scheme for the probing of intercultural relations. It identifies some of the important mechanisms at work, and the broad strategies that have been envisaged to make the highest and best use of these mechanisms or to counter their unfortunate consequences. Chapter 3 focuses more particularly on multiculturalism as a strategy adopted by countries such as Canada. It proposes a distillation of the different reactions to this strategy and a summary of what has been learned about its unintended consequences. It also sketches the broad contours of alternative scenarios that are still regarded as plausible ways to reconfigure the original multicultural strategy.

Part II tackles head on the challenges of optimizing diversity. Chapter 4 critically examines multiculturalism as federal policy in Canada, as a controversial way to "optimize," and underlines the limitations of such an approach. Chapter 5 investigates the difficult question whether there are limits to diversity. Chapter 6 studies the crucial "progressive dilemma" that has intensely occupied the intelligentsia in western democracies of late: the diversity–solidarity trade-off. It explores cosmopolitanism and compares it to multiculturalism in an effort to determine to what extent it provides a genuine alternative.

Part III examines the tools in good currency for regulating diversity, on the assumption that total laissez-faire might not be desirable or workable. Chapter 7 and 8 examine the two instruments mentioned earlier, moral contracts and citizenship. Moral contracts are shown to be enabling mechanisms and citizenship is shown to be, potentially, an umbrella strategy. Chapter 9 looks into the impact of the Charter of Rights and Freedoms, and the growing importance of adjudication in this issue domain. It shows that the hypertelia of the language of rights, and the high degree of judicialization and formalism it has entailed, might play a deleterious role and prevent our reaching the sort of reasonable accommodations that can be regarded as desirable.

The Conclusion suggests a modest and cautious strategy that would take full advantage of all these governing instruments and pave the way from multiculturalism to cosmopolitanism. It is would be built on a strategy that is much less static than conventional multiculturalism, and would make much greater use of the powers of intermediate cosmopolitanism and moral contracts.

Introduction: Diversity as Weasel Word and Multiculturalism as Questionable

Diversity ... is a watered-down, misguided ideal.—Raymond D. Boisvert

Coping with diversity cannot be meaningfully undertaken without some probing of what is meant by "diversity." The word is opaque and ideologically loaded, and has been used as a convenient label to connote very different realities and to underpin quite different programmes of action. First, some have used "diversity" as a picturesque word to describe the outcome of the great shuffling of population that has led to much more commingling of different cultural groups in many regions of the world, as a result of the reduction of transportation costs and the lowering of territorial barriers. Second, it has been used by others to connote the objective pursued by some countries, either wittingly or unwittingly, of increasing such intercultural migration in order either to recalibrate the age distribution in an ageing country, or to gain access to a higher level of creativity and innovation, through the greater social learning likely to ensue when different cultures and frames of reference are cross-pollinating. Third, the word has also been used to identify clinically the plight of countries being torn apart, or perceived as "losing their soul," as a result either of an unwelcome cohabitation of deeply different and hostile groups within the same territory, or of an unbridled invasion of external groups becoming established as isolated communities in the host society, and generating fractiousness and factions. In such cases it is asserted that, far from leading to more creativity and innovation, diversity is more likely to generate social friction and higher transaction costs. Fourth, "diversity" has also been used as a new code word for affirmative action.

This book will not argue in favour of any of these approaches, but rather will develop a mental toolkit to clarify the basic underlying issues, whatever one's view of diversity may be, and to forge the tools necessary if the governance of diversity is to be less destructive.

An X-Ray of Acculturation Strategies

The new demographic shuffling has led to a variety of reactions, which have taken many different shapes and forms across democratic countries. A whole range of different acculturation strategies have materialized, from attempts to completely assimilate the Other to actions aimed at generating complete apartheid. To sort out, in a rough way, the different families of reactions and strategies, I have suggested elsewhere (Paquet 1989a) a simple classification scheme for the intercultural relations that these strategies entail. This classification was inspired in part by the work of Nathan Glazer (1983). For the sake of convenience the strategies have been labelled "North," "South," "East," and "West", as represented in Figure 1, where the face of a clock has been superimposed on the cardinal points of the compass to facilitate the identification of mixed cases.

The "Eastern" model is not explicitly recognized by Nathan Glazer. It is the world of assimilation: the host culture perceives itself as being bound to absorb and digest the incoming or other group into its own original ethos. However utopian this may appear, it is not far from the condition aspired to by the early colonies in North America.

The "Southern" model is that of a segregated society where the different segments are divided along lines defined by customs, violence, and law to ensure that the different groups are allowed to pursue their separate existences in separate life worlds. This is not exactly what materialized in the Southern states of the United States, or in South Africa, but it is akin to these real-life experiences.

The "Northern" model suggests a competitive view of intercultural relations, where fragmentation is such that differences are somewhat pulverized and fluid, and often temporary, because they are linked to changes in wealth, power, education, and values. In this world of integration an open society subsists in which diversity is more in the nature of a continuum that does not challenge the existence of a common society.

The "Western" model is a world of balkanization, defined by a fragmentation of groups that acquire different, more or less crystallized

Figure 1. An X-Ray of Acculturation Strategies

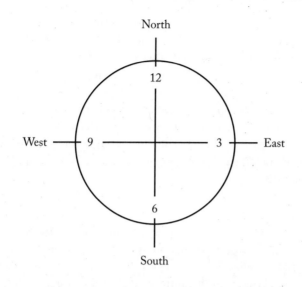

Source: adapted from Paquet, 1989a, p.88

identities, based on patterns of material and symbolic resources, and thereby generate some social distance among them. As a result there is a new social division of labour.

There is no reason to believe that one model should prevail and dominate the pattern of intercultural relationships in a particular country in perpetuity. Nor should one presume that these ideal types are the sole possibilities: one can imagine all sorts of combinations and amalgams of the four basic approaches, corresponding to all hours of the day, or all points between the cardinal points of the compass. One may easily see, for example, how patterns have varied from region to region in the United States, and from one historical period to another. Nevertheless, there has been a tendency for dominant patterns to be reified, under different labels, in the form of "models" that appear to be aimed at imposing a template, and thus excluding any evolution of a pattern that is claimed, for all sorts of reasons, to be the "right" one. Indeed, this is the very weakness of all of these models when they are reified.

Such reified versions of desirable arrangements tend to underpin many strategies for intercultural relations. This is also the case for "diversity" as an ideal. It is often defined as an ideal state in which each subcommunity is allowed to coexist with others, with full respect for all its idiosyncrasies, so that all can develop "into bounded, authentic, pure subcommunities" (Boisvert 2005, p. 124). This version of "diversity" translates into social fragmentation and emphasizes reification. A less static view would suggest that any demographic shuffling should trigger nothing less than creative interplay, a process through which transformation and change will occur, and what might be sought in intercultural relations is amalgamation, merging, and blending that go far beyond the arrested development, in the form of a rigid pattern, that is so often celebrated.

This underlines the dramatic opposition between model and reality, between the reasoning that often underpins policy stances and the messier realities that these models are superimposed onto. Much of this process of reification that has plagued the policy debates may be ascribed to reliance on the essentialist definitions of culture that are in good currency in the anthropological literature, in place of the more relational, pragmatic, and fluid notion of culture that appears to correspond to daily life.

While the essentialist view is purer and simpler, it does not fit well with the realities of our world, where each person is not the bearer of a simple and single culture, but has limited multiple identities that are the results of considerable mixing. Raymond D. Boisvert has stylized this contrast as an opposition between, on the one hand, multiculturalism, "with [its] emphasis on the episteme of an authentic essence rather than the praxis of contact, change, and transformation" (Boisvert 2005, p. 125), and, on the other, the more dynamic relational alternative that he labels "creolizations," an alternative that focuses on process, change, and action.

Human Rights Ideology as Reifying Machine

This crucial aspect of intercultural interaction has been dramatically affected by the new ideology of human rights, and by the legalistic and formalistic twists that it has inflicted on evolving strategies of acculturation. This ideology and the legalistic language that it entails have underpinned a growth in the expectations of the different groups, wherever they may happen to be, that they might be able to cohabit with the Other while fully retaining the features of their own culture, as a matter of "rights." A whole industry of "minority rights" has quickly injected an essentialist flavour into the intercultural equation.

While one may regard all these debates as quite legitimate—and they are—one has to acknowledge that the tendency for groups to articulate their wishes and preferences, specifically about retaining the purity of their original essence, in a language of rights and entitlements has led to a significant increase in the demand for "legitimate" deep diversity, in a world where people still want to live with "their own," but cannot (Dahrendorf 1988; Gauchet 2000). This judicialization—for the language of rights has triggered the emergence of all sorts of institutions to adjudicate whether these rights are respected or not—has heightened the degree of deep legitimized diversity of the essentialist sort. This in turn has made the whole process of intercultural relations (already plagued, as we shall see in Chapter 2, by forces that tend to crystallize the fragments into harder and denser enclaves) into one that has accentuated and celebrated these features.

Not only have the heightened judicialization and adjudication processes generated by the language of rights crystallized intercultural boundaries, they have also strengthened considerably the defence mechanisms available to subcommunities with which they can prevent the development of softer accommodation arrangements. The language of rights has transformed many "more or less" issues into "either/or" issues. Canada has pushed this process of reification further than most other countries by constitutionalizing its commitment to multiculturalism.

The Canadian Strategy: Proclamation, Assumption, Recognition, Charter, and Denial

This section is not meant to provide an overview of the Canadian strategy. There will be occasions in later chapters to do so. It is meant instead to identify some key steps in the construction of the Canadian strategy, which evolved from a mixture of apartheid and assimilationism, in the first half of the twentieth century, into quite a different direction in the latter half of the century.

This evolution has been ascribed to many forces, but it has crystallized around a certain numbers of important moments when bold statements were made that were meant to crystallize the strategy, often without much reflection about the implications and consequences of such proclamations. Moreover, additional rationalizations have blossomed after each of these moments into an intellectual gospel, intended to justify such particular stands ex post. As a result many unsubstantiated statements have now become a canonical view that it would be sacrilegious to attack.

In the beginning were some pragmatic moves by politicians to loosen immigration policy after the Second World War, for two reasons: first, to increase and enrich a declining and ageing population; and, second, to elicit the votes of the new wave of immigrants who were eager to bring their kin to their new country. These moves were presented as "progressive," a label that has been often sufficient to rationalize any policy regarded as desirable but not necessarily rationally defendable. They were most certainly electorally profitable, in a world where the restrictive immigration policies in vogue until the middle of the twentieth century were beginning to come under attack.

These moves also served the purposes of Pierre Trudeau, who was desperate to tame French Canadian nationalism and its separatist overtones. A commitment to multiculturalism and an immigration policy designed to promote diversity could be interpreted by cynics as a way to drown one particularly annoying intercultural interaction in a sea of many such interactions. A proclamation by Trudeau in 1971 launched what is now the familiar Canadian strategy: a more liberal immigration policy and a commitment to multiculturalism. The most fascinating aspect of what ensued is the manner in which this proclaimed strategy acquired intellectual respectability by being subtly theorized and not so subtly judicialized.

On the theoretical front, the first foundation stone came from John W. Berry's "multicultural assumption," which, simply stated, asserts that only those people who feel secure about their own cultural identity can accept those who are different. This assumption has become a foundational belief in Canada and has led to the second foundation stone: an extraordinary flourishing of the "recognition industry," which contends that it is only through the recognition of the cultural rights of "others," be they First Nations, non-mainstream old-timers or newcomers, that one can make them feel "secure," and hope to develop the basis of workable and effective forms of cohabitation. The powerful argumentation of this assumption by Charles Taylor and Will Kymlicka made recognition and "recognition rights" a cornerstone of the defence of multiculturalism in Canada. Indeed, in both cases, what was produced was a philosophical basis for a multicultural strategy that was then advertised and promoted around the world as a philosopher's stone.

On the legal front, the folkloric dimensions of the first wave of multiculturalism gave way to ever more formal if cautiously worded engagements that could only stimulate a hardening of intercultural frontiers, and an inflation of the demands for cultural rights and entitlements. The rights revolution paved the way for the recognition of minority rights, as the proclamation of 1971 became a national policy, crystallized most firmly in section 27 of the Charter of Rights and Freedoms in 1982. What Berry, Taylor, and Kymlicka theorized came to be the new constitutional gospel.

It is very difficult to overestimate the power of inertia supporting this double-barrelled intellectual and constitutional apparatus. Suffice it to say that, in our politically correct world, it provides a robust immune system guarding against critical thinking about the Canadian strategy. Those who have tried to express such thinking have seen their arguments summarily dismissed and their characters impugned. What has been most surprising has not been the wrath and bile of the "progressives" and the diversity entrepreneurs, but the sophistry continuously displayed to ensure that the Canadian strategy would not be seriously and critically examined. Every forewarning or questioning about the unintended consequences of the Canadian strategy has been met with obsessive denial and ad hominem attacks. Any negative unintended consequences have been discounted or nuanced into vapidity. The media have been relatively mute on these issues, but a large number of media gurus have conspired in the enterprise of national self-congratulation. It is argued in the rest of this book that, as a result, there has been an uncritical reification of the Canadian position on these issues—and that this may turn out to be a dangerous strategy to maintain.

More importantly, the Canadian strategy is now glibly exported wholesale to the rest of the world, as the enlightened way to deal with diversity, so much so that a senior columnist on the Globe and Mail can assert that Canada has nothing to learn from the traumatic experience of the Netherlands, without generating any negative reaction. The consensus about Canada's superiority appears to have immunized even thinkers who are usually critical from entertaining any doubt about its absolute wisdom. Consequently, at a time when, around the world, there is a great deal of reflection on the limits of the multicultural strategy adopted by Canada, there is very little debate about these issues in Canada itself, and whatever debates there are carefully avoid addressing the most difficult questions. Indeed, there appears to be an unconscious conspiracy to maintain the debates at the level of evasive thinking, ensuring that there will be no way to question frontally the Canadian strategy in good currency, that any sign of tension is dismissed, that any critical evaluation is ascribed to a mean spirit and an abandonment of Canadian values, and therefore that a meaningful debate about the best way to deal with deep cultural diversity will be avoided at all costs. This book intends to challenge that ethos.

The Precautionary Principle

Genocidal wars on several continents, intercultural tensions degenerating into violence in other modern democracies, adverse events flaring up in countries that have adopted similar strategies to Canada, and intellectual denunciations of the limits of the positions of Berry, Taylor, Kymlicka, and their co-thinkers have all begun to take their toll. Even the more nuanced evaluations of the Canadian multicultural strategy are beginning to admit that, while the situation is not yet catastrophic, there are signs of tension that cannot, or at least should not, be ignored. This level of concern may be sufficient for the principle of precaution to be safely invoked, yet this must be done with care.

If it appears that the unintended consequences of a certain strategy are generating negative results, a strong case can be made for not waiting until all the evidence is in to take precautionary action. Not to do so would be both imprudent and unwise. This book is therefore a call for more precautions. However, it should be clear that one of the downsides of the precautionary principle is that it has a tendency to translate all too often into judicial procedures. Too many cases where the precautionary principle has been invoked have been cases where it has been argued that certain responsible persons should have known, should have anticipated, should have taken action to prevent certain catastrophes. This can easily lead to a drift from an ethics of precaution to a fixation on judicial adjudication of what should have been anticipated. One can easily see that one may fall prey to indictment for not having been clairvoyant enough.

It should be made clear, then, that our plea for the precautionary principle is not one that would support its judicialization. What we have in mind is simply a need to break out of the present "mental prison" that prevents any critical examination of a strategy that might do irreparable damage to the fabric of the country. Our view is that there is enough circumstantial evidence for such a critical examination to begin now, and that is what this book will try to do.

PART I

Analyzing Diversity

1

The Problematique of Cultural Pluralism

From the dew of the few flakes that melt on our faces we cannot reconstruct the snowstorm.—John Updike

Betting on diversity is a moral and political act. It is "the celebration of human possibilities." This position is based on the beliefs that the best way in which individuals can make a good life for themselves is to have a plurality of values at their disposal; that cultural plurality is an asset; and that it is the role of the state to create the conditions in which diversity can blossom (Kekes 1993). However, this entails the necessity of imposing limits, for not all possibilities are reasonable. Differences breed not only social learning but conflicts. Particular identities rooted in cultural differences may generate tension. The challenges are to build new forms of identity that are likely to be workable, and to promote coexistence and cooperation in an increasingly pluralistic and interdependent world.

Promoting common citizenship and a sense of belonging in contexts where a mosaic of deeply different cultures and identities prevail is often mentioned as the panacea. This is more easily stated that done. This world of diversity is plagued with problems that prevent understanding and consensus. Both a loose problematique and a preliminary lexicon might provide ways to feed an intelligent conversation on these issues.

A Loose Problematique

Plurality is a general recognition that diversity is a new reality in modern societies and is the bedrock on which "modern culture" must be built. Yet these three words can be frustratingly opaque. What is "culture"? What is "diversity"? What is "plurality"?

The role of a problematique and of a lexicon is not to provide answers but rather to generate a toolbox that will permit the formulation of relevant questions. Without a framework and a clear vocabulary, or, at least, a clear view of the confused nature of the vocabulary in good currency, one cannot conduct a useful conversation. To help us map the territory, we have identified three major dimensions in a classificatory scheme, as presented in Figure 2.

The first dimension pertains to the dichotomy between material and symbolic orders. This notion has emerged clearly from the works of Raymond Breton, among others, and has contributed to a broadening of the debate on culture in Canada (Breton 1984). The insistence on the importance of the symbolic order allowed the discussion to escape from the traps of traditional analyses of interest groups' demands for material or financial gratifications, and to focus equally on problems of collective identity (traditions, customs, norms, and so on) that are embedded in the forms and styles of private and public institutions. It has reaffirmed something that is often forgotten: that the symbolic order underpins the workings of the material order and is also a prime target of government interventions (Tussman 1977).

Figure 2. The Main Dimensions of Cultural Pluralism

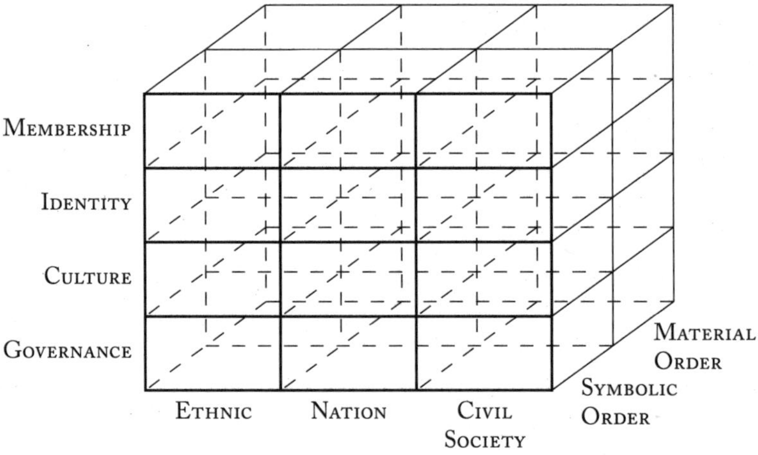

For Breton and others the construction of the symbolic order is as important as the construction of the material socioeconomy. Citizens traditionally have sought a certain concordance between their private way of life (their "culture") and the style of their public environment (their "national identity"). Their demands for status (recognition within the public space) will often be as vociferous as their demands for access to a good life. Governments of plural democracies must be increasingly involved in monitoring and understanding the symbolic order, both in response to demands by diverse groups, and as a way to temper the potentially destructive behaviour of different and often hostile groups by acting on their representations and perceptions. These more inclusive analyses have helped in providing interpretations built on acknowledging a shift of emphasis from "material" to "symbolic" ethnicity in the recent past, and on the growing centrality of competition for status (Gans 1979). Membership and identity have roots in both material and symbolic life. Naturally such dimensions either flourish through the development of culture and institutions, or fade away.

The second broad axis of the problematic gauges the increasing degree of tightness of a social arrangement: from membership, which may be regarded as a minimal set of conditions for belonging to a club (the difference between members and strangers), to identification/identity, involving the subjective recognition of some salient features as the basis for self-categorization, to culture, which represents a more or less "formalized" set of rules, laws, customs, and rituals, to institutions, which amounts to the development of a stable pattern of social interaction (Walzer 1983; Edwards and Doucette 1987; Roberts and Clifton 1982). The notions of membership, identity, culture and institutions are extremely difficult to define precisely. Some scholars have anchored essentialist definitions in certain selected traits. Others have insisted on some primordial features as determinant. A third group has defined these notions fundamentally in a relational way, as shared differences that are the results of negotiated arrangements (Drummond 1981–82). In the first two instances a number of ethnographic features are said to provide the basic or dominant characteristics necessary to qualify for membership (Nash 1989). In the last case membership, identity, and culture are in the nature of a persona, which is the result of a creative and interactive process through which relationships are constructed and evolve in a manner that makes them matter of conventions and agreements with outsiders (Goldberg

1980). In that sense, membership, identity, and culture may be regarded as increasingly complex, and stylized forms of arrangements or social capital (Coleman 1988). This symbolic capital simultaneously provides the basis for differentiation, structuration, and integration: it serves as a way to provide a basic partitioning based on negotiated differences, but also as a basis for assembling those disparate elements into a coherent whole (Porter 1979; Lussato 1989).

Since *de facto* heterogeneity may generate a segmentation of the social space into disconnected groups, and since such segmentation may well degenerate through multiplex relationships into cumulative processes accentuating and crystallizing such segmentation, an increasing degree of balkanization and anomie of the segments may ensue (Gluckman 1967; Laurent and Paquet 1991). Consequently, it is crucial that conventions be negotiated vigorously, and that the pattern of rights and obligations of each party be spelled out. Membership is going to be easier to negotiate than identity, and identity easier than culture, but corresponding to these different degrees of cohesion there is some sort of "moral contract" (Paquet 1991–92).

The third broad axis of the block identifies three complementary and yet intricately interwoven principles of social integration: ethnicity, nationality, and civil society. These are different grounds on which these moral contracts are negotiated or arrived at. The case of ethnicity used to be regarded as quite distinct because of the fact that membership was perceived as rooted primarily in physical characteristics and the material order. However, as ethnicity has tended to become more and more symbolic there has been a growing importance given to the symbolic order in defining ethnic boundaries. In that sense, ethnie, nation, and civil society are different ways of anchoring membership and identity that may be regarded as tending to become substitutes, or at least the basis for a complex compound, rather than being the basis of absolutely non-intersecting foundations. They are valid bases for discussing membership, identity, culture, and institutions, but, depending on what is the hegemonic or dominant terrain, the "moral contract" will contain a different set of collective rights and obligations. Determining the valence of each terrain becomes crucial.

DEEP CULTURAL DIVERSITY

Building a Lexicon

The ambiguity of a number of key concepts has always hampered discussion in the past, so some clarification may be useful at this time.

Pluralism is probably the most troublesome of these concepts. The word is used loosely, and there is no corpus stating clearly what a pluralist society is or what its fabric should be. We may approach it by way of the notion of *the open society*, developed and expounded by Bergson and Popper (Bergson 1932; Popper 1942), connoting societies that have escaped the dominance of holistic values and have managed to put the individual at centre stage. This has translated into the following characteristics: a private sphere for the individual, who enjoys freedom within that sphere; the principle of private property; the rule of law to regulate the relationships between individuals and states; and restricted power for the state, so that society is never allowed to become "closed" (Reszler 1990). A pluralist society, however, goes beyond this notion of negative freedom and calls for "an ensemble, composed of compartments freely agglomerated," in which the constituent parts retain a good portion of their original autonomy, and are regarded as "irreducible domains in permanent interaction," so that "each particular sphere finds its expression in a partial power" and there is a multiplication of allegiances corresponding to this division of powers (Reszler 1990).

At one extreme of the spectrum of pluralism, then, one may posit complete relativism and the cult of diversity *qua* diversity. This entails a multiplication of allegiances and a gamble on solidarity emerging as a result of a multiplicity of competitive focuses in the different cultural groups. At the other extreme, one may posit the unitary and closed society. One may imagine a gradation of intensities and interpretations of pluralism between these two poles.

Another central concept at the root of our notion of modern society is *liberalism*, with its central concept of individual autonomy that is meant to override, or at least firmly constrain, the emergence of any communal authority or cultural rights that may exclude non-adherents. Liberalism as a political philosophy provides an interpretation of what it means to belong voluntarily to a cultural community. Liberals, with their uncompromising defence of individual rights, have been somewhat hostile to group rights and even more to minority rights. Yet, in relatively more "enlightened" or "generous" versions of liberalism, nothing denies group rights, cultural rights or minority rights. All depends therefore on the notion of liberalism in good currency.

Thus, in Trudeau's Canada, it was felt that "liberal equality was incompatible with the permanent assigning of collective rights to a minority culture;" this notion of liberalism posited the "idea of collective rights for minority cultures as both theoretically incoherent and practically dangerous" (Kymlicka 1989), for these rights would be deviations from the strict principle of equal individual rights. Kymlicka has argued that this is a truncated understanding of liberalism. If separation is a "badge of inferiority" in certain circumstances, "in Canada, segregation has always been viewed as a defence of a highly valued cultural heritage" and thus cannot be regarded as a "badge of inferiority." Consequently, Kymlicka challenges the traditional view of liberalism and argues in favour of a broadening of liberalism to take minority rights into account. This is the same argument that Kolm has developed in connection with cultural rights (Kolm 1985).

At the centre of this reframing of liberalism is the value of cultural membership. This is a primary good for Kymlicka: in his view, if an individual is stripped of his/her cultural heritage, his/her development is stunted. This implies that a liberal view of equality need not be insensitive to social/cultural endowment: "members of the minority cultures can face inequalities that are the product of their circumstances or endowment . . . and . . . certain collective rights can be defended as appropriate measures for a rectification of inequality of circumstances." What is required is a set of constitutional provisions that would be "flexible enough to allow for the legitimate claims of cultural membership, but which are not so flexible as to allow systems of racial or cultural oppression."

While a liberal argument may be provided for cultural membership, the limits to be imposed on the use of such an argument are unclear. Some have used it to defend the equality of all minority rights, others have defended them only if they are rooted in shared projects, and others still would restrict its ambit to groups facing clear inequality of circumstances. Ralf Dahrendorf has referred to "wet" and "dry" liberalism to connote the looser and tighter versions of the liberal theory (Dahrendorf 1988). In a "dry" liberal system community rights do not exist, but in a "wet" liberal system they may. Yet these rights remain ill-specified and, given the divergence of views even among jurists on the question of the differences between private and public, or between civil society and the state, it is hardly surprising that so many incommensurable cases have been defended with equanimity on the basis of the same doctrine.

The debate on secession rights for minorities (Buchanan 1991) may provide a useful forum for the clarification of the terrain, but liberalism is likely to be a most unhelpful arbiter. Individual rights and collective rights have become so intermingled since the New Deal of the 1930s (Ackerman 1984) that any Solomonian effort to separate them, or to establish a definitive order or hierarchy in those rights *qua* rights, is bound to be futile (Bouchard 1990; Dumont 1990).

Liberal democracy's emphasis on rights and on *negative freedom*—protection against interference with individual choices—has led to a phenomenal reductionism. Democracy, which originally meant putting the active citizen at centre stage, through government of the people, by the people, for the people, has expropriated citizens of this central governing work, which was part and parcel of being a citizen, in "rights societies" (Tussman 1989). Participation and, with it, the emphasis on *positive freedom*—being able to do this or be that, and the duty to help others in that respect (Sen 1987)—has been virtually excised. The whole range of notions of membership, identity, culture, and institutions connotes a sense of participation in ethnie, nation, or civil society that has consequently remained rather obscure and underdeveloped.

Charles Taylor has argued that there is a cleavage between "rights societies," where the dignity of each individual resides in the fact that he or she has rights, and "participation societies," where freedom, agency, and efficacy come from the fact that the individual has a recognized voice. This participatory model obviously presupposes "a strong sense of community" (Taylor 1985). For different societies, this process of identification with the community may be more or less important a characteristic. Moreover, the participatory institutions embodying it may not be equally congruent with the ethnie, the nation or the civil society. Different degrees of allegiance and belonging may spell out a multiplicity of identities based on the relative salience of these different communities in the life of citizens. This plurality of identities, or the legitimization of "hybrid identities" based on a plurality of participations in ethnie, nation, and civil society, has not developed evenly across national territories.

The rationale for participation is the very same that underlies the notion of group rights. Denise Reaume has provided a persuasive argument for the participatory nature of a number of goods, such as the maintenance of a language community (Reaume in Lafrance 1989). This complements the argument put forward by Taylor. This approach makes sense both of group rights and of the obligation for a substantial number of the group to participate. Michael McDonald has used a parallel line of argument to show that the "sharing of *nomos* and narrative makes possible public spaces that are common property," and that rights to protect the existence, identity, and integrity of the communities sharing that *nomos* are as important as individual rights (McDonald in Lafrance 1989).

Culture connotes a whole way of life, so it would be unduly reductive to define it only on the basis of ethnicity, or with reference to an idealized and aseptic notion of civil society. Culture is more usefully defined in terms of communication. Social systems are those constituted as operating through communication. Culture is defined by how individuals and groups communicate through language and solve problems. Language is indeed a central operational common denominator, or the matrix on which culture is erected. Cultural values are underlying reference points in all these communication activities. Building on this communication notion of culture, *cultural identity* acts as a set of boundaries that, while facilitating communication within a community, may in fact frustrate communication with "the outside," with those who are not part of the cultural group. In an "open society" that allows for respect for diversity, social cohesion, and non-discrimination, language is a vector of communication, exchanges, and mixing (Bouchard 1999).

Fundamentally, each individual bases his or her own experience and action upon selections made by his or her ancestors to decomplicate reality. This *cultural heritage* enables each individual not to have to reinvent complexity reduction strategies anew in each generation, but it also requires that such choices and innovations be transmissible. As differentiation and diversity increase, the world visions of the different groups also become more differentiated and diverse, and the media of transmission also become differentiated. The challenge is to understand these different media of transmission, and the extent to which they may combine to ensure adequate learning, and complementary and not conflictive cognitive expectations. Moreover, while in traditional undifferentiated societies transmissibility was ensured through a shared construction of reality (community, religion, family, and so on), in differentiated societies the most significant media may be structures built on money, power, and other such factors, and one must be able to identify the relative efficiency of these different channels and their relative valence.

The Leverage of Cultural Diversity

As a general proposition, cultural diversity is regarded as a new reality that has to be taken into account in collective decision-making. It is also regarded by all, whether as a result of personal conviction or as a result of some degree of political correctness, as generally desirable. Yet the discussion dries up very quickly and drifts into generalities as soon as anyone tries to define, explicitly and verifiably, *how* cultural diversity is likely to improve the economy, society or the polity.

Indeed, as conversations proceed it generally becomes clear that, for many, diversity is primarily a constraint on social development, a problem to be managed. The arguments used indicate that the very fact of acting to preserve or maintain diversity—or homogeneity, for that matter—is regarded by some as an effort to stop the evolution of societies at a certain stage and to prevent the further development of heterogeneity—or, the other side of the same coin, to prevent the further erosion of homogeneity—instead of allowing the dynamics of evolution to prevail. While many observers are quite willing to bet on diversity, they feel that there is a need for the state to manage, or, at the very least, to monitor and accompany, this new reality, in order to prevent unintended consequences that might arise from such diversification being conducted too fast or without due diligence. For this latter group it is not reasonable to allow this process to proceed unattended. Indeed, this is perceived as being the case, not only because of the potential damage that it might generate, but also because of the fact that one cannot expect the highest and best use of diversity to emerge organically.

For yet another group of observers, diversity can only mean the end of consensus. Consequently, it must be tamed. While no one questions the reality of diversity, few would seem ready to accept unlimited diversity without significant safeguards, and yet very few feel strongly enough to make a specific case of the matter. This explains the cacophony, confusion, and malaise that erupted, for example, during the current debate on *accommodements raisonnables* ("reasonable accommodations") in Quebec when a bold group dared to put a specific proposal about such safeguards on the table. As for the degree of diversity that can be regarded as appropriate, given the nature of the safeguards, little consensus emerges except at the highest degree of generality: that the optimal degree of diversity might not be the maximum degree, and that *accommodements raisonnables* need not be specified, for they simply exist.

To the extent that governments and states have diminished powers, they lose both their roles as protectors of civilization and as promoters of a pluralistic society. There is obviously no longer any guarantee that governments and states will either accept the responsibility of shouldering these roles or be able to perform them well. We have seen recently a sufficient number of states that have been characterized by policies of ethnic cleansing and struggles against pluralism. The loss of state capabilities and will is significant in so far as it makes it impossible to envisage some of the counterstrategies capable of designing a tolerant approach likely to generate a decent society, a society in which institutions do not humiliate people (Margalit 1996). Such a society requires a state capable both of protecting civilizational values *and* of promoting pluralism. Between the suspicion of the state on the part of many in North America and the lionizing of the state by many Europeans there must be a *juste milieu*, a happy medium, a mid-Atlantic response.

Conclusion

Any discussion of the subject of diversity is marred by tiptoeing and groping. The issue of pluralism is fraught with sensitivities. Political correctness, as the late Supreme Court Justice John Sopinka remarked many times, is the most important enemy of free speech. Yet any such discussion generally contributes to bring several points of agreement to light.

First, we need a better lexicon with which to analyze the issues of pluralism more effectively and we also need public forums where these conversations can be conducted. Second, most of our assumptions about democratic governance are likely to be transformed by a commitment to pluralism. Third, there are limits to cultural diversity beyond which the social costs exceed the social benefits, and among the general public there is a tacit diffidence in the face of cultural pluralism when it is presented as boundless, or without precise limits. Fourth, in a mostly *ad hoc* way Canada has developed a multicultural strategy that appeared to be promising in its early years, but experience, in Canada and elsewhere, has generated some doubt about the adequacy of this prototype model, and further public discussion is now necessary in order to ascertain what plausible and workable alternatives to multiculturalism there may be to serve as strategies for dealing with deep diversity. Fifth, the state has a subtle role to play in these discussions. Finally, in the search for viable strategies with which to approach deep cultural diversity, the best is often enemy of the good.

Many of these propositions remain presumptions or hypotheses, but they serve as points of departure for further discussions. Some may prove ill-founded, others useful, still others false. Yet they are propositions that, we feel, readers must be able to critically appraise if they are to deal intelligently with deep cultural diversity and effective ways to cope with it.

2

Intercultural Relations:
A Myrdal–Tocqueville–Girard Interpretative
Scheme (co-authored with Paul Laurent)

*Distance lends, if not enchantment, anyway indifference, and thus
integrity.* —Clifford Geertz

A major change in the intensity of cultural interpenetration has taken place over the past one hundred years or so. In remote times and on remote offshore islands, primitive cultures had limited involvement with one another. This does not mean that "civilized societies" were ever homogeneous cultural units. Polyethnicity and cultural diversity were salient features of most civilized societies, a fate imposed on them by conquest, trade, and so on. More recently, however, after an era when cultural homogeneity was idealized, if not realized, "a shuffling process" has been activated that has resulted in a degree of cultural diversity, "which is, by now, approaching extreme and near universal proportions" (Geertz 1986). This "shuffling process" has led social and cultural boundaries to coincide less and less closely, and the social space to become more culturally diversified. Ironically, this real increase in cultural diversity and heterogeneity comes at the very same moment that the Enlightenment yearning for a world polity, whose citizens share common aspirations and a common culture (Rorty 1986), appears to have become the dominant ideal.

The dialectic between these two drifts—greater cultural heterogeneity and stronger yearning for a common culture—has been played out differently in different forums, such as (to take just a few examples) Belgium, Canada, the two parts of Ireland, Lebanon, South Africa or Switzerland. Yet intercultural differences have not been eliminated or eroded anywhere. Rather, they have crystallized ever more sharply through a process of cumulative causation, described at length by Gunnar Myrdal (Myrdal 1944). This has led to an uneasy coexistence between real differences and decreed egalitarian status. Alexis de Tocqueville argued that this sort of situation could only generate envy (de Tocqueville 1961). Such a surge of envy in turn could only give rise to intercultural violence, as René Girard explained rather well (Girard 1978). Consequently, only through the imposition of some shared conventions could envy be reduced and violence be controlled.

This chapter discusses the growth of cultural diversity, and the power of the "shuffling process" of the past one hundred or so years to generate a heightened degree of cultural diversity and interaction, as well as some cultural balkanization. Then it shows why societies decreeing equality as a norm have become more prone to generate envy. It then builds on the work of René Girard to show how intercultural envy can only trigger violence, and looks into the different ways that have been developed to manage intercultural interactions and contain this violence.

Cultural Diversity: The Myrdal Hypothesis

Polyethnicity and cultural diversity have been the hallmark of most civilizations. And yet, because of the long hiatus during which the ideals of ethnic homogeneity within a particular geographical territory and of national sovereignty conformable to ethnic boundaries prevailed as values in Western Europe (McNeill 1986), the essential cultural diversity of most civilized societies has come to be occluded. The duration of this hiatus may be the subject of some controversy, but the heyday of what one might call the cultural nationalist principle spanned a period in Western Europe from the latter part of the eighteenth century to the early part of the twentieth century. The roots of this particular nationalistic vision may be found much earlier, with elements of the nation-state in the sixteenth and seventeenth centuries (Braudel 1979), and this notion is still in good currency in some regions of the world.

Indeed, this vision of ethnic solidarity and national independence has permeated much of the consciousness of our contemporaries, even though it echoed only the perceptions of a time- bound and evanescent (Western) European ideal. For quite a long time now it has led even the educated classes to completely block out the historical record of cultural diversity. It is only of late that the polyethnic norm has been re-established and the norm of nationalistic homogeneity has come to be regarded as an ideology emanating from an historical episode.

It is not difficult to understand why advanced civilizations have clung to this ideal. Polyethnicity and cultural diversity are important sources of friction. Many societies would gladly wish them away. One of the fundamental results of polyethnicity and cultural diversity is the development of multiplex relationships, with simultaneous ethnocultural linkages in more than one context (Gluckman 1967). Culture and ethnicity are led to permeate the worlds of work, play, family, polity, and society, thereby generating a certain compactness of ethnocultural groups.

The shuffling process of the past one hundred years or so has heightened the degree of intercultural mixing within national boundaries, and has led to the accumulation of social capital within cultural communities through the development of networks of mutual aid, voluntary associations, obligations and expectations, information channels, and social norms developed by those cultural communities (Light 1984; Coleman 1988). These facilitating structures have also led to some early balkanization of the socioeconomy via the closure of social networks and the sanctioning of multiplex relationships. A dynamic cumulative process has ensued that has tended to reinforce rather than attenuate intercultural differences. Initially, cultural differences are the basis of higher costs of transaction among groups, as opposed to within groups. Such cost differentials lead to the accumulation of intra-group social capital in the sense in which Coleman uses the term (social networks, norms, trust, sharing of information, and so on, all tending as a matter of consequence to facilitate transactions), and this further increases the costs of transaction across communities, erects barriers to trade and communication, and triggers a next round of accumulation of social capital (Coleman 1988). The accumulated social capital tends not only to reinforce and legitimize existing intercultural differences, but also to immunize the whole system against any effort to change it by modifying one facet or one factor in the whole game. In fact, the multiplex relationships tend to act as a bond, confirming and strengthening the interethnic frontiers, and feeding a circular causation process through which the boundaries are hardened (Myrdal 1944, 1957).

Such social coagulation has been regarded by neoclassical economists as essentially temporary. Since the discrimination component inherent in these partial systems has been diagnosed as leading to less than fully efficient production and consumption arrangements, it has been argued that they could not survive long (Becker 1957). Consequently, the cultural mosaic might prevail in the short run, but, as a result of the competitive process, it would be likely to disappear in the longer run.

Yet cultural diffraction has proved resilient and, very much in the way of regional disparities and income inequalities, has continued to prevail over very long periods. Myrdal showed that, in all those cases, this is due to a process of cumulative causation at work (Myrdal 1944, 1957). To the extent that a social structure and social customs ensue, it becomes profitable to follow prevailing social customs, and to follow the caste code that characterizes the divisions of society (Akerlof 1976). The consequent more or less permanent balkanization of multiethnic societies is hardly surprising. It is characterized by fragmentation, multiplication of different rights and norms in the many cultural groups, increasing gaps between groups as their identities become rooted in different patterns of symbolic and material resources, and the deep-rooted dominance of different social customs. From such circumstances ensues what Nathan Glazer calls the Western pattern of organization of polyethnic societies (Glazer 1983; Paquet 1989a).

Egalitarianism and Envy:
The de Tocqueville Mechanism

This semi-permanent segmentation of the social space along ethnocultural lines through the Myrdal mechanism of cumulative causation, and the economic rewards for those following the prevailing social custom, has been at odds with the prevailing democratic and egalitarian ideology that has permeated the Western world in the aftermath of the Enlightenment. Liberty and equality have been hailed as the basic tenets of the new democratic creed, and they have become the foundations of the democratic symbolic order. Of these two basic values, equality is the dominant one in the democratic credo.

Alexis de Tocqueville showed that "democratic peoples . . . have an ardent, insatiable, eternal, invincible passion for equality; they want equality in liberty and, if they cannot obtain it, they still want it in slavery" (de Tocqueville 1961, Vol. 2, p. 104). At the core of his book *De la démocratie en Amérique* (first published in 1840) is a sort of sociology of equality in democratic societies. It argues that in this sentiment of

DEEP CULTURAL DIVERSITY

equality resides the basis of modernity and democracy. Equality in this sense is not only an observed fact, it is fundamentally an ideal, an "imaginary equality," an egalitarianism that drives democracy (p. 189). Indeed, de Tocqueville showed that not only is equality the dominant value in democracy, but "the desire for equality becomes ever more insatiable as equality increases" (p. 144). Even when an extremely egalitarian status has been realized in a society, "one may expect that each of its citizens will always perceive in his vicinity several positions that predominate over his, and one may foresee that he will obstinately turn his attention to them alone" (de Tocqueville quoted by Dupuy in Dumouchel and Dupuy 1979, p. 49). Contrary to what one might have assumed, greater equality generates, not less envy, but more.

This sort of passion for equality also applies to ethnic and cultural groups, and operates with all the more force when there is a coexistence of decreed egalitarian rights with considerable *de facto* differences in power, wealth, and other characteristics among the different groups. Strong resentment ensues (Scheler 1958; Paquet 1989b), leading not only to cultural jealousies, in the form of an innocuous zeal for the preservation of something possessed, but to envy, actual displeasure, and ill-will at the superiority of another person in happiness, success, reputation or the possession of anything desirable (Foster 1972). The dogma of egalitarianism, therefore, when coupled with the realities of the Myrdalian cumulative causation process and with the existing caste code explaining the preservation of intergroup differences, fuels intercultural tension and leads to explosive intercultural interactions (Dupuy 1985).

The rise of egalitarianism as a modern democratic dogma, combined with the concomitant acceleration of the demographic shuffling process, have consequently produced a heightened degree of tension, frustration, and envy in intercultural interactions. It has contributed to the accumulation of culture-specific social capital and to the further balkanization of modern societies. Moreover, in countries such as Canada, where multiculturalism has become a national policy, and where cultural rights have been entrenched in constitutional documents and ordinary laws alike, this process of segmentation has been accentuated and envy further promoted, when erected in view of the stark contrast between the formal equality of ethnocultural groups, decreed as norm, and the realities of intercultural differences in status (Paquet 1989b).

The transformation of the socioeconomic process over the past one hundred years or so has also fostered this passion for equality. In a poor society consumption is concentrated on basic material goods, but, when the standard of living increases, the demand for luxury goods and positional goods increases. Competition for positional goods is underpinned by a passion for distinction, for resources in absolute scarcity that bestow some relative superiority upon individuals. "The distinctive appurtenances of the rich then become squirrels' wheels for those below: objects of desire that the most intensive effort cannot reach" (Hirsch 1976, p. 66). The increase in the relative importance of positional competition has heightened the relative frustration of those on lower rungs, increased resentment, and made the whole socio-economic process more envy-driven.

Mimesis and the Genesis of Violence: Girard's Analysis

One of the most fascinating analyses of the dynamics of mimesis and envy in modern times has been proposed by René Girard. It is nothing less than an X-ray of these dynamics, illuminating the powerful forces unleashed by intercultural envy (Girard 1972, 1978, 1982).

For Girard mimesis is the central phenomenon, the only basis on which one may construct a theory of envy. Individual A wants something that individual B has, because B possesses it; A thereby imitates the desire of B. There are three elements in mimesis, then: the imitator, the imitated, and the object that the imitated has and the imitator wants to appropriate. In Girard's parlance, if A desires the object that B possesses because B has it, B is said to be "the mediator of desire." According to Girard, one may differentiate between internal and external mediation in mimesis, depending on the distance between the imitator and the imitated. The mediation is said to be external if the imitated is very distant, as with Don Quixote and his model knight, or Julien Sorel and Napoleon I. In these cases the imitated is truly simply a model. When the distance between the imitator and the imitated is reduced and is no longer insuperable, the imitator sees the imitated as an obstacle standing in the way of the object of desire, or as an obstacle to the realization of his desire. In the latter situation envy ensues (Orsini 1986).

Girard's analysis reveals that mimesis is the moving force behind envy and that the greater the state of "indifferentiation"—of limited difference and therefore limited distance between groups—the more envy is going to be unleashed. The closer the "model" the more it becomes an "obstacle," and the more intolerable it is that A might have something that B does not have. Therefore, a move towards greater equality of social conditions is bound to generate harsher competition and, as parties compete more fiercely for the same objects, violence emerges.

There is no reason to believe that there will not develop a "double mediation" between closer (not very differentiated) groups. Mimesis works not only upwards but downwards. René Konig has shown how bourgeois have often imitated proletarians or cowboys, for example by wearing jeans. It is therefore quite probable that, in a somewhat undifferentiated world, double mediation, through which each group develops its mimesis whatever its position on the social ladder, might generate uncontained violence (Konig quoted in Dumouchel and Dupuy 1979).

Violence is fed not only by competition between the imitator and the imitated, but by a passion for distinction that becomes exacerbated the more equality of conditions prevails. De Tocqueville stated it most clearly: "whatever general effort a society makes to render its citizens equal and similar, the particular pride of individuals will always seek out an escape to another level and will want to form, to some extent, an inequality from which it can benefit" (de Tocqueville, Vol. 2, p. 224). In this way inequality breeds envy, but equality fuels an equally potent passion for distinction that keeps the competition going and breeds violence: "the passion for distinction is joined with the passion for imitation" (Melonio 1986).

This mechanism is at work not only between individuals, but also between groups and cultures. The greater the intercultural differences in wealth and power, in the face of decreed rights to equality, the greater the envy and the resentment, as Tocqueville explained; however, the more successful the efforts to reduce these real differences in wealth and power, the more intolerable they become. Thus they generate more envy and fury and, ultimately, the passion for distinction is more forcefully unleashed. Hence we find ourselves in a double bind.

Hierarchy, and Devices for Reducing Envy and Controlling Violence

In compounding the three arguments presented above, one is led to a rather compelling conclusion. Cultural diversity is on the rise and is likely to lead to an increasing degree of cultural friction, through the development of multiplex relationships and the cumulative process of causation leading to cultural balkanization. This segmentation of the social space along cultural lines is developing at the very moment when democratic ideals are promoting the idea of a common and egalitarian culture. The rise of egalitarianism alongside the presence of resilient differences has provoked the omnipresence of mimesis, and has led to the double-bound mushrooming of envy, resentment, and violence between cultural groups. Multiethnic and multicultural societies have had to develop mechanisms to reduce the envy, and contain the violence, generated by mimesis.

G. M. Foster has examined in detail the various cultural forms used by persons who either fear the envy of others, or fear that they may be suspected of envy. These take a variety of forms, from concealment, denial, and sharing (symbolic or real) in the first instance, to reassurance and withdrawal in the second instance. There is also, however, a gamut of institutional devices to reduce envy and contain violence: redistributive mechanisms, but also diverse forms of encapsulation and segregation designed to mark boundaries between groups (Foster 1972). A typology of such cultural/institutional mechanisms appears to emerge from the literature we have referred to above.

René Girard has identified the main mechanism of this kind as the sacrifice of a scapegoat, a victim towards which the violence of the community is channelled, actually or symbolically, in order to drain the social system of its violence. Such sacrificial violence plays the role of a catharsis. It purges the community of its dissension by channelling violence onto a victim that has no capacity to seek revenge, and the vicious circle of violence is thereby broken. The sacrifice of the scapegoat is a mechanism of reconciliation for the community that can be repeated as a preventive measure through sacred and religious rituals. Girard shows that many of the interdictions and taboos developed by communities have the same basic foundation: an attempt to contain violence by prohibiting as transgressions behaviours or situations likely to fuel mimesis. He argues that this is the case with the incest taboo, for instance (Girard 1972, 1978). This mechanism, however often it may be shown to have been used as a stratagem for containing violence, does not deal directly with the root cause of envy and violence. It contains violence only by channelling and focusing it.

Richard Kearney has used this very interesting idea of a scapegoat mechanism to shed light on the dynamics of the intercultural conflict in Northern Ireland (Kearney 1979). He shows how Pádraig Pearse, James Connolly, and the other martyrs of the Easter Rising of 1916 still hold a central place in the symbolism of the Irish Republican Army, underlining the sacrificial nature of the event. Kearney suggests that such bloody sacrifices are seen as a way to regenerate the national community in Ireland. While this interpretation provides some insight into the nature of the situation in Northern Ireland and the mythology built around it, it also reveals the great limitations of the scapegoat stratagem in containing violence.

Girard has proposed as a second and more fundamental strategy one based on the Gospel, on a theology of renunciation, a mechanism to end violence by an unconditional renunciation of violence and an unconditional acceptation of a logos of love. The love of one's neighbour is proposed as a way to break out of mimesis through the imitation of Christ. This might be extremely effective as a mechanism to reduce envy and contain violence, but it appears to be extremely utopian, given what we know about human nature. In any case, it has never been effectively used as a way out of the bind of intercultural tensions in any circumstances with which we are familiar.

The scapegoat mechanism and the strategy of renunciation are the only devices that Girard explicitly propounds. The former represents an interesting way to analyze various literary and anthropological experiences, and the latter looks like an inspiring way out of the double bind, but neither appears to have much operational appeal.

Foster's review of violence-reducing mechanisms in different societies in the past is a better guide. What he calls "encapsulation mechanisms" have been used extensively to reduce envy and contain violence and they have taken a range of forms: from voluntary self-selection and agreed reciprocal insulation by certain communities, to coercive measures imposing forced segregation, through various mixed mechanisms triggering part-voluntary/ part-involuntary balkanization. These mechanisma have all been formed in the name of minimizing intercultural contacts and the possibility of making intercultural comparisons, thereby reducing envy and making violence less likely. This is not the place to survey all these mechanisms, but a few examples along the spectrum of devices might serve as illustrations.

For instance, Trevor Denton has studied the process of acculturation that occurred in Canada in the latter part of the eighteenth century when the British conquered what was then known as Nouvelle France or New France, a territory populated by persons of more or less recent French extraction Denton shows how a form of stabilized pluralism, with two cultures existing side by side but almost completely independent of one another, evolved by keeping face-to-face relationships to a minimum (Denton 1966). An implicitly agreed sociocultural division of labour and policies of limited intercultural contact acted as boundary-maintaining mechanisms that allowed both cultures to retain their autonomy, and dramatically reduced envy and violence. Other examples of negotiated encapsulation might be drawn from contemporary Belgium, Canada or Switzerland, with their segmentations of social space into portions, provinces or cantons with different ruling languages and cultures (Coppieters 1984; Cameron 1974; Steinberg 1976). Each of these cases represents a different stratagem to effect a certain degree of encapsulation in order to ensure intercultural peace. While the boundary-making mechanism is different in each case, and the degree of success in ensuring intercultural peace varies too, it may be said that each appears to have moderated the prospect of violence. In particular, Switzerland has shown how it is possible for minorities, however small, to have inalienable rights, and how the dilemma of majority will and minority rights can be solved by human ingenuity (Steinberg 1976, p. 188). In contrast, the most obvious case of coercive encapsulation was South Africa, where a segregation policy was followed, in 1948, by an apartheid policy. The objectives were similar to those pursued by other techniques of encapsulation of cultural groups: to reduce points of contact by increasing separation, in order to minimize friction and reduce the probability of conflict (Giliomee 1987).

All these techniques have been used and are likely to be used still more in the future, if Ralf Dahrendorf's diagnosis, made with reference to the 1980s, remains accurate for the early twenty-first century (Dahrendorf 1988, p. 156):

> More and more people (it appears) do not want to live in a multiracial or even a multicultural society. Furthermore, this

applies not only to cosy majorities but to the affected minorities as well. They demand their own niche, if not their own region or country. "Separate but equal" was a slogan much scorned by liberals in the 1960s; in the 1980s it has become very topical, and often separateness is stressed more than equality. There is a clamour for homogeneity which rejects all attempts to build civilized societies by having civil societies first and cultural differences within them second.

Dahrendorf concludes (p. 157): "Membership is not conceived as a matter of rights which can be extended, but of unchanging, ascriptive features which must be preserved against contamination by strangers." We are very far from notions of citizenship designed to make cultural diversity bearable.

Yet another strategy is the use of redistributive schemes, in other words the extensive use of sharing as a way to diffuse envy. This important device has been much used in both ancient and modern societies, but it is rarely used as the sole or even main mechanism. It is usually an adjunct to encapsulation. Contemporary Canada might be regarded as a good example of such a mixed solution (Hardin 1974). Such mixtures of encapsulation with redistribution combine physical segregation and social conventions, making certain differences bearable by ensuring that the gap between groups is not eliminated, but seen to be narrowed somewhat by explicit redistribution from those who are better off to those who are less well off. Several forms of taxation and income redistribution schemes are central fixtures in most modern societies. However, it would be unwise to restrict one's view of redistribution to such direct reshuffling of real resources. Regulation is an adroit way to tax and to bestow benefits on different groups. One may therefore identify many policies designed to attenuate perceived or imaginary differentials between cultural groups through regulations or through redistribution of symbolic resources (Breton 1984).

The logic behind such encapsulation and redistribution mechanisms has been to create social distance, either by force or by negotiation, while at the same time making that distance bearable by redistribution, concealment, or other means, and maintaining a nominal or at least rhetorical commitment to equality. However, since the root problem of mimesis is the ideology of egalitarianism, the radical solution that would reduce envy and contain violence is the reintroduction of hierarchy. Most of the social architects who have designed these encapsulation and redistribution mechanisms have gone to a lot of trouble to avoid admitting this, however, because egalitarianism remains too deep-rooted a foundational value to be openly questioned.

Much of this type of containment action is based on the premise that equality and differences are compatible, yet it has been shown that they are not (Dupuy 1985). This is at the centre of a most important double bind plaguing intercultural relations: as a matter of principle, equality denies differences, but we also know that what human are most afraid of is "indifferentiation," or loss of identity. Since they cannot have equality with differences, they must settle for differences with separateness, and therefore for hierarchy (Dumont 1983). The common denominator, therefore, in all the envy-reducing and violence-containing arrangements is the notion of hierarchy.

The acceptance of the principle of hierarchy runs so profoundly against the dominant creed of the day in intercultural affairs that it is crucial that these last statements about hierarchy be well understood. For both Dumont and Dupuy, hierarchy does *not* mean inequality. Rather, it means, first, segmentation; second, the recognition of a global order (as in the hierarchical opposition between right and left hand); and, third, the insistence that it does not represent a unique ordering, but rather a sort of complementarity, so that, as used to be said, the priest and the king have each their own sphere of prominence (Dumont 1983; Dupuy 1985). Egalitarianism leads to a negation of these three characteristics. Indeed, Dumont and Dupuy have shown that racism and other forms of social discrimination are unintended consequences of the individualist/egalitarian credo.

The answer is, therefore, not to chase after some elusive "different but equal" ideal, but to face the need to construct an order that ensures that different groups will be "different but united" (Dupuy 1982). Indeed, Dumont goes so far as stating that no recognition of differences can be anything but hierarchical: "recognition of the other as other . . . can only be hierarchical" (Dumont 1983, p. 260, cited by Dupuy 1985). Thus, all the exercises in social architecture one may undertake to reduce envy and contain violence fundamentally involve the creation of hierarchies. These social contraptions do not necessarily generate inequalities, but they clearly contribute to a slowing down of the process of growing "indifferentiation" that egalitarianism tends to fuel.

It may well be that none of the strategies sketched above is entirely satisfactory, but there is no reason to believe that they

DEEP CULTURAL DIVERSITY

will not continue to be used if Dahrendorf's diagnosis remains accurate. Conversely, attacking these contraptions may not be widely understood as tantamount to questioning the priority given to equality in democracies, but it really amounts to exactly that. As Dahrendorf suggests, separateness is the new dominant value, and it can only lead to a questioning of the house that equality built.

Conclusion

The intriguing results generated by the use of the Myrdal–Tocqueville–Girard interpretative scheme as applied to the analysis of intercultural relations pose interesting challenges to social theorists and liberals. Indeed, liberals, such as Dahrendorf, are concerned that current circumstances have given rise to what he calls "wet liberalism," which "abandons the great gains of a common floor of civil rights and entitlements for all in order to accommodate the separatism of minorities." He regards this as a "big step backwards in the history of civil society" (Dahrendorf 1988). This may be a somewhat romantic reaction. A more realistic assessment might be that the new notion of citizenship most likely to be a useful guide in this new world cannot be built simply on individual rights and equality, but must also incorporate collective rights and differential obligations (Paquet 1989a). A new moral/social contract, based not on "different but equal" but on "different but united" as the key principle, and giving its due place to the power of mimesis, might not be wholly satisfying for the "dry liberal," but it may be the only viable gambit. Such a contract would provide for hierarchies, separateness, and complementarities in institutional forms, in order to reduce envy and contain violence. Sociological imagination will be required to craft adequate and appealing institutions, but sociologists should be able to help, since sociology is, after all, an art form (Nisbet 1976).

The recent explosion of strong demands for the recognition of separateness in most of the countries in the Organization for Economic Cooperation and Development confirms that feelings of ethnocultural self-assertion are almost ubiquitous and that separateness is becoming more important than equality. This is a very dramatic social mutation, which poses quite a challenge if violence is to be avoided. "Dry" liberals may have to realize, sooner or later, that organic solidarity is easier to realize within hierarchical structures than within horizontal ones, and that the disappearance of organic solidarity has often meant a surge of anomie in social systems. Indeed, the risk of anomie, and thus of breakdown in the cultural structure, has been diagnosed by Dahrendorf as one of the peculiar features of modern societies. Re-reading Durkheim and studying societies such as Brazil — where the substantive "individual" is regarded almost as an insult because it refers to a person deprived of an organic link with the social whole — might turn out to be interesting new priorities for those interested in intercultural relations in coming years (Douglas 1986; Dupuy 1982).

Nevertheless, to effect a turn in the direction of separateness and hierarchy in discussions of intercultural relations will require nothing less than a revolution in the minds of liberals, a recasting of the problem of cultural diversity, a critical assessment of the passion for equality that has inspired them, and a decision to give mimesis its proper place in human affairs. It would be unwise to presume that this revolution will occur overnight. Many sacred cows will have to be slaughtered before such a turn can be effected. Let the slaughter begin!

3

Political Philosophy of Multiculturalism

Diversity . . . enshrines certain kinds of factionalism as a universal
good, just like liberty and equality.—Peter Wood

The purpose of this chapter is not to survey the history of multiculturalism, nor to critically evaluate it, but to try to put in place a framework for strategic analysis of the Canadian scene. It aims to do this on the basis of a few distinctions and some of the learning that has been accumulated in Canada and elsewhere along the way, in order to ascertain roughly what plausible scenarios might be envisaged now that pluralism, as traditionally conceived, has given way to multiculturalism.

Pluralism was for a long time an approach that pertained to three groups in Canada, defined by having either British, French or Aboriginal heritage. It would not be unfair to say that governing relations among them was difficult. Their deep cultural diversity did not lead to outright formal war or apartheid, but there was something of both in their intercultural relations. However, the significant waves of migration into Canada from all continents over especially the past fifty years have made the pluralist equation much more complex. Polyethnicity has become a reality now that more than ten million Canadians, out of a total population of around thirty million, are not from any of the three "founding peoples."

Multiculturalism, as an idea and a policy, was at first an innocuous symbolic gesture that emerged as an unintended consequence of the call by the Royal Commission on Bilingualism and Biculturalism, in its final report (1969), for a refurbishment of the status of the French-Canadian community. This forced the Liberal government of the day to provide some greater recognition for the other minorities as well. What might have been originally nothing more than an electoral ploy, or a cynical attempt to get beyond the inconvenient "founding nations" setting by shifting from a world of the few to a world of the many, then mushroomed into a public philosophy about nation-building. The media and the clerisy of opinion-moulders in these other ethnic groups played key roles in this process. The other ethnic Canadians who did not find their roots among the three "founding peoples" were bombarded with rhetoric exalting the irreducible differences between the points of view of those peoples and their own. These other Canadians were understandably bamboozled when they heard representatives of Quebec affirm the right to secede for fear of cultural cross-breeding, while representatives of English Canada demanded centralization in the name of egalitarianism and a fraternal duty to protect the rights of individuals belonging to threatened minority groups in Quebec (Robin, 1989; Buchanan, 1991). These wars did not make much sense to them, and generated considerable unease, which in turn generated lobbying. The notion of a Canadian cultural mosaic came to be more and more solidly implanted in the Canadian psyche as a much more apt metaphor, for all concerned, than the original triad was.

A Framework for Strategic Analysis

In the world of intercultural relations there are two playing fields. The first-order reality is the "material order," the flows of material resources generated under different technical, legal, social, political or economic arrangements. While there are no simple and unambiguous indicators of the ensuing welfare levels for the different communities, or of the economic surplus generated by certain agreed arrangements, the debates, speculations, and discords in this field are mainly about the production, allocation, and distribution of material and financial resources. Analysts chiefly search for technical-legal arrangements or rearrangements likely to maximize the overall welfare level, or the economic or financial surplus, and to ensure that it is not too unfairly distributed.

The second-order reality is the "symbolic order," the images of, and the conversations about, the material order or some features derived more or less clearly from it. It underpins decisions by different social actors, not only to act in certain ways, but to value goods or agency differently. Myths and values play an important role in shaping the representations and perceptions of social actors. While the symbolic

DEEP CULTURAL DIVERSITY

order may be boldly presumed by some to be a simple mirror image of the terrain of realities, this is most unlikely. Assumptions are boldly and often wrongly asserted, and distortions, generalizations, varying emphases, and sheer fantasizing are omnipresent in the construction of these representations. Action by the different stakeholders is often triggered by imperatives emanating from the material order, but action is generated much more often by second-order reality, by the representations that frame the first-order reality (Tversky and Kahneman 1981).

The historical context of Canada had prepared the ground for multiculturalism. As Hugh Thorburn explains, the existence of two linguistic and many ethnic groups in semi-separate portions of the Canadian space since the eighteenth century had made more or less unthinkable the simple assimilationist dream that underpinned the "melting pot" in the United States. In that sense multiculturalism may simply be regarded, and indeed is regarded by some, as an extension of an already existing and distinctively Canadian arrangement (Thorburn in Dwivedi 1989). As a significant portion of the Canadian population came to be drawn from new sources, and as two of the three "founding peoples" (but not the Aboriginals) saw their privileges confirmed somewhat by the Royal Commission on Bilingualism and Biculturalism, it became normal for opinion-moulders in the other Canadian constituencies to press government about, and alert citizens to, the need for some clarification on their status. In this context multiculturalism was a modest symbolic gesture offering heightened respect to these other Canadians. It also served the interests of Trudeau's government in providing a "liberal" alternative to the two-nation policy of the Progressive Conservatives under Robert Stanfield, a policy that was attractive to Quebeckers, but did not serve in any way these "other" Canadians.

The promulgation of the Charter of Rights and Freedoms in 1982 and, crucially, the entrenchment within it (section 27) of the requirement that it "be interpreted in a manner consistent with the preservation and enhancement of the multicultural heritage of Canadians," heightened the expectations of the "other" Canadians. The belief that they might not have to adapt their mores was nurtured, while the cultures of at least two of the "founding peoples" remained dominant in the overall text of the Charter.

There was no single response to this complex evolving situation from the ethnocultural field. Different communities have chosen different paths, some building on the Franco–Anglo separation, others being voluntarily or involuntarily led to different patterns of adjustment, from the conformity/assimilationism position to the segregated enclavic ethnic identity position, along the continuum proposed by Leo Driedger (in Dwivedi, 1989).

The symbolic order shapes the forum, as Raymond Breton points out (Breton 1984):

> The construction of a symbolic order . . . entails the shaping of cultural traditions: values and norms on the one hand; customs and ways of doing things on the other. Perhaps the most important component of this cultural way of life is that embedded in the forms and styles of public institutions . . . [that] become incorporated in systems of ideas that are symbolically reinforced in laws, official speeches and documents, constitutional provisions and their public discussion, advertisements, and other public relations behaviours.

Two central elements are at the core of the construction of representations by the different groups involved in public issues: the vision-distorting glasses that everyone wears because of the experiences in which they anchor their perceptions (Kahneman and Tversky 1979); and the attentional deployment of the group, whereby the structure of attention forms the network of communication between individuals and lies at the heart of the system of resource deployment (Berger 1989). The attention of the citizenry is the scarce resource that opinion-moulders compete for, and mobilizing the attention of the public is the way to frame and reframe problems and issues.

Far from being the locus of perfect competition between ideas and attention-grabbing issues, the forum is pregnant with important synergies. The media play on those and tend to dramatize issues to ensure that they remain in the forefront of the collective psyche. They draw on the sociocultural backgrounds of citizens, on their myths, sensitivities, propensities, and fears, to ensure that citizens are mobilized (Hilgartner and Bosk 1988). In times of pressure or crisis a sort of groupthink may even develop, a tendency for social actors to echo each other's views, and to accept such echoes as confirmation that proves both reassuring and comforting (Janis 1982). The media play a central role in this process. These representations have a determining impact on the sociopolitical multilogue and, in the case of issues as complex and contentious as multiculturalism, the perversion of the languages of problem-definition has often fed a cumulative process of discord under a veneer of mutual understanding (Laurent and Paquet 1991; Nielsen 1991).

The First Twenty Years of Multiculturalism

The gap between expectations and realities has generated resentment and frustration. Many Canadians, "new" and "old," have come to argue, first, that the multiculturalism narrative may have degenerated, unwittingly or not, into a containment policy (Paquet 1989b); second, that, intentionally or not, multiculturalism preserves the reality of the Canadian ethnic hierarchy (Kallen 1982b); and, third, that, as a result of the new ethnocentrism generated by the policy and the new rhetoric of rights that has been carpentered to underpin it, there has been a dangerous drift from unhyphenated Canadianism into ethnic particularism (Kallen 1982a) or, as others would put it, toward a "tribalization" of Canadian society (Spicer 1988). A quick survey of the literature less than twenty years after the original statement of the multiculturalism policy in 1971 (Thomas 1990) acknowledged a growing intolerance among Canadians, a certain degree of xenophobia and racism, and the strong sense that there was a need to develop a national inclusive identity.

While these tensions remained relatively benign in the early 1990s, there was also considerable complacency, because these tensions had not yet exploded into overt conflicts, as they had elsewhere. Instead, they generated nothing more than an ill-defined malaise about the need to specify limits to the expression of multiculturalism (Cameron 1990), about the danger that Canada, being unconcerned about integrating immigrants, might fall into a form of "Babelization," and about the need to foster the development of a "metaculture" based on some kind of authentically Canadian communal psyche. Fundamentally, this malaise remained very much unspoken and underexpressed, even if it was strongly felt. This was largely ascribable to the fact that any statement about the importance of constructing a "national" culture or metaculture was interpreted as essentially racist. In this context, establishing a hierarchy between the positive commitment to Canadian dualism in most parts of the Constitution and the "rhetorical flourish" (Peter Hogg) about multiculturalism in section 27 of the Charter posed quite a challenge. It appeared difficult to deny that a hierarchy existed, yet it also appeared to be politically incorrect to discuss it openly (Bastarache 1988).

In some countries, the ageing host population and the economic benefits from immigration had become the new dominant themes, but these were not in good currency in Canada. A report from the Economic Council of Canada (1991) had argued that what Canadians would gain economically from more immigration was very small. As for the social costs of such increases in immigration, the Council suggested that it was "cautiously optimistic, but that the risk is acceptable," though there were risks of social friction. It was further argued that adjustments in the existing multiculturalism policy "would pay handsome dividends." The nature of these adjustments was hinted at only obliquely, but involved a shift from the existing stance, where multiculturalism demanded too much adjustment by Canadians and too little by immigrants, to one where adjustment responsibilities might be more balanced.

The next idea to be discussed was that of a "moral contract" that might embody not only such an arrangement, but also a variety of measures introduced in order to ease the incorporation of immigrants into Canadian society, by combating prejudice, providing more information and training, and so on (Gagnon-Tremblay 1990). The elephant in the room was the decision of the Supreme Court of Canada in the Singh case in 1985. While everyone had been under the impression that Charter protections did not extend to those without the right of residence in Canada, the Court decided otherwise. As a result, anyone claiming refugee status at the border or a port was able to enter the country and enjoy all the Charter entitlements, such as a work permit, housing, legal aid, and welfare payments, until their case was heard. The hearings were held without any of the normal rules of evidence and claimants' statements were accepted as true, however farfetched they might be. A Nigerian claimant, for example, stated that he did not know how he got to Canada because a witch doctor had made him disappear and sent him here, and his claim was accepted (Francis 2002, p. 36). It is not exactly difficult to understand why Canadians became diffident about the new arrangements.

The unease of successive Quebec governments about the multiculturalism policy has remained strong ever since its inception. It has translated into greater support for a more integrationist model than in the rest of the country. In English Canada, meanwhile, critical comments about multiculturalism became strident on both sides, some demanding a more vibrant and decisive delivery of the promises made in Trudeau's statement (Kallen 1982a), others denouncing the debilitating effect of the policy on the national ethos (Brotz 1980). The proportion of Canadians who felt that "there are too many immigrants coming to Canada" grew from around thirty percent in 1988 and early 1989 to some forty-three percent later in 1989 (Palmer 1991). The sense of unease associated with the fragmentation of the Canadian social fabric became quite prevalent. It was felt that some erosion of the sense of community had been generated and had triggered an emphasis on mere "coexistence," thereby generating a "mosaic madness" (Bibby 1990).

A quick review of the press around 1990 also reveals that there were numerous "new" Canadians who denounced the "serial monoculturalism" that had been the result of the multiculturalism policy up till then. They did so because they felt that as a result "minority ethnics lose the opportunity to develop into their full citizenship as Canadians" (Sugunasiri 1990). It was observed not only that "multiculturalism as a response to the concerns of ethnic Canadians is illusory and gives false hope to those ethnic Canadians who seek to be part of the country," but also that multiculturalism was "insulting because it tends to denigrate the individuality of ethnic Canadians and instead defines them as members of 'different' groups," so that "it pays them to remain peripheral" (Meghji 1990). During 1990 there were numerous comments along these lines from members of ethnic minorities as well as from "mainstream" Canadians, leading to calls for a reframing of the policy (see, for example, *Winnipeg Free Press*, January 12; *Calgary Herald*, March 27; *Le Devoir*, November 10; and *Globe and Mail*, November 17).

In this context, the deliberate funding of institutions of ethnic maintenance was perceived as blocking the natural integrating forces at work and as fostering the "ethnicization" of immigrants. The prevailing policy — which continues to be that there is no official culture in Canada and that immigrants can carry on living with all their customs in Canada — could only be interpreted as using the concept of culture as a way to help ethnic entrepreneurs turn ethnic identities into institutionalized ethnies, or to pay people to "create institutions of otherness" (Harney 1988, p. 85). Indeed, recognizing the cultural identity of a minority group and promoting its maintenance through official financial support was seen by many as an indirect and Machiavellian technique to consecrate the exclusion of members of minority groups from the mainstream. In that sense the tension between national identity and cultural identity was clear. The definition of a *de facto* dominant national culture (or even of two or, more rarely, three "founding" cultures) could only amount to marginalization of the many other groups with different ethnocultural identities. National identity thus came to be seen as the foundation of a hierarchy (Oriol 1979), and as underlining both the unhealthy rapport between ethnic and national culture, and the disingenuousness of a policy that thrived on ambiguities and confusions.

Re-evaluating Multiculturalism since 1990

From the 1990s onwards a more systematic effort has been made, in Canada and in other countries, to theorize but also to evaluate the multicultural leap of faith. The results of this work have led to a significant questioning and tweaking of multicultural strategies all around the world, and to efforts to transform them dramatically. However, given the immense amount of political capital invested in these strategies and the high degree of political correctness associated with them, very often these modifications have been effected while keeping intact the explicit rhetoric defining the conceptual and policy thrusts.

The reasons for this two-level approach are that extraordinary expectations were created by the first twenty years of the multiculturalism ideology. Anything that could be seen as abandoning the policies based on this ideology could only generate significant setbacks at the polls in countries where important sections of the electorate were of recent foreign vintage. The crumbling of the *laissez-faire* multiculturalism philosophy evolved as a result of three sets of observations: challenges to the factual bases of multiculturalism; challenges to its theoretical bases; and the disgruntlement that multiculturalism generated in the citizenry. Yet these three factors could not have generated an effective revision of the multiculturalism strategy without the help of such dramatic events as the assassination of Theo Van Gogh. Even then an honourable face-saving explanation could be articulated and well understood by populations that remained crippled by a high level of political correctness.

The appropriate configuration of such factors materialized earlier in the Netherlands and the United Kingdom than in Canada, and this led to a dramatic volte-face. In Australia the synthetic cluster of forces had a less dramatic impact and therefore the evolution was much more modulated. As for Canada, it has remained crippled by a lack of critical thinking at all levels, and by a robust protective belt theoretically and practically built around the commitment to the "preservation and enhancement of the multicultural heritage of Canadians." It would not be unfair to say that a major segment of the intelligentsia remains in denial about the failures of this experiment. To this day a whole intellectual and political apparatus is geared to ensure that the celebration of multiculturalism remains alive and well, and is very generously funded by the federal government, whatever the facts or the citizens' views.

Nobody denies that *laissez-faire* multiculturalism has failed to help immigrants overcome barriers to full participation in society, that it has also failed to promote creative interchanges among all groups, or that it has instead encouraged parallel lives and socially disconnected enclaves. Moreover, it is also clear that the formidable conceptual apparatus brought forth to bolster the view that minorities would be more effectively integrated via a politics of recognition—a doctrine that has been propagated at great cost by the Canadian government—has been greatly damaged by lethal criticisms at the theoretical level, and that it has been accused, at the policy level, of having fuelled separatism and ghettoization (Joppke 2004). Indeed, in recent years Britain, the Netherlands, and Australia have all veered away from multiculturalism, *de facto* even if *sotto voce*, towards an explicit "true" integration strategy based on citizenship. Two major failures of multiculturalism have triggered this change. One is the fact that multiculturalism postulates, inanely, that all cultures are equal, despite the false and dangerous assumption, as Irshad Manji has put it, that just because human beings are born equal, cultures are taken to be so as well. The other is that multiculturalism has trivialized the notion of citizenship to such an extent that it prevents countries such as Canada from embracing the policy of emphasizing citizenship adopted by the Netherlands, Britain, and Australia as an alternative to multiculturalism.

Alternative Approaches

The "Hotel Canada" syndrome has generated enough unease that there has been subdued but continuous discussion over the last twenty years of alternative ways in which one might harness both the transformed sociodemographic fabric of Canada and the expectations manufactured by a generation's experience of the multiculturalism policy. The first family of suggestions is built around the denial that the present policy is problematic. The present policy is seen as enlightened and adequate, and supposedly needs no substantial change. At best, some cosmetic changes in some programmes might be tolerated. These suggestions are built around that misleading word "integration" (Berry 1991), on the grounds that the best way to facilitate integration is to maximize the degree of comfort for minorities by giving them maximum recognition. Integration is used here in the sense of "rapprochement," although in the late 1960s it clearly had the sense of "acculturation" (Morissette 1991). The term "incorporation" (Breton et al. 1990) is also rather ambiguous, but it most certainly also connotes the sense that the integrity of the incorporated is going to be maintained. Advocates of "rapprochement" or "incorporation" regard the two polar possibilities of complete separation or total assimilation as sufficiently abhorrent and unrealistic to bet on the present middle-of-the-road strategy.

A second family of approaches is still cautiously optimistic about the present state of affairs, but calls for significant adjustments to the present multiculturalism policy to be negotiated as part of a moral contract between Charter and non-Charter Canadians (Economic Council of Canada 1991; Gagnon-Tremblay 1990). These approaches call for mutual adjustment between the two groups, implying both that all cultures are not on par and that there are "official cultures" in Canada. Dominant or older cultures might have to accommodate the newly arrived, but there would no longer be any possibility for the newly arrived to be told that they do not have to adjust and modify their ways of living. The moral contract would be a negotiated agreement or convention about the nature of the mutual adjustments compatible with the maintenance of a certain "Canadian-ness," defined *ex ante*. It would call for continuing negotiations, and the definition of a new set of social armistices between cultures and ethnies, but it would shift the burden of adjustment much more onto newcomers, in contrast to the present arrangement. Whether it is explicitly recognized or not, this is the subtext of the recent debates about "reasonable accommodations" in Quebec and beyond.

A third way, branded "interculturalism," has become the form of pluralism adopted by Quebec to distinguish its policy from the present federal multiculturalism policy. The main difference between the two is the dual constraint of a hierarchy of cultures and a recognition that the intercultural process requires a greater degree of asymmetry. While multiculturalism has been defined by Lise Bissonnette as "a simple collage," she has defined interculturalism as "a gentle ecumenical embrace" (Bissonnette 1988). The degree of osmosis is much greater, but the asymmetrical nature of this osmosis is both more clearly understood and probably much more pronounced. Such an approach emphasizes the integrative capacity of the official cultures, with integration here having a sense much closer to gentle acculturation. For Quebec, "to be integrated is to become an integral part of a collectivity" (Morissette 1991). Other phrases used in connection with this third family of approaches are useful guideposts: *tronc commun* and *priorité au centre de gravité* give quite clearly a sense of a hierarchy of cultures, and the idea of the necessity for both "a common public culture" and "a territorial Quebec nationalism" that can transcend the simple anthropological sense of identity and ethnie, and suggest an asymmetrical moral contract (Harvey 1990a).

A fourth set of approaches gambles on a fusion of cultures to "actively create a new culture": this is transculturalism (Caccia 1984, Robin 1989, Tassinari 1989, Van Schendel 1989). The aim here is to break down the equation between language, culture, and nation, and form a coalition around a symbol such as language, allowing identity to be freed from domination either by a nationality or by a culture, and instead created by a multilogue among all those groups that have contributions to make. The "migrant identity" then evolves as a sort of transnational and transcultural cultural mixing. This fourth way is an optimistic gamble on change and creativity that redefines membership, ethnicity, culture, and nation, and asserts a dynamic conception of cosmopolitanism in opposition to the statism inherent in multiculturalism, whether in the form of "the Canadian mosaic," "the ethnic patchwork" or "the melting pot." It would be, not the end of nationalism, but rather the beginning of a new form of territorial nationalism, based on a renewal of civil society designed to replace the old nationalism based on ethnicity and state (Harvey 1990b).

It is unclear which of these four ways will prevail. Despite a mounting critical literature on assimilation and absorption, there is also a strong sense that a high degree of integration is desirable and a growing conviction that multiculturalism can only lead to an impasse (Spicer 1988, Paquet 1989b, Corbo 1991). Consequently, the current malaise is likely to generate greater efforts to integrate all ethnocultural groups more firmly into civil society. The fact that this integration will occur within the present language terrains, which serve as rallying points, seems to be fairly certain. But the extent to which the new emergent metaculture, which has yet to be constructed, will metamorphose the old and preserve the new, is still to be determined.

PART II

Optimizing Diversity

4

Multiculturalism as National Policy

Let us value the obstacles between human beings ... not in order that
they communicate less, but that they communicate better.
—Jean-Pierre Dupuy

Multiculturalism is a label for many things in Canada. It describes our multiethnic cultural mosaic, it denotes a policy of the federal government, and it refers to an ideology of cultural pluralism. As a Canadian policy it is one of the most daring initiatives of the past forty years, but it has been assessed in varying ways, ranging from being hailed as "enlightened" (Jaenen 1986) to being denounced as a "manipulative device used to perpetuate control over ethnic groups" (DeFaveri 1986) or as a policy that "undermines the foundation for national unity" (Kallen 1982a). These differences of opinion stem to a large extent from the vagueness of the language in good currency and the Rorschachian interpretations that this vagueness nurtures, but also from the difficulty inherent in the assessment of such a bold policy move. Our purpose is to deal with this complex question from the point of view of policy research and cultural economics. What is sought is some clarification of the underlying issues—for there is much confusion about this policy domain—and some provisional conjectural evaluation of the Canadian multiculturalism policy of the past forty years. We have to be satisfied with conjectures because it may not be possible to evaluate such a policy meaningfully except in the very long run.

Our approach emphasizes two major points. First, multiculturalism poses an ill-structured problem for policy analysts. Ill-structured problems have two characteristics: the goals are not known or are very ambiguous; and the relations between means and ends are highly uncertain and poorly understood. These ill-structured problems call for special policy research programmes (Ansoff 1960, Friedmann and Abonyi 1976). Second, the central feature of the multiculturalism policy has to do with symbolic resources and the reallocation of these resources with a view to generating equality of recognition and status. Economists have little experience with the analysis of the economics of symbols or of the sociocultural underground of truth, trust, acceptance, restraint, obligation, social virtues (Hirsch 1976). We shall argue that multiculturalism, as an operation of production and redistribution of symbolic resources, may have had positive effects on ethnocultural pride, and therefore on the efficiency of the economic system, but that such a policy has also a dark side that has been occluded and may be of even greater importance.

Consequently, any provisional and conjectural evaluation of this policy must be prudent because of the ill-structured nature of the problem, and somewhat inconclusive because of the limited development of the economics of symbolic resources. When dealing with such issues one finds oneself in what might have been the predicament of Alfred Marshall when he presented, at the beginning of the twentieth century, his disquisition on the social possibilities of economic chivalry (Marshall 1907).

In the next section we sketch the contours of what we call the paradigm of social practice, which we claim is called for in dealing with issues such as multiculturalism. The two sections that follow present two major characterizations of the policy of multiculturalism in Canada, as containment policy and as symbolic policy. The subsequent section looks at the dynamic that this policy has triggered. The concluding section gives some reasons for the necessary unfinishedness of the current policy, and mentions some of the pitfalls and challenges lying ahead.

Social Learning

Ill-structured problems pose great difficulties for policy research. Analysts must learn on the job about both the configuration of facts and the configuration of values, but they must also manage to learn from the stakeholders in the policy game and from the many groups at the periphery who are in possession of important local knowledge, for, without their participation, no policy can be implemented. Friedmann and Abonyi (1976) have stylized a social learning model of policy research to deal with these ill-structured problems. It combines a detailed analysis of four subprocesses: the construction of appropriate theories of reality; the formation of social values; the gaming that leads to the design of political strategies; and the carrying out of collective action. These four interconnected subprocesses are components of a social learning process, and a change in any one affects the others (Friedmann 1979). This paradigm of social practice in policy research in depicted in a graph by Friedmann and Abonyi that is reproduced in Figure 3 below.

Block B is the locus of dominant values that provide normative guidance either in the transformation of reality or in the selection of strategies for action. Theory of reality (block A) refers to a symbolic representation and explanation of the environment. Political strategy (block C) connotes the political game that generates the course of action chosen. Social action (block D) deals with implementation and interaction with the periphery groups (Friedmann and Abonyi 1976, p. 88). Together these four subprocesses come to life in concrete situations.

Traditional approaches to policy research focus on attempts to falsify hypotheses about some objective reality according to the canons of scientific experimentation. This is too narrow a focus for policy research when the ground is in motion. For the social practitioner what is central is an effort "to create a wholly new, unprecedented situation

Figure 3. A Social Learning Model of Policy Research

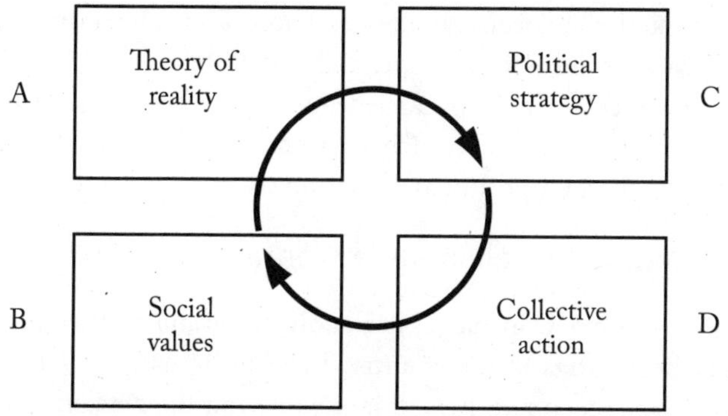

Source: Friedman and Abonyi 1976, p.88

that, in its possibility for generating new knowledge, goes substantially beyond the initial hypothesis." The social learning paradigm is built on reflection-in-action, dialogue, and mutual learning by experts and clients, that is, on an interactive or transactive style of planning. As Friedmann and Abonyi assert (p. 938):

> the paradigm makes the important epistemological assumption that action hypotheses are verified as "correct" knowledge only in the course of a social practice that includes the four components of theory, values, strategy, and action. A further epistemological commitment is to the creation of a new reality, and hence to a new knowledge, rather than in establishing the truth-value of propositions in abstraction from the social context to which they are applied.

When dealing with broad policy issues such as multiculturalism one must be aware of the limits of our tools. One cannot hope to produce anything more than incomplete answers. In the words of Alvin Weinberg, policy research confronts us with trans-scientific questions that cannot be answered by science because they transcend science. Engineering (physical and social) and many of the policy sciences are plagued with such questions: answers may be impractically expensive, the subject matter may be too variable for scientific canons to apply, moral and aesthetic judgment may be involved, and so on (Weinberg, 1972). What is required is a new understanding built on usable ignorance, and institutions should be designed with the ignorance factor in mind, so that they can respond and adapt in good time (Collingridge 1982, Ravetz 1986). Coping with ignorance requires a more transactive and transparent policy process, a deliberative dialogue designed to tap local knowledge, and therefore a change in the way in which policy research is carried out. It has been argued that the transaction costs of running such a system are higher, but the outcome is also more than proportionately improved.

Multiculturalism as a Containment Policy

The social fabric of Canada has been polyethnic and multicultural since the very beginnings of the country. The Aboriginal populations were displaced by French and British invasions, and the new ethnic groups occupied the whole of the territory. Despite some effort to stimulate immigration from other countries in the nineteenth century, in 1881 the population of both non-British and non-French extraction was a shade less than half a million, and represented only about eleven percent of the Canadian population. In 1981, in contrast, this group represented close to one third of the Canadian population (thirty-one percent) and totalled more than eight million people (Sheridan 1987). Only five years later the census of 1986 showed that this group represented thirty-eight percent of the population (Cardozo 1988). After the change in the immigration laws in 1967, the process of visible multiculturalization accelerated. While Asians represented twelve to thirteen percent of all immigrants before 1970, they now represent the bulk of the inflow of immigrants into Canada each year.

Multiculturalism is more than a reality in Canada, it is an ideal type. It has been said of Canadians in the nineteenth century that they had only "limited identities" and did not define themselves entirely and even primarily as Canadians. Rather, they identified first with their region or province, and then only in a limited way with the whole nation (Paquet and Wallot 1987). This reality of "limited identities" made it easier to accept and even to promote the legitimization of multiple identities. From being a country lacking a global identity, inhabited by people loyal first and foremost to regions or sections of the country, we have drifted into a celebration of ethnocentrism and the development of a mosaic ideal-type model of Canada, one in which distinctive ethnic collectivities would make up the country. Collective cultural rights, making all Canadians hyphenated Canadians with equal weights on each side of the hyphen, would ensue (Kallen 1982b). The positive valuation of ethnic segmentation that necessarily follows from these assumptions is not universally shared by all Canadians, but it is most certainly defended with lesser or greater vehemence by many stakeholders.

A soft version of this mosaic model became government policy in the early 1970s. The objectives of the multiculturalism policy as it was introduced in 1971 were fourfold: to support ethnocultural diversity for cultural communities that wished for it; to provide assistance to persons seeking to overcome cultural barriers; to promote creative interchange among ethnic groups; and to assist immigrants in acquiring one of Canada's two official languages. On the encouragement of ethnocultural diversity there were two schools of thought, some supporting the promotion of ethnic identity as being of intrinsic value (Burnet 1976), others suggesting that this would make Canada into some kind of ethnic zoo (Brotz 1980). There was also strong disagreement about the acquisition of one or other of the official languages, between, on the one hand, those for whom living cultures and languages are "inextricably linked," and who argued that the linguistic rights of ethnic communities and immigrants should also be recognized and guaranteed, and, on the other hand, those for whom assimilation into one of the two official languages groups was so essential that the egalitarian mosaic model had to be subjected to an overriding constraint.

If one had to find a label for this Canadian model, an apt description might be "contained pluralism" (Arnal 1986). It is a pluralism that is constrained in a variety of ways by a number of core Canadian principles, including bilingualism, democracy, and non-violence. Within this context multiculturalism is only one of many values officially enunciated and it is limited by all the others. Such important constraints imposed on the pure mosaic model have led many to argue that the policy of multiculturalism within a bilingual framework is nothing but a policy of appeasement and containment, designed to find an accommodation between the demands of non-French/non-British groups and those of French and Anglo-Canadians (Peter 1978).

The limited efforts to implement this new policy until the 1980s lent some support to this view (Lupul 1982). In 1972 a Minister of State for Multiculturalism was appointed and in 1973 an advisory body was established, later to become the Canadian Multiculturalism Council, to help the Minister to implement the policy, but little substantive progress was made during the 1970s. It was only afterwards that there was a growing institutionalization of the policy. In 1982 multiculturalism was consecrated in the Canadian Charter of Rights and Freedoms. In 1985 a Standing Committee of the House of Commons on Multiculturalism was created, and in 1987 it reported and recommended the creation of a separate department. In 1988 new legislation, the Multiculturalism Act, was passed and a full-fledged ministry to deal with multiculturalism was created. Efforts to help to fund training in non-official languages was acknowledged and some work was done on the issue of confronting racism (Stasiulis 1988).

If progress was slow on the implementation front and no all-out effort to move Canadian society towards the ideal cultural mosaic was attempted, this was due to a situation where power and opportunities were still largely shared by the "founding peoples," which could mount effective resistance. However, opposition was not restricted to them. Canadians in general were from the beginning only mildly positive about the idea of cultural diversity (Berry 1977). The political strategy of containment and accommodation by Canadian governments through most of the period since 1971 appears to reflect fairly accurately the state of mind of the nation.

Some cynics would go so far as to say that the objective of the multiculturalism policy has always been for the state to regulate the collective interests and goals of minority groups. In this sense the political strategy may be said to have worked rather well (Stasiulis 1980). However, this conclusion stems from an interpretation of multiculturalism that is too narrowly focused on multiculturalism as a social policy designed to eliminate discrimination and reduce income and employment inequities in a social system that is not free of cultural barriers. Progress on these fronts has clearly been very slow, even though this was most certainly one of the objectives of the original policy. Yet it would be unwise to reduce the multiculturalism policy to this dimension alone.

Multiculturalism as a Symbolic Policy

The Canadian policy on multiculturalism has been interpreted in many different ways. It is not only a social policy designed to eliminate inequalities among ethnic groups and to remove barriers to entry into the mainstream of Canadian life for those of non-French and non-British extraction. It is also, and maybe mainly, the purposeful construction of a mosaic of institutionally complete ethnic communities in Canada, as well as an effort to produce "symbolic ethnicity" with psychological benefits.

Reactions to these partial versions of the multicultural policy have been, on the whole, sceptical. If the goal is the elimination of inequalities, this policy was, arguably, unnecessary; the Charter of Rights and Freedoms, along with other instruments, could very well have taken care of the problem. If the goal is the construction of an ethnic mosaic, then the policy is, according to its critics, simply an unrealistic exercise in social engineering. If "symbolic ethnicity" is the name of the game, other critics have argued that it is an unwarranted activity on the part of the state, on the basis that the state has no business dabbling in the affairs of the mind or in the symbolic order.

Yet none of these partial characterizations fully captures the import of the Canadian multiculturalism policy, and most certainly none of them recognizes the central importance of symbolic ethnicity. This is much more than simple psychological gratification. Changes in the symbolic order often have fundamental effects on the framing of decisions and on the dynamics of society. What's more, the process of enhancing the status of ethnic minorities in Canada has acquired a logic of its own, which has blown away the containment of the 1970s. Some argue that the true significance of the multiculturalism policy is, therefore, to be found at the symbolic level, where it is truly revolutionary. It corresponds to some of the new roles of the state in the affairs of the mind in modern society (Tussman 1977, Lowi 1975), and contributes to the reconstruction of the symbolic system and to the redistribution of social status among linguistic and ethnocultural groups in Canadian society (Gans 1979, Breton 1984). In a nutshell, multiculturalism is an effort to regenerate the cultural-symbolic capital of society, to restructure the collective identity and the associated symbolic contents, and such efforts must be analyzed in terms of production and distribution of symbolic resources (Breton 1984).

Culture is a shared symbolic blueprint that guides action in what is perceived as an ideal course and gives life meaning (Roberts and Clifton 1982). Cultural identity formation is the result of a progressive crystallization of a new ethos, the sum of characteristic usages, ideas, norms, standards, and codes by which a group is differentiated and individualized from other groups (Banfield 1958). In a sense, identity formation occurs very much as capital formation does. Only if a new social contrivance proves to be a profitable economizing device for some will it emerge and persist.

It would be naive to expect a cultural identity to evolve organically in a vacuum. There are public goods and social overhead capital to this production process, as there are in other sectors. One cannot expect that such overhead capital (meta-rules) will evolve organically. The state may have a role to play and the optimal amount of coercion may not be zero. In the same way that the state is seen as being legitimately involved in the creation and sustenance of a monetary system and a political order, it is quite legitimate for the state to sustain the appropriate state of mind. In fact, the state is involved in many ways in shaping the institutions of awareness, in politics of cognition, and in managing the forum, that is, the whole range of institutions and situations of public communication (Tussman 1977).

Multiculturalism as a national policy is a granting of status and recognition to various ethnic communities. While this production and redistribution of symbolic resources may not translate into big budgets, one would be unwise to presume that they are unimportant. Multiculturalism involves redrawing mental maps and redefining levels of aspirations. This in turn modifies the frame of mind of these groups, though not always in a positive way.

It is true that status enhancement through multiculturalism might be presumed to have a positive impact by providing primary securities for ethnic communities, as well as confidence through helping to develop collective pride and redefining higher levels of aspiration. Multiculturalism might be expected to modify the framing of decisions by members of those communities and to engender an outburst of entrepreneurship (Light 1972, Paquet 1986 and 1988). This is a process that has been noted elsewhere. Some have even argued that the ethnocultural communities might take advantage of their intimate awareness and appreciation of cultural nuances to become go-betweens with Canada's foreign trading partners, and thus enhance the country's trade potential (Passaris 1985).

However, there is also the possibility that the multiculturalism policy might have the opposite effect and generate ressentiment in the very population it was meant to upgrade in status. This form of psychological self-poisoning is maximal in societies where more or less egalitarian rights coexist with considerable differences de facto in the power, wealth, culture, and other assets of different groups (Scheler 1958). Nietzsche understood the importance of spite and rancour in modern societies. A French word is necessary here, as Nietzsche clearly understood (Friedenberg 1975):

> ressentiment is to resentment what climate is to weather . . .
> ressentiment is a free-floating disposition to visit upon others the bitterness that accumulates from one's own subordination and existential guilt at allowing oneself to be used by other people for their own purposes, while one's life rusts away unnoticed.

Canadian multicultural policy has had an impact of this sort. An illustration of this outcome is provided by Bharati Mukherjee in the introduction to her book Darkness (1985). Mukherjee is a writer who was born in Calcutta, lived in Toronto and Montreal, and became a writer in Canada before moving to the United States. Her words are rather harsh:

> In the years that I spent in Canada - 1966 to 1980 - I discovered that the country is hostile to its citizens who had been born in hot,

moist continents like Asia, that the country proudly boasts of its
opposition to the whole concept of cultural assimilation . . . With
the act of immigration to the United States, suddenly I was no
longer aggrieved, except as an habit of mind. I had moved from
being a "visible minority," against whom the nation had officially
incited its less visible citizens to react, to being just another
immigrant . . . For me, it is a movement away from the aloofness
of expatriation to the exuberance of immigration. I have joined
imaginative forces with an anonymous, driven, underclass of semi-
assimilated Indians with sentimental attachments to a distant
homeland but no real desire for permanent return . . . instead of
seeing my Indianness as a fragile identity to be preserved against
obliteration (or worse, a "visible" disfigurement to be hidden), I see
it now as a set of fluid identities to be celebrated . . . Indianness is
now a metaphor.

Mukherjee, for one, has not found in the celebration of a fragile cultural
identity a basis for cultural equality, even though one of the objectives
of the multicultural policy was to respond to the status anxieties that
had been voiced. Far from breaking down "cultural jealousies," as Prime
Minister Trudeau had announced in 1971, the policy of multiculturalism
has led to some dissatisfaction within the ethnocultural communities,
to interethnic competition, and to heightened demands for more
symbolic capital (Breton 1986). Moreover, given the expectations
created by the policy, there has been considerable frustration at the
slowness of the process of "realization" of the cultural equality that had
been promised. Political leaders responded to these growing pressures,
especially in the 1980s, by legislating ethnicity as a feature of Canadian
life and by raising the level of multicultural promises once again, this
time from the preservation of cultural heritage to the enhancement of
ethnocultural communities.

The Dynamics of Multiculturalism

One cannot unambiguously predict the future of the multicultural
experiment that Canada has embarked upon. Nothing less than a research
programme paralleling the experiment—tapping continually into the
local knowledge at the periphery, in the ethnocultural communities,
and taking fully into account the values of the stakeholders, their
Weltanschauungen or theories of reality, and the dynamics of political
gaming—could offer any hope of leading to plausible conclusions. Yet
even in such quasi-ideal circumstances the amount of ignorance would
remain great, for the action hypothesis on which the multicultural

DEEP CULTURAL DIVERSITY

gambit is based can be verified only in the course of its unfolding. Even so, a few unintended consequences are emerging from the experiment and might be worth noting, if only to ensure vigilance. Our norm here is the one that E. F. Schumacher suggested for cartographers not knowing for sure if there is a dramatic fall down a river: if in doubt, show it prominently on the map (Schumacher 1977).

The first of these consequences is the growth of ethnocentrism in Canada. Some have referred to this development as a tribalization of Canadian society (Spicer 1988). As Claude Levi-Strauss put it (quoted by Geertz 1986): "loyalty to a certain set of values inevitably makes people partially or totally insensitive to other values ... a profound indifference to other cultures [is] ... a guarantee that they would exist in their own manner and on their own terms." Such impermeability does not authorize the oppression of anyone, but it does lead to a growing segmentation and to a drift away from unhyphenated Canadianism into ethnic bloc action. For even if segmentation is somewhat idealized in the mosaic model, most experts would agree that it leads to ethnic particularism and impedes national unity (Kallen 1982b).

The second notable factor is the resurgence of racism under a different name. As a result of the growth of ethnocentrism a new rhetoric, based on the right of each culture or ethnoculture to be different, has emerged. This rhetoric has led in turn to a sort of juxtaposition of ethnocultures, each claiming the right to be different but also to be equal. A whole literature from de Tocqueville to Louis Dumont (1983) has clearly shown that in any society a difference can only mean a value difference, and thus some explicit or implicit hierarchy (Taguieff 1987). In Canada, intentionally or not, the multicultural policy preserves the reality of the Canadian ethnic hierarchy (Kallen 1982b). A new differentialist neoracism is germinating here, as it flourishes in other polyethnic societies that have consecrated this illusory search for equality-with-difference (Taguieff 1987).

The third negative force at work is the permeating influence of envy in interethnic relations. It has been well-known since de Tocqueville that egalitarian societies, or societies claiming to decree equality, are more prone to envy. The equality among ethnocultural groups decreed by multiculturalism has provoked a heightened degree of interethnic group competition and animosity. Indeed, the sort of ressentiment described above by Mukherjee is at the very root of envy as symbolic behaviour (Foster 1972). This in turn poisons interethnic relations, as the success of group A is perceived by group B as a sign that the latter group has been injured or maligned. The zero-sum game syndrome looms large. Multiculturalism may claim to try to break down cultural jealousies, which in any case amount to only a rather innocuous zeal in the preservation of something possessed (as any dictionary indicates). But it has also been the source of envy, which (as again any dictionary would show) encompasses displeasure and ill will at the superiority of another person in happiness, success, reputation or the possession of anything desirable (Foster 1972). In his study of envy as symbolic behaviour Foster examines the socioeconomic and psychological conditions that breed envy, the cultural forms used by those who fear the envy of others, concealment, denial, symbolic sharing and true sharing, and the institutional forms used to reduce envy. One of these forms is a system of encapsulation, a device making use of the egalitarian principle to produce subsocieties "marked off from each other by social, psychological, cultural and at time geographical boundaries" (Foster 1972, p. 185). The balancing act between ethnocentrism and encapsulation as institutional forms, on the one hand, and envy/ ressentiment as state of mind, on the other, may become a vicious circle with a violent outcome, if they were ever to begin reinforcing each other in our society (Dumouchel and Dupuy 1979).

In parallel, one may tally growing evidence of tolerance, of a shift from juxtaposition to integration, and some signs of the emergence of a new modern concept of citizenship to replace old nationalities. However, at this time one can see only the harbingers of this new citizenship, based on collaboration and achievement rather than status. In any case, these features do not appear to have been fostered by Canada's multiculturalism policy. Proximity and closer personal contacts have eroded barriers, as they do in the "melting pot," and have led to some appreciation of other ethnocultures. While it is difficult to apportion success or failure to the restructuring of the symbolic order undertaken by the multiculturalism policy as such, some have argued that, if anything, this polity might have generated, on balance, more emotionally charged conflicts rather than fewer—conflicts ascribable to status anxieties for those at the top of the vertical mosaic, and to rising expectations and relative deprivation at the bottom.

Conclusion

Canada has faced the challenge of its polyethnic society by defining a multicultural philosophy within a bilingual framework. The national policy of multiculturalism has been translated slowly, but more and more influentially, into a set of institutions that have performed two very different sets of functions. On the one hand, these institutions and policies have helped cultural groups to overcome cultural barriers, and they have promoted some interchange between cultural groups. However, these efforts have been much less important than those that have fostered, on the other hand, the ethnocultural consciousness of cultural groups, and have encouraged institutions and organizations that appeal to such consciousness. As a result, it cannot be said that the multicultural policy has done as much as it might have to nurture an ethnic or race-relations policy in Canada. Rather, it has, up to now, emphasized ethnocentrism and segmentation, with important unintended consequences.

When important new resources appear likely to be channelled towards the implementation of the policy on multiculturalism, it might be useful to repeat a statement often made by Jean Burnet, one of the pioneers in ethnic studies in Canada. Burnet spoke about the need for more research of a different sort, action research, which would help in the redefinition of our multicultural policy in line with directions that are technically feasible, socially acceptable, implementable, and not too politically destabilizing. Such directions cannot be elicited from the centre, but need to tap the local knowledge. There is little point in encouraging specific consciousness among groups that have seemed dormant or largely assimilated for the sole reason that they are there. The continuing redefinition of policy directions is essential in any evolutionary policy domain, but if Canada's bold gamble on multiculturalism is to succeed, such a refocusing is essential now.

If, in the midst of this complex investigation, policy analysts were ever in need of a sextant to guide them toward what might be a sense of Canadian identity in the making, they could do worse than to reread the classic collection of essays Our Sense of Identity (1954), edited by Malcolm Ross. His introduction to the book contains the following gems:

> We [Canadians] kick against the pricks of our necessity. Yet, strangely, we are in love with this necessity. Our natural mode is not compromise but "irony"—the inescapable response to the presence and pressures of opposites in tension. Irony is the key to our identity. . . . Our Canadianism, from the very moment of its real birth, is a baffling, illogical but compulsive athleticism—a fence-leaping which is also, and necessarily, a fence-keeping. .

. . Ours is not, can never be, the "one hundred percent" kind of nationalism. We have always had to think in terms of fifty–fifty. No "melting pot." Rather, the open irony of the multi-dimensional structure, an openness to the "larger mosaic." . . . we can see vividly the actual movement from the dual irony to the multiple irony, from the expansive open thrust of the French–English tension to the many-coloured but miraculously coherent, if restless, pattern of authentically Canadian nationhood.

5

Are There Limits to Diversity?
(co-authored with Paul Reed)

All life's innovations ... have been unable to break through some set
ceiling on diversity.—Richard A. Kerr (2001)

Six sets of considerations define the problem area for this chapter. First, variety is a crucial factor in the development of complex systems, but that does not mean that maximum variety is optimum variety. There is a balance between the sort of variety that generates novelty and the need for a basic zone of security if efficient social learning and creative adaptation are to ensue.

Second, diversity was in the past a matter of accident. Globalization has accentuated the intermingling of populations, and most societies have become more or less polyethnic, multilingual, and so on. It appears that some societies feel disconcerted by such trends, while others embrace them as desirable goals, yet it remains unclear what diversity really means. Is it diversity of agents, of traits, of values or of interests?

Third, variety, like any "social chemical," cannot be examined in isolation, for it interacts with other "social chemicals." For instance, in Canada there has been an extraordinary growth of symbolic group recognition as a result of the Charter of Rights and Freedoms and other such developments. This sort of phenomenon has quickly translated into entitlements. This has meant that symbolic recognition has not been a substitute for material gratification, but a complement to it. This has had revolutionary effects, since diversity has become a lever underpinning and legitimizing seemingly unbounded social demands upon the state.

Fourth, variety appears to be perceived as undermining other social characteristics, such as belonging, identification or commitment. Indeed, it is widely presumed that there may be a trade-off between these desirable social features and variety-cum-diversity. This entails that there is a celebration of diversity, but only as long as there is no sense of threat to these other values. As soon as diversity requirements appear unbounded and of necessity threatening to those other values, there is a slippage in support, even though it does not always dare to show its face.

Fifth, there is a great confusion about the complex relationships linking social capital, social cohesion, and diversity. Social cohesion has been used too often as a proxy for uniformity, and egalitarian actions have therefore been propounded as the source of social cohesion/uniformity. In fact the creation of social capital as a label for civic solidarity, organized reciprocity, and social networks based on trust may be facilitated by a certain degree of commonality and security, but it can also emerge from conflict, since social learning is enhanced by diversity and contrasted perspectives.

Finally, we are confronted with a major problem of vocabulary. We do not have a language of problem definition that is satisfactory. Too many words, such as "diversity," "identity" or "belonging," stand in the way of meaningful dialogue and limit our capacity for analysis by setting multiple traps, of which political correctness is probably the most dangerous, as it has become impossible to raise questions about any of these icons without being accused of bigotry.

Diversity is a source of social energy, but it is also a source of dissipation of social energy. Interaction with evolving contextual factors has made diversity more than a matter of nominal recognition, respect, and tolerance of otherness. It has translated into a legitimate tool to generate group rights, balkanization, and entitlements. As a result diversity has become associated with the erosion of certain basic values, but the trade-offs that diversity imposes on a society are not easily discussed. Indeed, the very notion of governance of diversity—the intentional use of instruments to ascertain how much is too much, and to ensure that such a threshold is respected—is challenged as politically incorrect. This is a remarkably naïve position to adopt. Diversity in this perspective would not be a matter of choice but a matter of fate. Refusing to govern diversity appears to be blessed with the name of virtue, while any effort at attempting to manage diversity is immediately perceived as an effort to limit it and therefore is chastised as a sign of latent fascism.

DEEP CULTURAL DIVERSITY

It is our view that the governance of diversity is a central challenge facing pluralistic societies and that no responsible society needs to accept being shaped by faceless external forces. The question is, how is this job to be done?

Governance in the Face of Pluralism

Governance is defined as effective coordination when resources, information, and power are widely distributed. Diversity entails of necessity a greater degree of variety and pluralism, and therefore causes new difficulties in arriving at effective coordination. On the other hand, pluralism and variety are also, undeniably, sources of innovation and wealth creation. It is a question of costs and benefits.

Plural societies are societies characterized by diversity, but also by an explicit recognition that individuals and groups are motivated by different priorities, and that they can legitimately have different value systems. To pursue their different objectives and goals they require positive freedom, that is, the capacity and the opportunity to actively and effectively pursue these values, and the elimination of the constraints or unfreedoms that would prevent them from doing so. Plural societies also deny that there is any overriding value. This entails the inevitability of conflicts, and the need to develop reasonable and effective conflict resolution mechanisms based on some meta-credo, however minimal, that the disputants may share. While the plurality of conceptions of the good life increases the range of valued possibilities, not all possibilities are reasonable, so there is also a need for limits, and for the justification of such limits as excluding unreasonable possibilities, or unreasonable ways of pursuing them, or ways that might simply maximize conflicts.

The governance of diversity entails the harnessing of the forces at work in defining the desirable degree of balkanization and mixing involved in the fabric of an efficient and decent society. True variety is not simply additive layers or groups of individuals living in totally separate worlds, as if in a quilt. Such a patchwork generates apartheid societies that are neither plural nor diverse in a true sense.

If the degree of interaction between groups cannot be zero, it may vary greatly according to the different regimes in place. A regime is a set of explicit or implicit principles, norms, rules, behaviour patterns, arrangements, decision-making procedures, and institutions around which actor expectations converge. It is neither orderly nor systematic, but reveals some internal consistency and technical proficiency. The mechanisms or techniques of collaboration are guideposts, moral contracts, conventions, and the like that are at the core of the regimes. They are not only the processes through which coordination occurs, but also the ways in which, implicitly, the limits beyond which one is not allowed to proceed are defined.

De facto, the set of rules in good currency and generally acknowledged are defining limits, in very much the same way that the speed limit on the road implicitly spells out what is regarded as the tolerable death toll. However, there is often a gap between the rules and the state of mind of the population. Rules are defined in the light of sanctimonious discourses that do not always take into account the unintended consequences of what appear on the surface to be reasonable rules. Good governance entails a process of guiding that is transparent, inclusive, participative, and fairly effective, through the crafting of mechanisms in keeping with the dominant logic of the regime, and is likely to generate a capacity to transform as circumstances change.

Limits to Diversity through a Contract of Citizenship?

Are there limits to diversity? If so, what are they? These two questions are related but different. It may well be that one can agree that there are notional limits to be respected, but that they cannot be defined precisely, only taken into account and acknowledged through mechanisms that the deleterious effects of their being exceeded, and it may also be the case that there is no consensus about the need to design a governance system. As for the role of citizenship, either as a basic ligature that might serve as a gauge to determine if such limits are exceeded, or as a mechanism to ensure the requisite basic necessary security zone, it has at least the benefit of making a taboo topic debatable.

On the question of the existence of limits to diversity, it is fair to say that there is a certain consensus. In principle most observers accept the idea that excessive diversity would generate chaos and make the task of coordination impossible. However, it does not follow that there is agreement that such limits are definable, or that mechanisms should be put in place to ensure that they are not exceeded. Most observers have been satisfied to admit that such limits exist, but then refuse to go any further, on the grounds that defining them would entail some form of exclusion. Moreover, the debates about such limits have proved so divisive and ideologically tainted, with so much nastiness and disingenuousness thrown in for good measure by those who feel that any limit to diversity is a form of racism, that the majority of observers have been satisfied to transfer the debate onto the terrain of citizenship.

What, then, is citizenship? Some see citizenship as legal status, others see it as participation in governance, and still others see it as belonging. These ideal types are presented in Figure 4.

At one apex of this citizenship triangle is the liberal notion of citizenship, rooted in the notion of legal status, which remains prevalent in the Anglo-Saxon world. On this view citizenship inheres in individuals, who are seen as the bearers of rights, and is couched in a language of rights and entitlements. Individuals are required to do very little, if anything, in order to become or remain citizens. Citizenship as legal status minimizes participation requirements, expects little sense of identification, and emphasizes the centrality of negative freedom, understood as protection against interference with individual choices.

At a second apex is the civic republican view of citizenship, which is largely couched in terms of duties, and defines citizenship as a notion with a high valence given to practice and participation: the citizen is a producer of governance. It calls on individuals to become members of the community, to participate in the culture and governance of the

Figure 4. The Citizenship Triangle

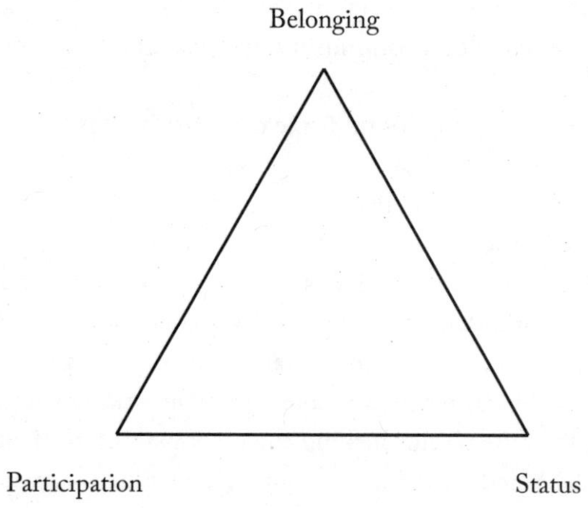

community. This concept emphasizes positive freedom, predicated on a person's being able to do this or that, as well as the duty to help others in that respect.

A third apex emphasizes neither status nor participation, but the process of belonging. In this zone of the triangle what is of central importance is the recognition, respect or esteem given to the individual and his circumstances. There are two important variants of this polar case: one in which recognition is simply acknowledgement of basic characteristics that are already there; and another that focuses on the "construction" of status and differences by activism designed to transform the symbolic order (Tully 2000, Markell 2000).

These three ideal-type conceptions are meant merely to illustrate the broad range of widely available notions of citizenship. One may find countries anchoring their notions of citizenship all over the terrain of the citizenship triangle, corresponding to different mixtures of status, participation, and belonging. In any concrete real-world situation citizenship in a plural society is a transversal mix of these three components (Paquet 2005b). Indeed, any concrete notion of citizenship condenses some of these dimensions and represents a nexus of moral contracts that deals with these different dimensions in a particular way. Consequently, citizenship may cover a whole range of possible meanings, with all sorts of intermediate cases giving different weights to each of these dimensions. Accordingly, instead of being absorbed into a simple, formal, and legal linkage between the citizen and the state, the citizenship relationship has evolved into a looser but more encompassing covenant, covering a web of relationships both among members of a community, and also between them and the state.

Finally, the proliferation of multiple citizenships has heightened the complexity of these arrangements and has generated a whole new set of problems for persons or organizations purporting to hold membership in many clubs at the same time. This has led both to ugly abuses of power—as when a group of citizens, such as Japanese Canadians after 1941, has been branded by a paranoid state as likely to collaborate with the enemy—and to individuals and organizations using a "citizenship of convenience" to take opportunistic advantage of all possible entitlements while shirking the responsibilities of citizenship. This should have led to debates about meaningful arbitrages among competing allegiances, or at least to the emergence of a dominant logic acting as a lodestar to guide collectivities in such choices. However,

DEEP CULTURAL DIVERSITY

not all countries have had the fortitude to deal squarely with such problems. Many have found it politically incorrect to even raise these issues.

There are daunting challenges in eliciting the requisite participation and engagement for a society to thrive and prosper when faced with a more and more variegated population in a more and more turbulent world. The mixture of negative and positive freedoms likely to provide the optimal integration—capable of providing ample possibilities for differentiated citizenship while ensuring the minimal rules of engagement necessary for the society to succeed—need not necessarily have evolved organically. One must therefore identify the ways in which the state may, wittingly or not, influence the terms of integration. The central challenge is to use the contract of citizenship as a terrain on which to construct the terms of integration, identifying the limits to diversity only in this oblique way.

Canadians as individuals are inclined to be both much more demanding in their definition of citizenship than Canadian officials tend to be, and to be much more willing than bureaucrats and politicians to craft de facto workable terms of integration. They define integration not only in terms of a bundle of formalized rights and freedoms, but also in terms of responsibilities, attitudes, and identities. Yet public officials, for whom pragmatism is generally the dominant value, claim to have no concern about defining any such set of expectations about the terms of integration for newcomers, on the grounds that one cannot ask anything from newcomers that one does not require explicitly from the native-born. Making additional demands on newcomers is branded automatically as a sign of intolerance, chauvinism or racism. As a consequence officials are not very concerned about ensuring that newcomers are provided with the requisite help to make them capable of participating fully in the host society. Officials also tend to feel that they have no legitimate basis for refusing to modify Canadian ways in response to requests by newcomers who claim that such ways constitute a discriminatory stance against them.

The result is not only a lack of debates in Canada about the limits to tolerance and diversity — except in Quebec, and there only of late — but a natural drift, as jurisprudence cranks out case after case, towards a refusal in official circles to recognize that there are any limits to diversity at all. This is no longer pluralism but a leap of faith, implying that, if some limits should prove to be necessary, they will emerge organically. This is quite a gamble, since the required terms of integration are in fact likely to emerge only from a continuous renegotiation as expectations and environments change, as well as from an explicit articulation of rights and responsibilities, of the limits to tolerance of the host society, and of the obligations upon newcomers to adapt. This is the challenge that Canadian leaders refuse to confront.

Their refusal is understandable, but it is not inconsequential. The lack of a clear notion of the responsibilities of citizenship can only lead to fuzziness in the definition of the limits of tolerance. More than any other factor, it is the very reluctance of Canadian governments to foster debates leading to a clear articulation of what the guideposts are in this fuzzy land that generates the most concern among those who favour tighter controls on immigration to Canada. The danger in this unwillingness to establish clear conditions of admission and clear terms of integration is that it has allowed extreme forms of erosion of trust, as significant groups have found it opportune to take advantage of Canadian benefits without accepting any of the obligations that constitute the other side of the moral contract of citizenship. This can only lead in the longer run to action that generates greater exclusion than would otherwise be desirable as a result of such abuses, and both "old" and "new" Canadians are, consequently, bound to be worse off.

However frustrating and ineffective the "official" Canadian way may, appear, by radical standards, it may well be that it is an efficient, even truly attractive strategy for polyethnic, multicultural, and plural societies in general, wherever they do not have the capacity to orchestrate the sort of open and vibrant debates that Australia, for example, has seemingly managed to conduct in a legitimate and peaceful way. In our context, it is as if the Canadian way entails a delegation of the task of developing workable terms of integration to civil society and to local neighbourhood groups. Raymond Breton has underlined the importance of this "social" approach in a paper on this issue (Breton 2003). Indeed, Australia may be wholly unrepresentative as to the capacity of most societies to deal with citizenship issues in transparent, wide-ranging national debates. Canada, with its crab-like, oblique, and local mode of operations, may come much closer to standing in for what is observed generally—a fractured and somewhat disconcerted socioeconomy, incapable of anything but ad hoc arrangements. As a result, the slow, scattered, unfocused, minutely incremental, and locally based approach that Canada has been known for, a process largely based on civil society and on local initiatives, may not be an

DEEP CULTURAL DIVERSITY

unreasonable strategy for most countries. Unwittingly, then, Canada may have invented an approach that can be used by many small nations to engineer the right strategy for preserving their cultural identities in a globalized world, while allowing their component communities to maintain both their integrity and their capacity to be heard.

In this context, the decision by the Quebec government to create the Bouchard–Taylor Commission and thereby to generate a society-wide multilogue on these issues may be a bold initiative that leads to some robust debates on new terms of integration. It may, however, turn out to have been a divisive move that, in its futile search for a golden rule of integration that is not achievable in society at this time, leads to a greater degree of frustration, as neither newcomers nor old-timers find, in or after this failed attempt, anything that they would regard as workable terms of integration.

Conclusion

The Canadian approach (outside Quebec) is characterized by a two-tracked strategy. On the one hand there is a cacophonous public forum, poorly managed by governments, where the powers of disconcertion are modulated by a systematic avoidance of general, ambitious, and all-encompassing debates about citizenship, the terms of integration of new immigrants, and the governance of diversity. On the other hand, difficulties are resolved in situ most imaginatively, even if in an ad hoc manner. Limits to diversity are identified locally as being quite different from place to place and from time to time. These limits are less a matter of concern, as they have recently become in Quebec, than a matter for discussion and resolution, in schools, churches, and workplaces. These are the locations for social innovations that may push back the limits to diversity case by case, but do not hold the key to unbounded diversity across the land. Some of these innovations may be exportable, others not. The challenge is to ensure that dealing with the limits to diversity does not remain a taboo topic. Otherwise, one may well stumble blindly into abysses that might have been avoidable.

Whether the more ambitious and all-encompassing approach adopted by Quebec will do better than the approach used in the rest of Canada remains to be seen. Tackling incompletely theorized domains, in a world characterized by little taste for robust discussion, lack of courage by politicians, and a very high degree of political correctness may turn out to generate explosive results.

Relying on local experiments is not without dangers either. The recent initiative, at the school board level in Toronto, to institute segregated Afrocentric schools in a city wher close to half the population has been born out of the country, may have a devastating effect on the terms of integration in Canada if it were to trigger a wider movement toward generalized segregation in public institutions. This would generate deeper fault lines between religious, racial, and linguistic groups, and might engineer a cascading effect on public institutions throughout the country that moight transform the fabric of Canadian society in a most unfortunate way.

This comes to show that neither broad sweeping multilogue in the public sphere nor the reliance on local initiatives by civil society can be regarded as strategies without perils. Vigilance is therefore required.

Diversity, Egalitarianism, and Cosmopolitanism

Diversity as fraternity lite.—Raymond D. Boisvert

C anada, like many other countries, has chosen to cope with diversity by adopting an official policy of "laissez-faire multiculturalism plus." This has meant allowing deep cultural diversity to crystallize, helping it to do so with some financial support, and conferring enormous moral authority upon it, chiefly through the provision in the Charter of Rights and Freedoms that the Charter itself has to be interpreted in "a manner consistent with the preservation and enhancement of the multicultural heritage of Canadians."

Laissez-faire multiculturalism plus thus strengthens and institutes deep cultural diversity, which entails not only consecrating it as a primary good, but also some hardening of the membership–governance axis (see Figure 2 in Chapter 1) in order to promote nations and ethnies to a foundational role. The additional thrust of the human rights ideology and of financial support for multicultural activism has helped a particular regime crystallize in Canada and in kindred countries that emphasizes the differences among diverse groups, the place and rights of minorities, and the centrality of recognizing the identity of such groups. These characteristics tend to promote the emergence of multiplex relationships within which each of these dimensions reinforces the others. The emphasis on difference, identity, and recognition can only ensure that minorities develop an entitlement mentality and are "invited" to make use of the full power of the Charter to proclaim and enforce group claims.

It is hardly surprising that a certain apartheid ensues, however much it may be suppressed and denied, and even though it was not necessarily the objective pursued. In fact much theorizing over the past thirty years has suggested that consolidating the symbolic recognition of minorities and their legitimacy was a meaningful way to foster integration. This "multicultural assumption" (Berry) is indeed the foundational premise of the first three families of approaches referred to in Chapter 3. Yet this emphasis on diversity has not led to any reduction in the emphasis on equality and egalitarianism, which remain pillars of modern 'progressive' social democracies. In this chapter we raise two questions. First, are multiculturalism and egalitarianism compatible? Second, if there is a dilemma involving multiculturalism and egalitarianism, is there a way in which one might escape it through cosmopolitanism?

Multiculturalism and Egalitarianism

One of the consequences of defining diversity as a primary good has been that it has been pursued as such. This could only mean that it might at times be pursued to the detriment of other objectives, such as freedom, efficiency or equality. There have been debates, for example, about whether the multicultural approach might limit the freedom of the members of various groups; about whether the tribalization it generates might, on the positive side, provide beach-heads from which to conquer foreign markets, but might also, on the negative side, underpin the emergence of segmented labour markets in the host country; and about whether the balkanization of the host country's population might reduce the degree of effective solidarity underpinning the redistributive schemes of the welfare state. None of these trade-offs is insignificant, and it can reasonably be asserted that, in most cases, the determination of the nexus of costs and benefits attached to the multicultural approach is complex, and does not necessarily lead to any consensus.

Probably the most sensitive trade-off for those who claim to be progressive is the one between multiculturalism and solidarity. Since progressives are clearly of the opinion that both these goals are absolutely desirable, they would face a serious dilemma if it were to be discovered that the multicultural approach generates lower levels of social cohesion and solidarity, and might thereby undermine the egalitarianism-driven welfare state. This question was raised explicitly by Brian Barry (2001) and generated a heated debate. The main points in contention were aptly synthesized by David Goodhart (2004) in response to a more specific question: "is Britain becoming too diverse to sustain the mutual obligations that underpin a good society and a generous welfare state?" The issue has since received a fair amount of attention (Banting and Kymlicka 2006; Banting et al. 2007), and a synthesis of the recent findings emerging from work done by a consortium of Canadian researchers on this general theme has recently been prepared by Keith Banting (2007).

Banting's nuanced summary directly tackles the two central questions: are there deep tensions at work between heterogeneity and redistribution, and between recognition and redistribution? The results of inquiries addressing the first question indicate that, on the basis of the empirical work done by the research team, "there is no evidence ... that countries with large immigrant populations have greater difficulty in sustaining and enhancing their historic welfare commitments. But large increases in the foreign-born population do seem to matter" (Banting 2007, p. 7). As for the second and much more difficult question, there seems to be no support for it as a bald claim, but there is an admission that "there are more localized circumstances where particular forms of recognition erode particular forms of redistribution" (Banting 2007, p. 10).

The debate reached a climax in the summer of 2007 with the publication of Robert Putnam's paper "E Pluribus Unum: Diversity and Community in the 21st Century." On the basis of a study of more than 30,000 people and more than 40 communities across the United States, and after normalizing the data to standardize for all sorts of extraneous factors, Putnam came to two clear conclusions: that more diversity means lower social capital; and that diversity, at least in the short run, seems to entail less social cohesion—less volunteer work, less charity, less voting, less involvement, less belief that citizens can make a difference.

Given the time lags that might be involved in the generation and disappearance of social tensions, the empirical work on these difficult questions leaves them unresolved for the long run, and the debate continues. But, even though the empirical work does not provide robust support for the hypothesis that there is some tension and trade-off between recognition and solidarity, as measured by redistribution, it remains quite difficult to believe that an increase in symbolic recognition, and therefore in separateness, does not reduce solidarity. Consider, for example, the extraordinary resistance to any symbolic recognition of Quebec as a "distinct society," or the general apprehension generated in Canada by the slogan "different but equal."

Indeed, much anecdotal evidence appears to reveal that the sharper and the more publicly celebrated the symbolic recognition of separateness, as in the case of French Canadians or Aboriginals, the more the sense of belonging and trust is eroded (Banting et al. 2007). One can choose to ascribe such antagonism to history, but it would be simplistic to discard separateness as a root cause. It is clear that, if recognition and separateness are clearly encouraged by the multicultural approach, it can only generate a weakening of the social fabric over the long haul. How can the determination to remain apart generate anything different, whatever the multiple regressions suggest?

The worst aspect of the formalization and judicialization of differences that the multiculturalism approach encourages, and of the parallel insistence that there is no such thing as Canadian culture or that it is "thin" at best, is that these developments foster a certain civic malaise. They shape a certain way for minorities and immigrant groups to think about their problem, to bet on their difference, to play the "humiliation card," and to demand more equalization. Indeed, one of the dirty secrets that nobody wishes to face is that the virtuous circle of more solidarity generating more redistribution generating more solidarity is broken. Recognition of separateness cannot but generate less solidarity, however much time it may take to be revealed in statistics, and this can only translate into less willingness to indulge in egalitarian intercultural redistribution. This is the recent news. We already knew that interregional and intergroup laundering of money, and other redistribution schemes, have long since ceased to generate national solidarity, if they ever did, except in the sermons of the progressives for whom such redistribution remains an article of faith. Wall-papering over the cracks and making Panglossian declarations that no U-turns are required may reassure some, but they hardly amount to a reasoned way to react to growing tensions.

The fundamental problem raised by the debate around the trade-off between multiculturalism and solidarity is that it has been haunted by the spectre of egalitarianism, which remains the reference point. Consequently, since this reference point is non-negotiable, no trade-off is possible with the other absolute—identity and recognition of separateness. Indeed, the conclusion of Banting et al. (2007) is built on the reaffirmation that the search for equality is the road to intercultural peace and prosperity. Putnam's recommendations do not emphasize redistribution, but they seem equally underwhelming: linguistic training, more forums for intercultural interaction, stronger

DEEP CULTURAL DIVERSITY

interethnic ties as a step to integration some day—more of the Berry–Taylor "reasonable accommodations" stuff—and some education about short-term pain generating long-term gain (Putnam 2007). This calls for a re-reading of de Tocqueville, whose sociology of equality, as we saw in Chapter 2, offers quite a different message. Recognition, bridging, and redistribution may reduce the differences, but the smaller the differences, the higher the tension.

What has to be debunked is the sacred character of egalitarianism, which needs to be replaced by a weaker and softer notion more likely to lend itself to trade-offs. "Equability" may be a more useful reference point. Merriam–Webster defines "equability" as "lack of noticeable, unpleasant, or extreme variation or inequality." The term may serve as a reference point in finding the right balance in the practical search for openness, inclusiveness, and high performance, since it appears to capture well the sort of balancing act that is required. Yet it is a word that is not in good currency in Canada, where words such as "equity," "entitlement," and "egalitarianism," all much more legalistic and reeking of non-negotiability, are the reference points most often quoted. This often results, as we shall see, in inclusion claiming to trump all other concerns, and in legitimacy trumping effectiveness. Nevertheless, "equability" would transform the doctrinaire position of the progressive intelligentsia by moving us from an "either–or" to a "more or less" framework. Instead of requiring staunch denials that there is any possibility of a trade-off between equality and diversity, it would foster a discussion in which both terms were open to some accommodation. This would pose the challenge of how much egalitarianism may need to be abandoned in order to accommodate a requisite but not absolute degree of separateness and recognition. Equability would thus raise the possibility of acceptable inequalities. On the other side, however, the notion of recognition remains more or less an absolute. Consequently, one may not be able to proceed further without some relativization of what multiculturalism has tended to absolutize.

Cosmopolitanism as the Way Out

One way to resolve this second conundrum may be to start from the other end of the spectrum. Starting from a position that emphasizes inherent differences, separate status, fractured lines, divisions, and "recognized" reified identities means having to find ways to overcome these differences, both inherited and nurtured, for deep diversity appears to have to be tamed. Instead, one might prefer to build on a loose notion of "cosmopolitanism." This would connote a vague notion of worldliness, of readiness both to accept that differences, however profound, are not so very important, and to accept that one has to live with largely unacclimatized evolving groups. The consequence would be that a civil-society-based regime might allow us to economize on all those integrative constructs based on nations-cum-ethnies that have, up to now, proved beyond our reach.

Yet "cosmopolitanism" is a tainted word. It has been used by many to connote quite different realities, from the way of life of the successful, who cut the links to their original communities to partake in the exclusive networks of supranational elites (Bauman 2001, Chapter 4), to the lifestyles of those vagrants not bound to any country, and characterized by a certain rootlessness and footlooseness as they move around the world (Rosenau 2003, p. 122). This is a particularly cavalier and dismissive way of addressing what is in fact an alternative way of dealing with "the other." K. A. Appiah (2006) has rehabilitated the concept of cosmopolitanism by defining it as a meshing of two strands: the idea of obligations to others, and the idea of taking interest in them and learning from them (p. xv). The reasonable cosmopolitan relates to the other in a way that is neither utopian—for treating all human beings as equals is both unnatural and unrealistic—nor entirely disconnected, since regarding strangers as belonging to another species is also unacceptable, except to bigots. Cosmopolitans follow a third way. They presume that "all cultures have enough overlap in their vocabulary of values to begin a conversation" (Appiah 2006, p. 57). This does not presume that there will be agreement, only that there will be a conversation. Cosmopolitanism is "connection, not through identity, but despite difference" (p. 135). In this sense, cosmopolitanism is the obverse of multiculturalism, which wishes to establish connection through building stronger separate identity claims, and argues, as Charles Taylor and others have done for decades, that more robust recognition will make connections easier.

Let us agree from the start that radically strong cosmopolitanism is unreal, and that the idea that each of us has equal responsibilities to all persons around the world is utopian. At the same time, radically weak cosmopolitanism, or boutique cosmopolitanism, based on the most superficial interest in exoticism and the like, is anodyne. What we might call intermediate cosmopolitanism is neither anodyne

DEEP CULTURAL DIVERSITY

nor superficial. It asserts that "all persons have a negative duty . . . toward every human being not to collaborate in imposing an unjust institutional order upon him or her" (Pogge 2002, p. 89), and it adds that, while special "thicker" relationships can increase what we feel we owe to closer associates (family, compatriots, and so on), they cannot decrease what we owe to everyone else.

Such an intermediate cosmopolitanism provides an interesting reference point through which one might wish to appraise other strategies for coping with deep cultural diversity, such as multiculturalism. It is important to have such a reference point, since, without one, no meaningful benchmarking is possible. Indeed, having two such reference points—cosmopolitanism and multiculturalism—might be even better than having one.

Two clarifications are necessary at this point. First, our intent is not to promote one perspective or another, but to deconstruct what appear to be the foundations of two philosophies that have been immensely influential in determining how deep cultural diversity has been dealt with. Our analytical emphasis therefore will be more on differences than on similarities. Second, our point is not to pitch either approach against the other in the form of a binary choice. Rather, it is to suggest that there is a whole range of plausible positions to be explored along the spectrum between the multicultural approach, based on essentialism and difference, and on a nation/ethnie base, and the cosmopolitan approach, based on reciprocity, indifference to difference, and on civil society.

For multiculturalists, grosso modo, culture, nationality, and identity make solidarity and trust possible. These in turn produce genuine deliberation and therefore constitute a requirement for genuine democracy. Multiculturalists tend to reify culture and identity somewhat, and are led to call for cultural rights to formalize the entitlements that flow from them. This may be said to lead to an overstatement of differences and to an inflation of the rights to recognition of these differences. Such hypertelia generates a hardening of the boundaries, a flourishing of ethnopolitical entrepreneurship to reinforce them, and a weakening of citizenship. There are, however, differences of opinions about the extent to which these consequences are determining (Kymlicka 2001, Brock 2002).

Conversely, cosmopolitanism tends to promote a transcultural approach that emphasizes less the variety of group cultures than the cultural variety of individuals, and their multiple and limited identities.

Instead of consecrating the "coexistence of non-communicating vases" and identity politics, it promotes a mediated solidarity between strangers, emerging from our shared humanity, and based on the equal worth of individuals and a high degree of impartiality of treatment, all claims arising being subject to rules that all can share. These presumptions avoid the dangerous trap (identified by Irshad Manji, among others) that is set for those who make the false assumption that, just because human beings are born equal, cultures are too. In fact, as Michael Ignatieff put it aptly, "without this fiction—that human similarity is primary and difference secondary—we are sunk" (Ignatieff 1999, p. 70). What must be avoided, at all costs, is losing sight of the fact that we are individuals and that we must see others as such as well, since what would follow is the turning of individuals into, as Ignatieff puts it, "carriers of hated group characteristics" (Held et al. 1999, Wilson 2006). John Keane (1998) refers to the "new civilians" as those individual bearers of such a basic identity that they refuse any primary marker by sole virtue of being a person belonging to a particular group.

One of the key elements brought to light by comparing the multicultural approach to the cosmopolitan approach is the fact that the multicultural approach, very much like assimilationism, assumes that majority and minority cultures are bounded and are in rivalry. It insists on a separate minority existence, and, in Canada, on the maintenance and enhancement of that separateness. The cosmopolitan approach does not presume that cultures are different, but rather that individuals partake in a variety of cultures. As a result, the cosmopolitan approach perceives the multicultural approach as threatening for citizenship, and prefers to pave the way to experiments with forms of true integration via a refurbished notion of citizenship. Indeed, citizenship is seen in the cosmopolitan approach as a most useful conduit to serve as a cauldron in which both majorities and minorities are transformed. One may therefore suggest that the drift towards citizenship as the way in which some countries, such as the United Kingdom, the Netherlands, and Australia, are trying to cope with the challenge of deep cultural diversity may well amount to developing some workable new covenant inspired by cosmopolitanism.

This new reference point is built on concord, or what Aristotle called homonoia, "a relationship between people who . . . are not strangers, between whom goodwill is possible, but not friendship . . . a relationship based on respect for . . . differences" (Oldfield 1990;

Paquet 1999a, p. 203). The new reference point will need to be built on a strong rationale and a robust institutional infrastructure for concord. Raymond Boisvert has attempted to capture the result of this sort of exercise. In his view diversity can only be tackled by fraternization, or what he calls creolizations, a dynamic process of creative interplay based on amalgamation, merging, and blending (Boisvert 2005). This squarely and resolutely challenges the silo-style coexistence and separateness that the multicultural approach invites. Whether this alternative approach, based on trust and a capacity to interact with strangers in a positive and limited but exploratory and learning way, is workable is a legitimate question. It most certainly appears to hold more promise, and to present less risk, than the present multicultural strategy for decision-makers in, for example, the United Kingdom and the Netherlands.

In a fundamental way one is sent back to the questions raised by Michael Ignatieff more than twenty years ago. In his book *The Needs of Strangers* (1984), Ignatieff explored ground zero of human obligation to the claims of strangers, searching for a language of the good that might answer these questions, but leaving his readers' appetites unsated. Some twenty years on K. A. Appiah (2005) has attempted to provide a language to deal with these questions in what he calls a "wishy-washy version of cosmopolitanism" (p. 222). This is rooted in two concepts of obligation that draw on Ronald Dworkin's distinction between morality and ethics. Morality has to do with what we owe to others, ethics with what sort of life it is good for us to live; morality involves duties to persons with whom one has "thin" relationships, while ethics involves duties to oneself and to those with whom one enjoys "thick" relationships (p. 230). There are complex trade-offs between these normative registers, but it would be unwise to assume that one should always dominate the other. As Appiah puts it, "moral obligations must discipline ethical ones" (p. 233), although, again, there is no absolute. What one is faced with is a series of "imaginary communities" that call for more or less "thick" relationships, more or less special responsibilities, and more or less partiality. These communities span the territory between perfect strangers and the self, and somewhere along the continuum the moral becomes ethical and vice versa.

Whether imaginary communities generate "thick" or "thin" relationships is an open question. Whether such relationships benefit from being formalized and discussed in the language of rights is also an open question. Yet these relationships need not be completely theorized. Most of the time they get resolved in practical ways, rather than through agreements on basic principles or as instantiations of some general concept or other. Moreover, the very notion of "community" may be said to inhabit a much wider range than what comes to mind when one refers to geographical contiguity. George Saunders's notion of "fluid nations" (explored in Appiah 2005) echoes the fact that imaginary communities are limited only by the resourcefulness of imagination. Men who fish or persons who make excellent strudel are also communities, and Saunders has a field day savaging the arbitrariness of the ways in which communities sort themselves and the absurdity of categorical chauvinisms (Appiah 2005, p. 238). What is most paradoxical is the way in which the multicultural approach has succeeded in bestowing rights and entitlements on some communities, while other equally meaningful communities have failed to acquire any.

Whatever the attractiveness of the cosmopolitan idea, it has acquired an unrealistic and utopian image in Canada. "Cosmopolitan," like "liberal," has become a word that connotes ideological stances in the organizational culture, and it would be naïve to presume that the market for ideas can operate as a perfect market under such circumstances. The organizational culture operates as a robust filter. The organizational culture is defined by the ideas, customs, and values that have been nurtured or have proved useful over the decades, and that continue to be regarded as making up an appropriate appreciative system. It is both enabling and limiting, echoing both a set of readinesses and capacities, and a set of mental constraints or taboos that prevent the system from choosing certain options when faced with unforeseen challenges (Vickers 1965).

The organizational culture in Canada may be roughly gauged as standing somewhere between the communitarian ethos of continental Europe and the individualistic ethos of the United States, in much the same way as in the United Kingdom, Australia, and certain other countries. On the criteria developed by Hampden-Turner and Trompenaars (1993), Canada is regarded as soft universalist, individualistic, somewhat risk-averse, inner-directed, short-term-oriented, and biased towards equality. The narrative in good currency is much marked by risk-aversion and soft egalitarianism. This explains Canadian centralizing pressures and state-centricity, and the focus on risk-pooling devices and redistribution mechanisms. It also explains the soft Hegelian tendencies that have made it difficult to get rid of the crippling epistemology of the state (often spelled with a capital "S") as a transcendent fundamental societal "organism" with moral purposes that transcend those of its individual citizens. Consequently, a so-called "progressive" filter prevents Canadians from unshackling themselves from the mental prisons of "state" and "nation" as dominant frames, despite their basic individualism. As a result, even though there are no reasons not to experiment with cosmopolitan ways, the soft communitarian mindset has blocked that perspective and generated a fair degree of false consciousness.

Multiculturalism, the Charter of Rights and Freedoms, and the North American Free Trade Agreement have been possible largely because they were mini-coups d'état. The population was carried through each of these mammoth changes without properly understanding their real effects. When special commissions and referendums focused the attention of the citizenry on institutional changes, as proposed in the Meech Lake and Charlottetown Accords, risk aversion in the face of significant gambles and a fundamental attachment to "equality," even when it was grossly unfair, led to massive rejection.

Becoming a cosmopolitan will not be possible without some cultural change. The dynamic conservatism of the organizational culture and persistent local patriotism will be able to sabotage any move away from tribalization, state-centricity, nations, and ethnies. This is why so many, in Canada and elsewhere, are still "closeted cosmopolitans," and why becoming a cosmopolitan will require denouncing many of these "mental prisons," battling against tribalism, and "halting the habituated practice of capitulating to the arbitrary glib and specious ends of the labellers and categorizers" (Hill 2000, p. 159ff). Moreover, "to come out" will require a serious questioning both of the degree of state-centricity in Canadian governance and of the seductions of soft egalitarianism in a world that is de facto willing to settle for no more than equability. This is the "satisficing" approach proposed by Harry Frankfurt (1988, pp. 134–58) but, twenty years on, the point has not yet been made with sufficient punch to knock out the egalitarian ideology (Kekes 2003). That would require a major transformation in the mindset of Canadians.

However, one may suggest that such a transformation is already under way, although there is a significant cultural lag by the intelligentsia and the politico-bureaucratic class behind the population. This has been clearly exposed during the debates about "reasonable accommodations" between "old" and "new" Canadians, about the Chaouilli decision, and about the need to re-engineer the state and to recalibrate the welfare system. Much of the blurring is likely to become unscrambled over time, but one cannot expect the state to be helpful in this process. The Taylor–Bouchard "consultation commission" set up by the Quebec government in February 2007 to help clear up the imbroglio generated by the debates over *les accommodements raisonnables* is co-chaired by two fervent communitarians. It is unlikely that anything will emerge from it that will challenge the mindset in good currency.

Conclusion

This world in transformation may provide very useful opportunities for intervention. In a book published in 1986 Hubert Reeves evoked an event that occurred in 1942, when forest fires caused by bombardments in the Soviet Union forced about one thousand horses to jump into Lake Ladoga, the largest lake in Europe, in order to save their lives. Even though very cold air had swept over the area in the days before, the water was still liquid. However, while the horses were swimming towards the other side of the lake it suddenly froze. By the next day the horses, with only their heads above the surface, had all become ice monuments in the middle of the frozen lake. According to Reeves, the explanation of this phenomenon is rather simple: when the drop in temperature is too rapid water does not have time to congeal into ice and remains liquid at a temperature below zero, but this is a quite unstable state and it can take very little to trigger a process of very rapid ice formation.

In the first decade of the twenty-first century nation-states are in just such an unstable state, which explains why a revolution might be effected quickly. In a way, it might take much less effort than had been anticipated to effect such a reframing as the exploration of the cosmopolitan approach would entail. What specific factor or event might trigger this mutation is not entirely clear, but it may already be said that it is likely to be the result of a deliberate investment in possibilism (Hirschman 1971). This would mean the discovery of paths, however narrow, leading to an outcome that appears to be foreclosed on the basis of probabilistic reasoning alone, in an approach built on the possibility of increasing the number of ways in which the occurrence of change can be visualized. How might such a trigger be pulled? A little disturbance may be sufficient and it may well be that, as Jason Hill put it, "a single solitary effrontery does leave the world changed" (Hill 2000, p. 162).

Part III

Regulating Diversity

7

Moral Contract as Enabling Mechanism

*Well-functioning societies make it possible for people to achieve
agreement when agreement is necessary, and unnecessary to achieve
agreement when agreement is impossible.*
—Cass R. Sunstein (2005, p. 2)

"Diversity" is a complex and essentially contested concept. It
can also be a taboo topic. While most modern societies are
becoming more diverse in a factual sense—more heterogeneous,
polyphonic, multiethnic—it is clear that all are not embracing an
objective of maintaining or enhancing diversity as an ideal *per se*
(Dahrendorf 1988, Paquet 1989a, Scott 2003). Indeed, a whole range
of countries make no secret of their objective of either assimilating and
dissolving diversity into the host culture, or succeeding in developing
a new homogeneity around some new values as a result of cultural
competition and demographic blending, thus eliminating diversity.
Other countries are more tempted by some form of consensual
apartheid or oligopolies as a basis of new social equilibriums.

The fact remains that, in any democratic society that is open to
massive demographic shuffling and has become more diverse, the
formation of identity groups is inevitable. They are also legitimate,
since they represent the voice of "shared identity" and echo something
that goes beyond the pursuit of self-interest. Yet such groups also carry
social expectations. It is therefore useful to probe alternative views
about the relationships between diversity and identity, and about the
ways in which identity groups relate to democracy.

To do so I argue that a viable arrangement must be built on an
implicit and explicit moral contract. I also hint at the directions in
which it would appear to lead democratic societies.

Betting on Moral Contracts

The challenge of implementing a "different but equal" strategy and the need to head off the dynamic of ressentiment create a "prisoner's dilemma" type of problem: a problem of mutual distrust. Native-born citizens have legitimate expectations that some of the trust and social capital that have been built over generations will not and should not be dissipated. Newcomers have legitimate expectations that there will be some accommodation to take their needs and preferences into account, since they make a contribution to value-adding. As the assumptions on which the host community is based are challenged, sometimes seemingly without any limit to such external displacement of internal core values and institutions, there may be a reflex closing of the mind to the demands of the new groups. As the demands of the new citizens are denied, a growing sense of alienation and exclusion is bound to emerge. As a result the two groups become mutually antagonistic, and collaboration becomes more and more difficult. We know that the economic, social, and political costs of such antagonism are large.

Dealing with this conundrum requires that the problem of moral distrust be engaged directly. Most of the time this is not resolvable through the orthopaedic interventions of the law, but instead requires negotiated soft arrangements, conventions, and moral contracts that establish the basis for parallel mutual expectations. This is the way in which prisoner's dilemmas are usually resolved (Paquet 1999a, Chapter 12) and it is the general thrust of the argument that one may detect behind the protracted discussions that have led to the emergence of "interculturalism" in Quebec (Paquet 1994b).

The challenge of negotiating moral contracts is daunting for many reasons. First, such negotiation entails a loose clarification of expectations on both sides that may not appear at first as unduly constraining. One can imagine a wide range of moral contracts, more or less binding on both established and new citizens. However, to the extent that culture means anything, it means a capacity to establish differences, to accomplish some integration of these differences, and to succeed in determining some hierarchy for this more or less diversified and more or less integrated complex of values (Lussato 1989). This is quite an arduous task.

Second, the very informality of these "contractual" arrangements leaves them open, not only to genuine misinterpretation, but also to sabotage by those intent on using this very vagueness to pursue other political or electoral objectives. Indeed, deception is the Achilles' heel of moral contracts. The systematic misuse of the languages of the Charter of Rights and Freedoms in particular, and those of human rights in general, to camouflage one's own preferences or desires as entitlement imperatives, has provided much evidence for the profuse deployment of deception in aid of ideological pursuits in high places, in Canada and elsewhere (O'Neill 2002, Paquet 1996-97, 2001b, 2004 and 2005abc). Moral contracts, to be of any use, need to establish a hierarchy among values, yet hierarchy and differentiation are mortal sins for the egalitarians. Therefore one major epistemological blockage to be overcome is the resistance to recognizing that legitimate differences and hierarchies need to be debated and negotiated.

One cannot and should not seek refuge in some transcendent political sphere where, supposedly, everything and everyone would become undifferentiated, and decisions would be taken by disembodied citizens. Culture and identity entail differentiation and hierarchy. Immunization from sabotage and deception is never complete, but open critical forums may help to expose such destructive initiatives, and fail-safe mechanisms may deter miscreants from wanting to stall the debates for fear that a worse outcome might automatically ensue.

Moral contracts are not only for establishing guidelines on what newcomers may expect, but also for setting limits to the accommodation of diversity, since certain basic tenets of the host society cannot withstand the anomie-generating pressures emerging from a diversity without limits (Paquet and Reed 2003). Both constraints and limits would be determined through some *principle of precedence*, with some constraints being regarded as taking precedence over others in the definition of viable arrangements. Deep cultural diversity cannot be managed otherwise.

Donaldson and Dunfee's integrative social contracts theory (1994) has defined different layers of moral contracts developed from the shared goals, beliefs, and attitudes of groups of people or communities. These social contracts serve as tools with which to measure the moral performance of organizations and illustrate what is meant by the principle of precedence. The moral contracts that Donaldson and Dunfee propose are at three levels. First come "hypernorms," such as the basic obligation to respect the dignity of each human person, which are at the core of constitutional arrangements and apply generally to all concerned. Next come "macro social contracts," providing conditions under which different communities can develop their activities at the

Figure 5. Integrative Moral Contracts

HYPERNORMS
Primum non nocere
Personal freedom
Physical security and well-being
Informed consent
Political participation

MACRO MORAL CONTRACT
Moral free space
Free consent and right to exit
Compatibility with hypernorms
Respect for international agreements
Priority rules

MICRO MORAL CONTRACTS
Not lying in negotiations
Honouring all contracts
Hiring preferences for the native-born
Contract preferences for local suppliers
Providing safe workplaces

Source: Adapted from Fritzsche 1997, p. 44.

micro level, contracts that best serve the different communities and are congruent or at least not in contradiction with the hypernorms. Finally there are "micro social contracts" to guide action at the operational level.

Fritzsche (1997) has sketched the different layers of moral contracts pertaining to different relationships, and illustrates somewhat the sort of guiding norms, values, and rules pertaining to them in Figure 5.

Discussions at these three levels cannot be conducted in isolation. We are faced with three-level games in which negotiations are carried out by somewhat different stakeholders at each level, in ways that have to ensure not only the basic coherence of the overall game, but also compatibility between the different levels, and adherence/conformity by lower-order arrangements to the norms of the higher-order conventions. These different moral contracts are like Russian dolls: the lower-order ones must fit with and into the higher-order ones. They must all be debated and negotiated. For instance, imposing a hiring preference in favour of the native-born may be contentious, but it may have to be confronted, in the same manner that immigrant networks sometimes act as self-selection machines in certain types of occupations or organizations. The important aspects of these contracts are optimal (not maximal) clarity, relative stability, and realism. These are basic parameters for the definition of mutual expectations. It must be ensured that they cannot be whimsically modified or mischievously interpreted, but they also must correspond to reality. There is no point in proclaiming that X can be expected by newcomers when, blatantly, X in fact cannot.

The fundamental stewardship function of defining moral contracts requires that certain design principles in institutional architecture be agreed on and that certain ranking priorities be respected. On the design front, Ostrom (1990, p. 90) has identified a few of the elements that appear to account for the success of some governance arrangements and thus provide some guidance about the sort of mechanisms that are likely to be effective: clearly defined boundaries; congruence between rules and local conditions; wide participation by those affected by operational rules; monitoring; graduated sanctions when rules are violated; rapid and low-cost mechanisms for conflict resolution; and the right of appropriators to devise their own institutions for implementation.

As for priorities in decision-making, Donaldson and Dunfee (1995) have proposed a set of priority rules within the context of their integrated social contracts framework. First, when it is agreed that there are no adverse external effects, transactions within a community should be governed by the community's norms. Second, the community's norms should be applied as long as they have no external adverse effects on other individuals and communities. Third, the more extensive the community that is the source of the norm, the greater the priority that should be given to the norm. Fourth, norms essential to the maintenance of the socioeconomic environment should be given priority over those that are potentially damaging to that environment. Finally, where multiple conflicting norms exist patterns of consistency among the alternative norms provide a basis for prioritization.

These design principles and priority rules are provided only as examples of the kinds of general guideposts that might be required to ensure the appropriate stewardship of a world that is otherwise self-governed as much as possible, a stewardship steered by the principles of participation, subsidiarity, multistability, and continuous organizational learning through relational leadership. The central question has to do with the ways in which one might set out to engineer such governance-cum-stewardship.

Diversity is another name for the cohabitation of identity groups that have important differences in their norms. Hundreds of years of human experience have shown that neither abolishing these groups nor elevating them to a dominant position is a solution that holds promise for sustainable and constructive coexistence. What has to be accomplished is the development of a *modus vivendi* among such groups that recognizes their legitimacy, but also recognizes the legitimacy of host societies' concerns about the preservation of their own values, as well as the legitimacy of some basic values inherent in any democracy.

New Directions

The proposed pyramid of moral contracts entails a hierarchy of principles. Micro contracts must honour macro contracts, and both micro and macro contracts must respect hypernorms. This hierarchy is obviously subject to constant deliberation and negotiation. There is no reason to believe that optimal arrangements will evolve organically, or to believe that relinquishing final authority on such matters to the courts will work. Indeed, the courts have often made decisions that violate the precedence of hypernorms in intercultural issues, as, for example, in the Julia Martinez case (Gutmann 2003, pp. 44ff). There may, then, be a need for conventions to ensure a reasonable *modus vivendi*. Such conventions will take the form of moral contracts defining mutual expectations, providing for systems of incentive rewards likely to promote peaceful and creative coexistence, and at the same time preserving the integrity of the social entity. This in turn entails both a hierarchy of norms and certain limits to the accommodation of diversity.

To be architects and stewards of collaborative regimes one must count on processes that move stakeholders past defensive and adversarial postures, and nurture collaboration. Common obstacles to collaboration are the historical and ideological barriers of stakeholders: power disparities, cultural norms, different perceptions of risk, the technical complexity of issues, institutional incentives, and so on (Gray 1989). *Technologies of collaboration* are the ground-level processes and structures of incentive rewards meant to overcome these barriers and nurture social learning. The word "technologies" here refers to techniques and social processes that help to increase the exchange of knowledge, generate trust and commitment, and ensure more effective coordination. They provide guideposts that shape the expectations, incentives, and reward systems that induce cooperation, as well as the conventions, moral contracts, and regimes of accountability that are necessary for cooperation to prevail and survive. The most useful technologies of collaboration include forums and public spaces, loci for dialogue and multilogue, capacity- and competence-building, and schemes for the exchange of information. These are all mechanisms, capable of generating the reframing of issues, which is the key to social learning. The points of view of different stakeholders are informed by what Schon and Rein (1994) call "frames," underlying structures of beliefs, perceptions, and appreciations that are different from group to group. These frames are usually tacit, exempt from attention, and immune from appeals to facts or reasoned arguments. Without reconciling these frames little progress can be anticipated in collaborative debates, but this also entails the blurring and blending of perspectives (Tacher and Rein 2004).

The *social imaginary* defines the moral order: what is and is not acceptable. Reframing entails nothing less than a paradigm shift in mindsets on the part of all those involved, in order that they recognize the new drivers that are likely to be useable as lever points. This requires challenging a number of deeply rooted but "unreasonable" assumptions buried in the social imaginary that, often, one is not aware one is making. A few examples follow.

The first is the false sense of the all-pervasiveness of culture as DNA. In the context of today's diversity we are all hybrids composed of a basket of limited identities, and no longer the simple expressions and consequences of singular cultural imprints. To allow the myth of one cultural identity to prevail is quite dangerous and can lead to an erosion or attenuation of individual rights.

The second is the sacralization of consensus. It is not because there is an agreement that such agreement makes sense. False consciousness and poor judgement may lead to agreements that can only generate unacceptable outcomes. For instance, the consensual apartheid between aboriginal groups and the rest of the population in many countries has led to disastrous outcomes, despite the high-minded speeches about the right to cultural survival that is purported to inspire such arrangements.

The third is the thwarted notion that civic equality must guarantee egalitarianism of outcomes. This has led to all sorts of equalization-inspired interventions that have squelched the dynamism of the targeted.

The fourth is the false dichotomy between symbolic recognition and material entitlements. In fact, entitlements are entitlements and they end up always being entitlements to real resources. The quest for symbolic recognition is only a stratagem to get access to real resources.

The fifth is the idolizing and lionizing of the language of human rights as a stratagem to inhibit democratic conversation, and to claim absolute priority for one's particular wishes and desires. As Michael Ignatieff puts it: "the tendency to define anything desirable as a right ends up eroding the legitimacy of a defensible core of rights . . . We need to stop thinking of human rights as trumps and begin thinking of them as a language that creates the basis for deliberation" (Ignatieff 2001, pp. 90, 95).

All these assumptions (and there are many others) are part of the "social imaginary," the process of intermediation through which a society sees its collective life and makes sense of its practices (Taylor 2004). This common understanding defines common practices and the shared sense of legitimacy. Negotiating the shape that the social imaginary will have defines the repertory of collective action at the disposal of a given group in society. This intermediation machine shapes the legitimate expectations of the different groups and the sort of moral contracts that might be regarded as acceptable. It defines the horizon that people in a society are unable to think beyond. In order to construct new moral contracts, capable of generating new forms and technologies of cohabitation, one may need to transform the social imaginary, to define a new terrain of mutual expectations.

In the case of Canada a mental revolution is necessary if the social imaginary is to be modified. It is not so long ago that official recruitment agencies for new immigrants could say, without being challenged, that immigrants could bring their own culture with them as they came to Canada, because Canada had no culture of its own. It is not surprising that, on the basis of such bizarre expectations generated by the false advertising of government agents, newcomers have come to expect that they could impose all their mores on the old communities, or even that the very idea of a moral contract with immigrants came to be regarded by federal bureaucrats — as when it was proposed by Monique

DEEP CULTURAL DIVERSITY

Gagnon-Tremblay, then Quebec's Minister for Cultural Communities — in 1990 — as an unacceptable and fascistic contraption. Yet the social imaginary has to redefine citizenship as a privilege that calls for shared and agreed limitations, and assert very firmly that, unless the appropriate conditions are met, the privilege will not be granted. Otherwise, no moral contract is possible. The whole debate about Madame Gagnon-Tremblay's proposal turned sour because the very idea was not considered permissible. Before one can suggest new mechanisms to promote "diversity within bounds" it will have to be established that the very notion of bounds is legitimate.

As it stands, the Canadian social imaginary, rooted in egalitarianism and the idolatry of human rights, is incapable of accepting the idea of designing mechanisms to limit the accommodation of diversity within certain bounds. Indeed, the very idea that the absence of safeguards is neither fully understood nor regarded as a legitimate thought may be the major source of anxiety about diversity and multiculturalism among native-born citizens, and therefore the cause of their reluctance to pursue the experiment of further increasing the degree of diversity (Paquet and Reed 2003).

Conclusion

It was not the purpose of this chapter to spell out the contours of a new citizenship capable of shaping a viable road to governable diversity. Our only objective was to propose an arena for engaging public discussion of such a prospect. We have provided a framework for looking at integrative moral contracts, and argued for a recognition that one may be able to develop the requisite mechanisms only if one is also able, in parallel, to modify the social imaginary.

It should be clear that only a major epistemological coup will succeed in transforming the social imaginary, yet such a coup is unlikely. *Natura non fecit saltum* ("Nature does not make a leap"). Consequently, the only hope is to use the oblique ways of bricolage, putting in place innocuous mechanisms likely to generate incrementally the cumulative causation that one is looking for. Tipping-point leadership is the only way.

8

Citizenship as Umbrella Strategy

*Liberalism is a doctrine about the external organization of society. It is
silent on the more important question: how shall we live?*
—Michael Lind

Pluralism is a world view that defines societies as fragmented and
discontinuous, composed of different complementary/conflictive
parts or spheres that are incommensurable and therefore cannot be
reduced to a single logic. In plural societies there is a constant and active
process of reconciliation, harmonization, and effective coordination
of the logics in these different spheres, in order to ensure a minimal
degree of coherence, resilience, and effective learning.

Citizenship is a covenant based on the principles, reciprocal
privileges, and reciprocal responsibilities that define ways of living
together. Therefore, in a plural society, citizenship cannot be anything
but plural, that is, limited and multiple, for the citizen in such a world
has multiple and limited relationships, and multiple, limited, and
overlapping identities (Cairns 1999).

However, many political scientists and jurists are critical of this notion
of limited and multiple citizenships. To bring commensurability to the
incommensurable they routinely reduce this rich and variegated nexus
of principles, privileges, and responsibilities connoting citizenship to
a common denominator, for the purposes of governance, by granting
politics a transcendent role. Through a sleight of hand they invent a
projection of the n-dimensional socioeconomic reality that citizenship
synthesizes onto a single transcendent plane where all agents are
defined as equivalent and equipotent, and make it the sole locus of
citizenship. The citizen becomes a rational being operating on the
transcendent plane of politics, a sort of lowest-common-denominator
soul inside every agent. In such an ethereal world there is a denial of

diversity, no possibility of considering any differences, and a refusal to establish lucid and responsible rankings among dimensions. This reductionism is even presented as the essence of democracy, with the implication that, without the transcendence of politics, democracy would not prevail (Gauchet 1998).

I argue in this chapter that plural societies need a much richer notion of citizenship. The argument is developed in four stages. First, I describe in a cursory way the stratagem of the "public sphere" as a sanitized locus for agent–state intercourse and show the limitations of the strategy on which politics has built its purported dominion. Second, I develop a broader notion of citizenship, rooted in civil society and in the notion of moral contracts, and show how it is likely to be better adapted to pluralist contexts. Third, I consider, briefly, the different ways in which Canada and Australia are drifting towards this "umbrella" position.

The Perils of Transcendent Politics

Plural societies are societies that explicitly recognize that individuals and groups are motivated by different values, and that they can legitimately have different value systems. To pursue their different objectives they require positive freedom, encompassing the capacity and opportunity to actively and effectively pursue these values, and the elimination of the constraints or unfreedoms that prevent them from doing so. Moreover, plural societies deny that there is any constantly overriding value (Kekes 1993, p. 19). This entails the inevitability of conflicts and the need to develop reasonable mechanisms for conflict resolution based on some core credo, however minimal, that the disputants may share. While the plurality of conceptions of a good life increases the range of valued possibilities, not all possibilities are reasonable, so there is a need for limits, and for the justification of such limits as excluding unreasonable possibilities, unreasonable ways of pursuing them, or ways that might simply maximize conflicts.

The central strategy of many political scientists and jurists in the face of "plural" societies has been to focus on finding complexity-reducing devices for the purpose of governance. One much-favoured stratagem has been to adopt the reductive assumption that there are only two sectors, the private sphere and the public sphere. According to this device, there is a private sphere relying on a right to privacy and a public sphere where individuals interact under the aegis of the state. It is in

DEEP CULTURAL DIVERSITY

this public space that citizenship is nested and the citizen participates in a restricted way, through representation in a legislature, to give a voice to the general will. For those who defend such a dichotomy the two spheres represent the private and public faces of the lifeworld of individuals. Groups and communities are simply considered as insignificant symbolic markers, while citizenship pertains to the public sphere and is dominated by state–agent relations.

This occluding of communities, and the emphasis on the private–public dichotomy and the vertical notion of citizenship associated with it, are both altogether too Manichean and unduly reductive. The real plural world is much more complex and is characterized by deep diversity. It is filled with communities, real and imagined, there are many more than two spheres, and they all overlap to such an extent that it is of little use to build any analysis on the assumption of tightly compartmentalized spheres, however many one may count (Janoski 1998, Paquet 2000a and 2001a). Consequently, citizenship cannot be restricted to a "public sphere." State, market, private, and public spheres, and others in the material and symbolic orders, overlap to such a significant degree that it is unreasonable to limit the ambit of citizenship to the sphere of the state. Indeed, as T. H. Marshall (1964) would put it, the nexus of privileges and obligations defining citizenship has evolved sufficiently that it has invaded all spheres.

Moreover, citizenship cannot be reduced to state–agent relations. At a certain level of generality political scientists and jurists recognize that citizenship is fundamentally a dual relationship, being both *vertical*, between the members of the political community and the political authority and the state, and *horizontal*, among members of the community. Yet they overemphasize the former relation to such an extent that the notion of citizenship becomes totally absorbed into it (Cairns 1999, Jenson and Papillon 2000). This bias toward the vertical is based on the special importance of the public sphere, and of politics and the state within it, through the process of political representation. Politics and the state are purported to play a transcendent role as the agent of transfiguration of society (Gauchet 1998, p. 112). There is a quasi-doctrinaire belief that this is necessary since only politics, through the process of conflicts among parties and other collective adversaries, can lead to a meaningful taking of the common good into account. For those holding such a view the state is the centre of the public sphere and the privileged locus of conflicts between power groups. Consequently, any relativization of the role of the state can only be regarded as a deplorable erosion of the political, even though the state is said, by the same persons, to have generated a "primacy for the representation of actors over and above the resolution of the problems that they pose" (Gauchet 1998, p. 123).

It is our view that in a modern, pluralist socioeconomy there is no privileged or transcendent locus of conflict, and, therefore, that the valence of politics and the state is considerably overstated. In a more realistic approximation of the socioeconomy, horizontal (community) relationships are as important or perhaps even more important than vertical ones. A reduction in the relative importance of the state and politics, a disenchantment of the political, a drift towards reducing the intermediate role of the political, or its implosion or reconfiguration in new sites—all this means a shift from government to governance (Paquet 1999b).

"Governance" may be defined as effective coordination when resources, information, and power are distributed. In the context of governance, citizenship means the ensemble of principles, reciprocal privileges, and reciprocal responsibilities that defines the nexus of moral contracts sketching out these privileges and responsibilities. These contracts constitute the necessary social technologies of coordination capable of bringing forth the good life in all its various senses for the different agents.

The perils of maintaining a fixation on the state and politics are clear. Since citizenship is a nexus of relationships dominated, not by the state, but by a much richer array of relations throughout the socioeconomy, the fixation on the political can only rob the notion of citizenship of much of its meaning.

Determination of foundational moral contracts is difficult, being fraught with Manichean dogmas and nasty discussions that reveal the full powers of naïvety and political correctness. Ethnos has become the target of many attacks because it is a source of exclusion. Indeed, the dichotomy between "bad" ethnic nationalism and "good" civic nationalism has become a mantra. Any connection between government and an ethnocultural nation upon which the nation-state is based has come to be regarded as "xenophobic, nativist, and even fascist" (Lind 2000, p. 44). In its place, the politically correct conventional wisdom has proposed a sort of civic nationalism as "progressive because it is committed to a political ideal." This represents a subtle but futile stratagem to capture the "psychological economies of scale" of the nation-state without having to pay the price of ethnocultural commonality broadly defined. Unfortunately, it seems that "the ethnic nation is the largest community with which ordinary beings can have an emotional attachment" and that civic patriotism is simply an abstract construct (Lind 2000, p. 46).

So far, at least, all attempts to completely exorcize ethnocultural dimensions have failed the test of reality, for ethnocultural nations and nationalisms thrive. There has been a recent attempt to salvage the paradigm of civic nationalism by insisting that ethnocultural dimensions may be factored in, but only as subsidiary or secondary features. These features are regarded as being important only at the symbolic level, as a support system for the "liberal-civic-nationalist" citizen whose "liberalism" remains the only fundamental value. Michael Ignatieff, for one, underwent a minor conversion in this respect between 1993 and 2001 (Ignatieff 1993, 2001). This has led to the emergence of a form of "boutique multiculturalism," a multiculturalism that one can invoke only in respect of inconsequential matters. For, as soon as there is an effort to leverage or parley these ethnocultural values into anything significant ,the dominant liberal view of the individual without ethnocultural qualities is used forcefully to trivialize the ethnocultural dimension (Fish 1999).

The analytical block proposed in Figure 2 (in Chapter 1) leaves a great deal of room for a wide variety of complex notions of citizenship anchored in quite different terrains. This captures the central fact that citizenship as a set of ligatures is an essentially contested concept about which reasonable persons may never agree (Gallie 1964) because it is a multidimensional concept, and different persons may legitimately put more emphasis on one aspect or another within the analytical block. What crystallizes as the relevant notion of citizenship is a set of ligatures or moral contracts defining a transversal syncretic entity within the analytical block, a mixture of principles, reciprocal privileges, and reciprocal responsibilities that provides citizenship with its broad diffuse base and its syncretic unity.

Terms of Integration and Emergent Transversal Citizenship

In the process of defining citizenship as ligatures of all sorts, it is easy to understand how different groups may focus on different cells of the analytical block. Ethnic membership may be regarded as the essential feature by some, while others may elect to emphasize symbolic identity in civil society exclusively. In a world characterized by considerable spectrality—multiple memberships, limited identities, a mélange of ethnic/national/civil society identification and cultures, layered governance structures, and a fluid boundary between the symbolic and the material world—citizenship is unlikely to be captured in one cell or dimension of the block. Indeed—and this is our main argument—citizenship is a transversal concept (Paquet 1989a, 1994a, 1994b).

This means that citizenship might be regarded as a nexus of ligatures defining a covenant or pact cutting across the block, across the many boundaries, and attempting to reconcile in an evolutionary way the many different perspectives that coexist, within a given society or at the intersection of many societies, through a nexus of fluid "moral contracts" (Paquet 1991-1992). Moral contracts are more or less informal arrangements and conventions that embody values and norms on which people agree. They define mutual expectations, legitimate entitlements and obligations, and the corridor or boundary limits within which people have agreed to live. Only such a transversal notion of citizenship based on moral contracts can capture the array of ligatures capable of meeting individuals' complex needs for autonomy and belonging, their needs for responsibilities and for opportunities for participation in an active democracy, and the challenges of a spectral society with its new type of sociality based on weak ties. This notion of citizenship need not be univocal, since there are multiple citizenships anchored in different terrains, and there may be citizenships differentiated in degree and in kind.

For instance, one can easily imagine a basic set of minimal norms corresponding to basic citizenship, but also differential levels of rights-cum-obligations that individuals and groups might choose in order to equilibrate their entitlements with the sort of responsibilities they are willing to accept (Paquet 1989a). In the same manner, in a world of limited identities and multiple citizenships, one can imagine layers of citizenship corresponding to different pacts entered into by individuals or organizations. These may echo either different degrees of rootedness, complementary ensembles of commitments, or, in some cynical scenarios, flags or passports of convenience that can be used alternatively or strategically by individuals or organizations depending on circumstances.

In this context, the multiplication of citizenships has called for some ordering, strong or weak, if the notion is not to be trivialized. The notion of primary and subsidiary citizenships connotes a sense of priority among the different limited affiliations. This ordering may or may not be embodied in a formal legal arrangement. At best, it would correspond to an always emergent and never fully crystallized meta-moral contract defining the relative valence of the different ligatures that make up individuals' and organizations' citizenship.

Over the past few decades the dynamics of the debates about citizenship have led to an evolution of the concept. From the original formulation of T. H. Marshall (1964), emphasizing the development of citizenship entirely in terms of rights—civil rights in the eighteenth century, political rights in the nineteenth, social rights in the twentieth—it has evolved towards a conception in which ever greater importance is given to participation, belonging, and symbolic recognition. Moreover, there has been a tendency for the notion of citizenship not only to change the valence of these three components, but also to react to the ever greater "liquidity" and complexity of modern societies (Bauman 2000), both by an increase in the degree of "informality" in the normativities embedded in the moral contracts, and by a multiplication of the contracts dealing with these more complex relationships (Paquet 2001a). Thus, instead of being absorbed into a simple, formal, and legal linkage between the citizen and the state, the citizenship relationship has evolved into a looser but more encompassing covenant, covering a web of relationships among members of the community, but also between them and the state.

Finally, the proliferation of multiple citizenships has heightened the complexity of these arrangements and has generated a whole new set of problems for persons or organizations purporting to hold membership in many clubs at the same time. As we have seen in Chapter 5, this has led both to ugly abuses of power and to irresponsible opportunism (see also Cohen 2007).

The emergence of the loose covenant that ensues from the developing notion of citizenship faces many challenges. Jenson and Papillon (1999, 2000) have identified some of them. One may underline a few of these challenges as a way of probing the process of construction of citizenship that is under way in most countries.

The first challenge has to do with the increasing diversity and spectrality of the populations. It appears that nothing less than a recognition of differential and asymmetric citizenships can do the job in a world where diversity and spectrality entail a multiplicity of limited identities that may be complementary or competing (Van Gusteren 1998, Paquet 2000b). Unless one can define some rank ordering among these attachments, citizenship becomes meaningless.

The second challenge has to do with the multiplication of the sites of citizenship. While the power and legitimacy of the nation-state appear to have been lessened, there are reasons to believe that this proliferation of sites of power is even more important when the ethnocultural basis of a society has become more diverse. When new entities at the supranational and infranational levels, become meaningful actors, and alliances and joint ventures blur the old distinction between the state sphere and the rest of society, one must either firmly re-establish the state sphere and salvage the old notion of citizenship, or transform the notion of citizenship to deal with the new realities (Paquet 2000a). This latter route calls for citizenship to be broadened, and for new social ligatures and arrangements to be negotiated. While different groups may wish to obtain symbolic recognition, others may want some political autonomy or a portion of the economic surplus. This is true for groups at the local and regional levels, but it is particularly so for ethnocultural groups.

The third challenge has to do with the evolving nature of solidarity. The old notion of citizenship associated with rights has been driven to extend rights to cover all sorts of social entitlements, on the grounds that social equality and political equality are linked. This has often been discussed in complete ignorance of citizens' responsibilities, and has often been rooted in the basic assumption that only the state can be trusted to take action with a view to the common good. This has led to a strong emphasis on redistribution as a way to ensure that the so-called collective rights of communities are honoured, and to a reiteration of the importance of a strong central government as a source of redistribution, for only such a government can bring the requisite resources to the centre and redistribute them to lessen inequality. However, it is far from clear that redistribution, whether of material or of symbolic resources, is the best way. A return to the principles of insurance might be a more appropriate response in a world of weaker ties and greater turbulence, where what one wants to encourage is a more efficient allocation of risk-taking through a wider use of risk-sharing. Such a shift in focus may be all the more important if one accepts, even if only in part, the argument of René Girard that reducing inequality by redistribution may increase the danger of envy and violence (Laurent and Paquet 1991).

The final challenge to be underlined here has to do with participation in the governance process. Again, this may take two forms: either opening up the political process through stratagems of inclusion, or accepting that citizenship does not necessarily have to be restricted to the political. This latter approach would require a broadening of the notion of citizenship to encompass more than individuals and communities, and the design of appropriate mechanisms to define and enforce the rights and responsibilities of these other "organizational entities" (Paquet 1998). There are daunting challenges in eliciting the participation and engagement that are required if a society is to thrive and prosper when faced with a more and more variegated population in a more and more turbulent world.

The mix of negative and positive freedoms likely to provide optimal integration—integration capable of providing ample possibilities for differentiated citizenship, while ensuring the minimal rules of engagement for the society to succeed—need not necessarily have evolved organically. One must therefore identify the ways in which the state, wittingly or not, influences the "terms of integration."

Umbrella Strategy

The idea of an "umbrella strategy" is derived from management literature. It pertains to strategies that set out broad guidelines and leave the specifics to be worked out in practice (Mintzberg and Jorgensen 1987).

There are two fairly distinct traditions in the literature on citizenship. One emphasizes a conception of citizenship as status and is couched in a language of entitlements, while the other emphasizes citizenship as practice and gives rise to a language of duties. The former tradition, usually labelled liberal individualism, has been dominant in the Anglo-American world, where citizenship has generally been regarded as a status that individuals born into this world acquire as a right. They do not have to do anything to become or remain citizens, unless they feel that the status is threatened, which is why it "requires the endorsement of civil law for its protection . . . [both] from the predatoriness of other individuals and from the arbitrariness of governments" (Oldfield 1990). In the latter tradition of civic republicanism, as Oldfield explains:

> it is by acting, by public service of fairly specific kinds, that
> individuals demonstrate that they are citizens. This public service
> relates to what it is necessary for citizens to do in order to define,

establish, and sustain a political community of fellow-citizens.
... It is action ... which is both constitutive of citizenship, and
constitutive and sustaining of the community of which the citizen
is member.

While many have celebrated the restorative qualities of citizenship
(Dimock 1990), others have defamed it as myth, as a "rhetoric of
complacency whose result is to reassure those who cannot bear the
moral complexity of a market society that they are sensitive and superior
beings," and therefore as a form of "moral narcissism" (Ignatieff 1989).
At the core of this conflict is a crucial disagreement about the dynamics
of participation. For some it is the desire to engage in the practice of
citizenship that is crucial, and citizens have to be inculcated with an
attitude of mind, mores, codes of moral and civil conduct, and the like
so that a virtuous circle may be created in which participation breeds
participation. Others believe that such a circle cannot be created.

The refurbished notion of citizenship envisaged here is clearly
more active than passive, and directed towards the private and social
arenas, not only to public ones. It therefore focuses on the problem
of community membership, and tries to construct conditions of
active membership based less on ethnic or national ascription than
on commitment and achievement. As such, it should take precedence
on all other sets of rules, since it addresses the very admissibility and
admission of the member into the community. Identity defined on
such a basis does not stem from national or ethnic roots, which are
communitarian but exclusive, nor from a liberal pluralism that verges
on atomism, but is based on a notion of "positive freedom" and on
loyalty to a negotiated notion that, in the words of R. M. Smith
(1988):

> if we may ... conceive of a liberal polity not as a neutral umpire for
> subjectively valued pursuits, but as a shared endeavor [sic] to create
> institutions and policies that will increase all citizens' personal and
> collective capacities for deliberative self-governance, we may better
> support feelings of meaningful community membership.

This refurbished notion of citizenship can accommodate any mixture
of communitarianism and liberalism negotiated in a social contract.

There has been a recognition that citizenship in a polyethnic
and binational society such as Canada's is not easy to develop.
Besides simplistic ministerial references to "linking citizenship to

cultural diversity," little has been done to determine what this sort of citizenship might be. We already know that active citizenship in contemporary liberal democracies is at a low ebb (Parry 1989). To develop it in a fractured context can only be more difficult, which is exactly the challenge faced by the European Community (Aron 1974) and its successor, the European Union. Yet the concept of citizenship is far from clear (Barbalet 1988, Oliver 1991). It has been regarded as a weasel word by many observers and interpreted diversely according to ideology. Still, the very malleability of the concept makes it attractive as a *negotiated* ensemble of rights and obligations. Citizenship creates a "community under law": it is not a "goal in itself but a means toward enlarging the life chances of men" (Dahrendorf 1974). It is a central concept of political democracy that has escaped from the shackles of ethnie and nation, and has led to a balance of rights and obligations based on a commitment to working together (Kelly 1979, Janowitz 1980).

The construction of citizenship has been a bizarre story in Canadian history. The term does not appear in the Constitution of 1867, and in the Charter of 1982 the notion has been trivialized (the word "citizen" appears in only three of its thirty-four sections). It has become clear through the Supreme Court's interpretations of the Charter that *almost all of its provisions* apply to any human being who happens to be in Canada or subject to Canadian laws (Garant in Colas et al. 1991). This has meant that any notion of a "moral contract" between "new" Canadians and the host society has been short-circuited by the decision that anybody happening to be in Canada is *de facto* a person under the Charter. In that context it is sufficient to sneak in to the country to become such a person, a bizarre extension of the spirit of the Charter. It follows that it may now be necessary to redefine what is meant by a Canadian citizen. Meanwhile, in Quebec, where the notion of citizenship has been a matter of some debate for years, there has been an oscillation between *ius soli*, as in France, and *ius sanguini*, as in Germany. The refusal to credit any notion of nation or ethnie led Pierre Trudeau to suggest a notion of citizenship entirely based on a certain "will" or "civic sense," which would be quite compatible with the Supreme Court's approach, but is different from the communitarian notion of citizenship coinciding with ethnicity that emerged from the Quebec nationalist movement (Beaudry in Colas et al. 1991) and may be too close to the pole of atomism.

Citizenship becomes a crucible in which a new identity is always in the process of being forged when it is understood that any identity or citizenship is always in transition, and therefore integration without assimilation becomes a concept that is not an oxymoron. Citizenship as an inclusive concept may therefore be constructed politically in the same manner as the exclusive concept of cultural communities has been constructed (Fontaine and Shiose in Colas et al. 1991). In that sense the conditions of citizenship may be negotiated in a manner that would recognize both the *diversity* of the social fabric and the need for some *unifying* concept to provide a linking force. Up till now multiculturalism as a national policy has emphasized the pluralist forces at the cost of minimizing the centripetal bond. The notion of citizenship would recognize the patchwork quilt of the social fabric without losing sight of the need to channel the energy of this varied group in a well-defined direction. Whether or not Canadianism can mobilize the "limited identities" that characterize people all over Canada is unclear, but negotiating "moral" contracts about what binds Canadians together and keeps them going may be neither impossible nor unhelpful.

The tendency for citizenship to be inclusive has meant that any need to ration citizenship rights has been perceived as a form of racism. Yet indiscriminate civic inclusion can only translate into a form of anomie that destroys any possibility of identity, culture, and effective collective action. The revolutionary character of citizenship is ascribable to the possibility of generalized inclusion, but that does not mean that generalized inclusion is desirable, or that lack of screening is going to translate into a better society. Indiscriminate civic inclusion may not be without its discontents (Eckstein 1984). Often this translates into unreasonable expectations, then disillusionment, *ressentiment*, and violence.

Whether or not a new notion of citizenship might generate a workable social contract may depend on the possibility of recognizing that citizenship need not connote egalitarianism. In a multiethnic and binational society meaningful membership may not develop without a sense of hierarchy. "Different but equal" is an impossible gambit: this antinomy is at the core of a most important double bind that plagues intercultural relations. Equality denies differences (Laurent and Paquet 1991). Already such a hierarchy has been institutionalized imperfectly by creating political categories of people, as members of cultural communities, who are neither fully citizens nor really aliens.

This is a case where politics has produced political categories that have then become social categories (Fontaine and Shiose in Colas et al. 1991). There is no reason to believe that citizenship might not become such a negotiated political category.

It was just such a gamble that Trudeau's policy attempted to realize (Beaudry in Colas et al. 1991), but the strategy has been effected in a manner that has not succeeded in eradicating the multiple identities in Canada, because it has failed to generate any cohesive Canadian identity. Such an identity may not be easy to develop. It would probably have to be built around a priority language—French in Quebec, English in the rest of Canada—and therefore would effectively generate some hierarchy between the groups that speak the respective priority languages and other groups (including Anglophones in Quebec and Francophones elsewhere). It could only be built around those two axes via a negotiated contract spelling out not only the rights and obligations of all citizens, but also the conditions of membership and the exact nature of the adaptation expected both from new members and from the host society. The foundations on which one might be able to develop this Canadian notion of active citizenship are discussed at length in the theoretical literature (Kelly 1979, Janowitz 1980, Colas et al. 1991).

The notions that separateness is becoming the dominant value, that loss of identity is the central fear of most human beings, and that one cannot have equality and differences (for equality denies differences) have generated a solution that entails differences and separateness, and therefore hierarchy (Dumont 1983, Laurent and Paquet 1991). This in turn raises the questions of the rights and duties of minorities or other groups that are not assigned a place at the top of the pyramid. Even if the new moral contract that underpins the notion of citizenship does not confirm a generalized egalitarianism, it appears that it cannot legitimize any type of full-fledged hierarchy either. Yet separation would call for social distance and hierarchy *within bounds*. Membership does not necessarily entitle all members to the same life chances, but different entitlements or obligations cannot be so wide-ranging that they tear the social fabric.

What is necessary is the evolution of a sort of *civil theology* embodied in a number of standards, guidelines, and agreements designed to ensure the protection of minorities and cultural communities through political means complementary to the Charter of Rights and Freedoms (Leslie 1986). In particular, a Citizenship Act designed to limit or develop what, for the time being, is implicit in section 27 of the Charter about the rights of members of minorities and cultural communities might be beneficial.

Musings on Australia and Canada

It is only since 1947 in Canada and 1948 in Australia that members of these societies have been able to claim citizenship of them. Before that time these persons were either British subjects or without citizenship. One may reasonably ask whether this discontinuity made any difference. The answer is not clear. It obviously entailed the creation of some symbolic capital around the new label, but it is fair to say that the relabelling did little to effect the instant crystallization of a new identity in either country. It only triggered the process of learning about what it meant to be a citizen, for true citizenship always remains, of necessity, something that is emergent in an evolving world.

The process of social learning since citizenship became possible has been experienced quite differently in Australia and Canada: Australia has tackled the issue more openly, frontally, and transparently. In Canada the birth of citizenship came just a few years after a very divisive fracture in Canadian society created by the Conscription crisis (Laurendeau 1962). This crisis split Canada along ethnic lines right at the height of the Second World War, when the federal government tried to escape from a promise that had been made to Quebec that it would not invoke conscription, a *quid pro quo* for Quebec's agreement to support Canada's participation in the war effort. The crisis was so traumatic, with the jailing of some of Quebec's leaders, that it had a chilling effect on the postwar debates in Canada. In Australia debates and documents registered progress in the emergence of a syncretic notion of citizenship. In Canada the debates were muffled, the arguments were less vibrant, and the documents were not very clear as markers.

A preliminary examination of the two experiences suggests that the Australian approach has led to faster progress toward a clear definition of the meaning of citizenship. Most certainly the issue has received in Australia more attention, has generated more debates, and has led to a much sharper sense of what constitutes the nexus of moral contracts making up citizenship. Yet one should not conclude too hurriedly that the Canadian way has proved dysfunctional. A closer examination reveals that the slower process of social learning in Canada was not only well-suited to the Canadian circumstances and ethos, but also was not necessarily unhelpful in dealing with ever more complex citizenship issues. A strategy of small steps and *ad hoc* measures suited a country that does not have the robust debating culture of Australia.

In this section some hypotheses are put forward about the different routes that these two countries appear to have followed over the past sixty years, about the different nexuses of moral contracts that have emerged in consequence, and about the paradoxical efficiency of the Canadian approach.

One might suggest the following differences between Australia and Canada as deserving investigation. First, there are the contrasts between the importance of "citizen commitment" in Australia and its relative unimportance in Canada; between the centrality of discussions about the moral contract embodying this commitment in Australia and the diffidence about any such discussions in Canada; and between the sense of the limits to tolerance that results in Australia from these discussions and the almost unlimited tolerance that prevails in Canada because no norms have been agreed upon, so a convention of no norms has emerged by default. Second, while there is a carefully constructed bottom-up social cohesion built on commitment in Australia, there is a top-down mechanical social glue supposedly generated through redistribution of resources in Canada. Third, there is a capacity and a taste for robust national debates in Australia, but in Canada there is a "sociality of consensus," and a taste for obfuscation, irony, and bricolage, in the public sphere. Finally, there is a certain differential in the degree of political correctness, which is higher in Canada than in Australia, seriously stunts social debates in Canada, and is a source of differential social learning between the two countries.

From the "White Australia" policy of yesteryear to the "commitment to Australia" expected from citizens today, there has been significant clarity in Australia's position. In Canada, on the contrary, much has been done to equivocate. Canada's immigration policy was almost as quasi-racist as Australia's sixty years ago, without being stated as bluntly. There is still great difficulty in Canada even today in accepting that this ever was the case. The hypocritical policy of obfuscation about an era when soft but effective discrimination was in force is easy to understand and is ascribable to the Quebec factor. It is not possible to debate openly the rights, responsibilities, values, participation, and other factors underlying the moral contracts of citizenship when a significant segment of the Canadian population is of a different ethnocultural extraction and has not been persuaded that such moral contracts are internally acceptable, or provide for the identity and lifeworld of communities. Indeed, as a result of the Quebec factor the conditions for becoming a Canadian citizen have had to remain strategically ill-defined. At first, admission was based on opportunistically defined norms, rooted in no clear principles. Then it evolved toward the present situation where any person putting one foot on the tarmac at any Canadian airport is automatically granted almost all the rights of long-term Canadian citizens except the right to vote.

The recent granting of a "Canadian citizenship" to Nelson Mandela by the Parliament of Canada has gone further and expanded the definition of "citizen" to include someone who meets none of the standard criteria for citizenship. Whatever the merits of this particular individual, the Canadian Parliament admitted into "our community of fate" someone who has only the most tenuous possible reciprocal relationship of obligation with other members of our community. Through this gesture it all but declared that there are no firm conditions for becoming a Canadian citizen and did much to establish that it is simply an honorific title.

Canadians as individuals are inclined to be much more demanding in their definition of citizenship than Canadian officials. They define it not only in terms of a bundle of formal rights and freedoms, but also in terms of responsibilities, attitudes, and identities. In contrast, as we have seen in Chapter 5, officials claim to have no concern about defining any such set of expectations for newcomers, there is a lack of debates in Canada about the limits to tolerance and diversity, and Canadian leaders refuse to confront the notion that there may be any obligation upon newcomers to adapt. In stark contrast, Australia has spelled out the content of the "Australian Compact," consisting of seven basic principles based on "commitment" that Australian citizens must accept (Australian Citizenship Council 2000, p. 82):

- to respect and care for the land we share;
- to maintain the rule of law and the ideal of equality under the law;
- to strengthen Australia as a representative liberal democracy;
- to uphold the ideal of Australia as a tolerant and fair society;
- to recognize and celebrate Australia as an inclusive multicultural society;
- to continue to develop Australia as a society devoted to the

well-being of its people;
* to value the unique status of the Aboriginal and Torres Strait Islander peoples.

Moreover, the community consultations conducted by the Australian Citizenship Council revealed that it was perceived by a majority of respondents that "Australian citizenship should be valued emotionally rather than purely as a way of gaining certain legal rights and responsibilities . . . [and] should also signify a commitment to Australia and to shared civic values" (pp. 92–93).

Australia has also chosen to establish clear limits on immigration. They are defined in terms of acceptance of the basic structures and principles of Australian society — the Constitution, the rule of law, parliamentary democracy, English as a national language, equality of the sexes, and so on—as well as of the responsibility to accept the right of others to express their views and values, and of an overriding and unifying commitment to Australia, to its interests and its future.

While Canada remains reluctant at the federal level to develop any such "moral contract" defining the responsibilities of citizens, the matter was explicitly raised and discussed by the Liberal government of Quebec in December 1990. Through Monique Gagnon-Tremblay's report on immigration it stated clearly the basis of the moral contract that it wished the newcomers to accept: recognition of French as the language of public life, respect for liberal democratic values and pluralism, and so on. This was not well-received by the Canadian federal government and Quebec governments have since fought for these principles without much success. Of late the creation of a separate Quebec citizenship has been proposed as a way to clarify these requirements.

The contrast between the ethos of Canada and the ethos of Australia is less closely related to issues of citizenship, yet it underlines the fact that the social learning process has evolved differently in the two countries. First, the sort of social glue that is regarded as binding the citizenry together is quite different in Canada than it is in Australia. While Australia builds on the commitment of members of society, from the bottom up, to construct Australian identity and commonalities, Canada has proved unable to follow this route, and instead bets on interregional and intergroup redistribution schemes as the foundation of citizenry. This is done on the basis of the assumption that egalitarian rights yield belonging (Vipond 1996). This has generated, maybe unwittingly, an instrumental view of citizenship as a way to get access to the privileges of being a member of the society. Some observers (Banting 1999) argue that Canada's perspective is not strictly instrumental, but this is most unpersuasive. They also suggest that the only way to generate solidarity is by such laundering of money, but this is also questionable, even though it may understandably be regarded as a defendable stratagem to generate social cohesion if all else fails.

Canada has also developed a sociality of consensus that has made public debates and harshly critical appraisal of opposing views unwelcome, because they are likely to be both painful and divisive. This most un-Australian *modus operandi* has led to undue restraint in public debates and greater timidity about tackling difficult policy issues (Caldwell 2001). This modest satisficing approach and the omnipresent search for appropriate compromises have had important positive effects on the socioeconomic performance of the country. Some, such as Joseph Heath, even say that it is a particularly apt approach that has generated a very successful society (Heath 2001).

This oblique and timid approach to crucial policy issues has been strengthened considerably by the extraordinarily high degree of political correctness that has marred public debates in Canada. A few years ago the late Justice John Sopinka of the Supreme Court of Canada even suggested that political correctness in Canada had become the greatest enemy of free speech. It is most certainly a powerful enemy of vibrant debates on issues such as citizenship. Canadian timidity has stalled the process of social learning by suppressing or stunting national debates. For instance, one is not allowed to discuss the required transformation of the costly and inefficient health care system in Canada, because medicare is purported to be part of the social glue that forges Canadian citizenship. One is allowed only to pay homage to the Canada Health Act as an untouchable icon, despite its inadequacies.

The fact that public debates are more robust and that political correctness is less crippling in Australia has accelerated social learning there, making it possible to generate national debates on many fundamental aspects of society, even on the possibility of becoming a republic. In Canada such debates have not been possible very often, and the painful experiences with the Meech Lake and Charlottetown Accords have made such initiatives unlikely in the future.

Finally, a great deal has been done explicitly in Australia, as, for example, in Switzerland too, to root citizenship in sites at the local and state levels. This was part of a process intended to ensure that membership of society was felt from the bottom up. Citizenship has been an active and emotional commitment built in consort with local authorities. Australia has used citizenship as an integrative feature involving state and local authorities, and has chosen to promote explicitly the involvement of local and state authorities in the liturgy of national celebration, especially at the time of public ceremonies to confer citizenship.

In Canada, in contrast, the federal government has hijacked the citizenship file. It has forcefully defined citizenship as a status bestowed passively by the federal government, as the monopoly agent entitled to do so. Citizenship has therefore degenerated into a federal gratification. Moreover, to the extent that citizenship has come to be used as a federal instrument of Canadian unity, and as an instrument of propaganda by the federal government to promote its view of the good life in the federation, this was bound to generate reactions on the part of fragments of the population that had different points of view about what the good life is. Indeed, this is now happening. Quebec, being unable to find a place to locate its identity, its participation or its sense of belonging within the federal discourse, is searching for a new site where it might be easier to do so. This has led to the recent proposal for the construction of a Quebec citizenship that would attempt to articulate separate rules of the game.

In both Australia and Canada the notion of citizenship has not yet fully crystallized but is still emerging. However. the nature of the moral contracts also appears to evolve quite distinctly in each case. Canadian citizenship is fundamentally anchored in the notion of legal status and gives scant attention to participation; Australia emphasizes the participation dimension. Both countries pay attention to belonging, but in a starkly different manner. In Australia belonging is an emotional force to be emphasized as the foundation for commitment and participation; in Canada belonging is looked upon with suspicion, for it is an echo of subnational communities (national, ethnic, or other) that evokes emotional forces likely to undermine the integrity of the "national" political collectivity. Belonging is not abstract but visceral and in Canada belonging is feared because it is seen as pertaining primarily to sub-Canadian communities. Yet outbursts of emotion on the occasion of Canada Day reveal the depth of this untapped "national" resource.

Another important difference is in the relative importance given to the vertical and horizontal relationships, between state and citizen, and among citizens, in the definition of citizenship in Canada and Australia. In Canada the emphasis is clearly on the vertical dimension and citizenship is rooted fundamentally in the entitlements of the citizen in relation to the state. The social glue integrating the groups is supposed to emerge from the interregional, intergroup and interpersonal redistribution of resources, effected top down by a centralized state. This has bolstered the instrumental notion of citizenship as a one-way contract to gain access to certain rights. In Australia citizenship more truly emphasizes relationships among Australians and the commitment to other members of the community by citizens themselves. There is some hostility to the instrumental notion of citizenship, and a strong emphasis on an emotional commitment, on the recognition of obligations, and on an agreement to actively participate as a condition of entry.

Australia and Canada have both explicitly recognized the constraint of diversity in some formal way. However, in the case of Canada, there has been a greater reluctance until very recently to accept primary communities such as Quebec, or Aboriginal groups, because of the very size of the Quebec fragment and the multitude of small Aboriginal groups, for it might entail a significant balkanization of the country. In Australia the existence of aboriginal communities has been acknowledged, and there has been a genuine attempt to reconcile unity and diversity through a composite citizenship. Canada has been nervous about following the same strategy, so it has done so, in general, in a rather timid way, though sometimes in a bold way locally, as in the case of the establishment of Nunavut (Paquet 1999b).

The debate about the nature of the "civic" deficit has been robust in Australia since 1995. It is still inert in Canada. Instead of doing as Australia has done, and dealing forcefully and explicitly with the need to square the circle—to ensure national unity while fully legitimizing the diversity of the civil society and fostering community participation—Canada has allowed the debate on citizenship to remain moot and less explicit.

Despite the differences in approach, both countries are still grappling with some important challenges that are likely to materialize in each country in the form of moral contracts defining:

• how a multiplicity of citizenships and some order among
  these different allegiances are recognized;

　　　　　　　　　　　　　　DEEP CULTURAL DIVERSITY

- how citizenship can accommodate some priority among the multiplicity of allegiances to different ethnocultural or subnational communities within a nation-state;
- the degree of ease of entry and the power to deport, it being understood that the easier entry is, the more powerful the instruments of expulsion might have to be;
- how communities can be provided with a democratic voice in the governance of the country, either through some form of self-government or some sort of effective community representation;
- how differentiated citizenship might be used to reconcile the multiplicity of allegiances and the different levels of commitments;
- the focus on "recognition" and the redistribution of symbolic resources, and the extent to which it can be a substitute for the sharing of real resources or protection against real contingencies; and
- the requisite mixture of status, participation, and belonging in a world of multiple and limited identities through an explicit recognition that "ethnos" may well forge the largest possible site of belonging (Lind 2000).

The narrow interpretation of ethnicity as a static entity, instead of a form of cultural practice, has led to a very narrow definition of community and to a demonization of ethnicity. What is required is a capacity to recognize the social need for difference and a democracy of communities deriving from it, while not mandating that this should be the case for all communities, and therefore running the risk of balkanizing the country (Howard-Hassmann 1999).

The Canadian ethos appears to make it more difficult than in Australia to face squarely the need to explicitly negotiate the terms of integration for citizens and newcomers, and to determine what these terms might be in the new world of citizenship. Yet the task is clear: what is needed is a nexus of moral contracts that, first, ensures the requisite degree of rights, obligations, participation, and identity necessary for the country to prosper; second, ensures that all the stakeholders retain their basic freedoms (political, economic, social) as a way to increase their capabilities; and, third, defines the appropriate trade-offs between these two sets of priorities.

The more timid and gradualist Canadian way is not necessarily an inferior strategy, since it fits the Canadian ethos. However, it entails a complex and somewhat erratic process of social learning, where progress comes most of the time by fits and starts, locally, and by trial and error, rather than as a result of broadly debated revolutionary transformation. This often means that social learning is fractured and slower. This fundamental Canadian conservatism could prove extremely costly in an evolutionary learning sense.

However, this way of gauging the opportunity cost of the Canadian way may be somewhat unreasonable, for it presumes that Canada has the choice of doing it otherwise. While theoretically such is the case, in practice it is not. Compulsory debates imposed on a Canadian citizenry that has neither a taste for them nor a capacity to sustain them does not represent a meaningful alternative. Canada can no more adopt the Australian way than the Swiss or the Japanese way in defining its moral contracts of citizenship. Even if Canada has to face many of the same challenges as these other countries—globalization, growing polyethnicity and multiculturalism, and so on—it is forced to confront these challenges with a different habitus (Bourdieu 1972). This habitus constitutes Canada's idiosyncratic propensity to deal with issues in a particular way that has been inherited from its history and experience.

Canada's habitus is its organized reaction capability, its way of seeing, the sum of its dispositions, and it has to be taken as given, at least in the intermediate run. Changing it amounts to changing Canada's culture. The peculiar Canadian habitus is undoubtedly a source of slower learning and of a diminished ability to confront these challenges head on. Yet Canada is condemned to deal with these challenges in ways that are congruent with its habitus.

This particular way is not without some advantages after all. However frustrating and ineffective the Canadian way may appear by radical standards, it is not only efficient (as argued by Heath), but, as discussed in Chapter 5, may even constitute a truly attractive strategy for polyethnic, multicultural, and plural societies in general. Canada is slowly moving towards a supranational and community-based federalism, while fruitless "official" debates continue unabated in a manner that appears very unpromising. This modest and oblique way to get there is obviously a roundabout way of tackling the unity–diversity problem, but, in many cases, it may be the only practical way to proceed. This social technology to square the circle is exportable, and citizens of most small and medium-sized countries may well come to the conclusion, when they reflect on it that, in this sense, "they are all Canadians" (Paquet 2002).

Conclusion

Whatever the drift in the multiculturalism policy, and whether it is reshaped by a large number of limited but complementary agreements embodied in a Citizenship Act, may not be the essential issue. The central problem is that the debate about multiculturalism has revealed problems with the underlying Canadian social contract.

The bond between generations, between social groups, between regions, instituted in a variety of programmes intended to embody solidarity, has shown signs of strain. The multicultural fabric of the country is only one dimension where such strain has materialized. Everyone is conscious that without cooperation little possibility exists of developing a successful socioeconomy, yet, for want of glue, the country shows signs of tearing at the seams (Valaskakis 1990, Grimond 1991). Rethinking citizenship has already begun in polyethnic and pluricultural societies as a way of bringing about a solution to the generalized prisoner's dilemma that plagues such societies (Wihtol de Wenden 1989). Whether it succeeds in bringing about a social optimum is not the issue. What is at stake is public management of the transformation of modern communities into postmodern societies.

For the time being no public philosophy appears capable of providing the necessary inspiration for the reconstruction of new solidarities. There is a crisis of nationalities, of social programmes, and of regions and territories within national boundaries, and there are extreme tensions among generations. Unless a new notion of citizenship can bring about new principles on which to rebuild our community, anomie will continue to run amok and what took a few generations to build, in terms of trust and social capital, will be quickly dissipated. In this reconstruction the multiculturalism debate is, in a sense, exemplary, and its solution may also hold the key to many other crises plaguing Canada and other pluralist societies.

However, the difficulty in conducting an honest debate about these issues may be more acute with respect to multiculturalism than elsewhere. Any questioning of the wisdom of the policy is branded as racist so quickly that many have simply abandoned the forum. The result is not less *ressentiment* but less open airing of deeply felt concerns. This is probably the most important impediment to revision of a policy broadly regarded as unfortunate in some of its consequences and impact, despite the generous spirit from which it blossomed.

Australian and Canadian citizenships are good examples of emergent idiosyncratic realities. These complex institutions are the results of ongoing interactions between values and environment. The sort of social armistices and moral contracts embodying the workable notion of citizenship at any moment, and the sort of adaptive learning process defining the dynamics of the terms of integration over time, are different from one society to another.

This chapter has suggested that the syncretic notion of citizenship may be usefully analyzed through a prism that reveals its complexity, its fundamental transversality, and its essentially emergent nature. A two-stage process has been sketched to identify the basic dimensions of interest, and to suggest the mixture of ligatures that appears likely to be useful for comparing different types of citizenship. These templates have been used to contrast the Australian and Canadian ways of evolving notions of citizenship. In the Australian case the nexus of moral contracts defining citizenship appears to have been arrived at through more vibrant national debates, and to have elicited a more explicit and proactive set of moral contracts. In Canada a more *ad hoc* and pragmatic process, avoiding national debates, has generated a more tacit and passive set of vague arrangements. While the former experience appears to be more satisfying from an intellectual point of view, it depends on the existence of a national ethos and habitus that carry the capacity to underpin such national debates. Canada's ethos appears to be unable to promote and support such robust debates without generating divisiveness. We are therefore led to conclude that the slow and erratic road to citizenship adopted by Canada might be a usable model in our postmodern world. While one might deplore Canadians' incapacity to conduct a "high road" debate on such issues and bemoan the *ad hoc* nature of citizenship construction in Canada, the extraordinary excesses and violence that appear to ensue when such broad national debates are engineered or simply experienced in contexts to which they are unsuited seem to favour the more modest Canadian way.

This conclusion should not be interpreted, however, as condoning the centralized mindset that underpins the federal "liberal constitutional project" (Carter 1998) in vogue in Canada, nor its top-down, heavy-handed, arrogant efforts to stifle the voices of communities and to use citizenship as a way to smother deep cultural diversity. Removing the taboos attached to the critical evaluation of multiculturalism and accepting that many sacred cows, including egalitarianism, may have to be slaughtered in the process constitute useful first steps in the right direction.

The Charter as Governance Challenge

*Democratic nations are at all times fond of equality, but there are
certain epochs at which the passion they entertain for it swells to the
height of fury.*
—Alexis de Tocqueville

As Guillermo O'Donnell (1998) reminds us, governance in Western-style democracies is a balance among democracy, liberalism, and republicanism. Such a balance is required because any one of these principles carries a risk, were it to become completely dominant, of triggering a drift into a tyranny of the majority, a tyranny of the rich, or a tyranny of the elites. Such governance is also fundamentally a balance among the legal, the political, and the sociohistorical, and, again, some balance is required among these complementary elements if good governance is to ensue, for the hegemony of any one of these families of regulatory mechanisms might have significant and crippling unintended consequences—reification, whimsicality or inertia (Gauchet 2000).

Regardless of the nature of the mixed regime that prevails at any one time, a significant public sector apparatus exists, embodying the constellation of government and state arrangements corresponding to what is perceived as required in terms of coercion under conditions of time and space. This public sector apparatus differs from place to place, and evolves over time, wittingly or not, in response to internal and external pressures.

In the past twenty-five years modern democracies have experienced a broad range of reforms in the organization of all sectors, private, public, and social, in their institutions, and in their interactions. This has resulted from pressures generated by globalization and accelerated technological change, but also, and most importantly, as a result of greater cultural diversity, heightened expectations among citizens, crises in the public finances, new ideologies, and so forth. These pressures have eaten away at many basic assumptions upon which the more traditional forms of governing were built. The most important of these eroded assumptions are the notion that the state must dominate governing (state-centricity) because the public sector can do most things better and more effectively than the other two sectors; the fixation on "one size fits all" uniformity in the delivery of public services; and the notion that a firewall should be erected between the public sector and the rest of society.

As a result there has been a refoundation of the process of governing. Governing has been drifting from "Big G" government—a state-centric, centralized, massively redistributive regime—towards "small g" governance, which is more decentralized, network-based, and only prudently redistributive, and in which the state acts mainly as an *animateur* or catalyst in normal times. The deep cultural diversity of modern societies has called for more differentiated services to be delivered in different ways, often mixing private, public, and social, depending on issue domains, priorities, and preferences. As a result the boundaries of the different sectors have become blurred, and distrust of both the sociohistorical and the political has generated a significant new eminence for the legal.

The Impact of the Charter on the Rise of Möbius-Web Governance

This emerging new regime has been called "Möbius-web governance." Möbius-web governance is characterized by a mixture of formal and informal structures, and by processes that are multidirectional (vertical, horizontal, and transversal). The dynamics of such hybrid and baroque arrangements are intricate, and overlap over several levels in such a way as to form, in the words of James N. Rosenau (2003, p. 397), "a singular weblike process that, like a Möbius strip, neither begins nor culminates at any level or at any point in time." Such a regime of governance requires that authority be dispersed and decentralized. Its newly minted transformed public sector, the "strategic state" (Paquet 1996–97), is in the process of replacing the old welfare state.

This drift toward Möbius-web governance has not proceeded smoothly and linearly, but by fits and starts, with chance events, such as (in the case of Canada) the introduction of the Charter of Rights and Freedoms or the signing of the Free Trade Agreement with the United States and Mexico, acting in important ways to accelerate, delay, or even derail the emergence of the new regime, and the evolution from the welfare state to the strategic state. In the same way that, as Hubbard and Paquet (2007) have argued, the Gomery affair has had a negative impact on the evolution of Canadian governance, it may be said that the Charter, on a grander scale, has had a paradoxical overall negative impact in the past twenty-five years on the evolution towards a new governance regime and the strategic state.

Gauging the precise impact of the Charter on the drift of the whole institutional order, and on Canadian governance in general, is a perilous exercise for two reasons. First, it is not clear that there is sufficient information and relevant speculations already available to provide a composite portrait of the emerging Möbius-type governance and the strategic state. It may threfore be difficult to calibrate the precise degree to which the Charter, and the effervescence of adjudicatory bodies that have emerged in parallel (Paquet 2006a), have slowed the drift toward this elusive destination. Second, twenty-five years is a very short time span in the life of a constitutional document such as the Charter, so the full and definitive impact may not have been felt yet.

That being said, whatever we know now is no basis for even cautious optimism. The idolatry of rights, exacerbated by the Charter, has had deleterious effects on the balance among the legal, the political, and the sociohistorical, to the detriment of the political. This hypertrophy and absolutization of rights has underpinned the radicalization of an egalitarian utopia that fuels indignation in the face of any clear facts suggesting that we have not yet reached such a utopian state of affairs; a consequent crippling of the discussion of many complex issues calling for a "more or less" compromise into palavers about black-and-white radical solutions; and an impatience with the process of deliberation aiming at constructing wise compromises, and thereby a tendency to replace the democratic conversation by processes of adjudication. This has clearly slowed the drift from "Big G" to "small g."

The Argument in Synopsis

Like all such bills or charters of rights, the Canadian Charter was originally purported to protect its citizens from their governments by ensuring *negative freedom*, freedom from restraint for the citizen. However, through various means, of which judicial activism is the central one (Leishman 2006), the Canadian Charter has morphed into a machine producing entitlements, and therefore into an engine that forces governments to accept new responsibilities, often imposed on them by the courts, in the name of an interpretation of *positive freedom*, which is claimed to be required for one to have the capacity and ability to fully accomplish one's potential. Much of the activism around the Charter is anchored in one feature regarded by some as the main feature of positive freedom: egalitarianism.

As a result of this *Charter twist*, groups have begun to express more readily their wishes and preferences, and therefore to call for a redistribution of resources in their favour, in the language of "Charter rights" instead of the traditional language of needs. This has been done more and more in the name of egalitarianism, and it has been argued that the massive redistribution required by egalitarianism calls for centralization, since resources have to be brought to the centre if they are to be redistributed. This sort of state-centricity, which stands in sharp contrast to the philosophy of subsidiarity that imbues "small g" governance, has been strengthened by the imperium of the courts, but also by the family of adjudicators and commissars charged with the tasks of guarding privacy, protecting the official languages, monitoring access to information, and so on. These commissars have become the final moral arbiters and enforcers of the "new entitlements" born out of the combination of an abuse of the language of rights, the emergence of a fundamentalism of entitlements, and a despotism of political correctness. In that sense the Charter has become an impediment to the blossoming of decentralized and distributed governance.

Whether this is simply the temporary result of Canadian inertia, the lack of restraint of some Charter-enthusiastic utopian officials or the lack of courage of elected politicians—a matter that jurisprudence might correct in due time—is unclear. Cynics say that this toxic mixture is more likely going to be a poisoned legacy that will create permanent damage to the fabric of society.

To understand more precisely the ways in which the Charter has reinforced certain features of the old order, and weakened support for some alternative futures, one needs to develop an appreciation of the societal context into which the Charter grenade was lobbed. It is not possible to focus on all aspects of this broad context, and I shall concentrate on intercultural relations as a particular domain where it is possible to illustrate and gauge the impact of the Charter.

Until the latter half of the twentieth century cultural markers were traditionally transferred vertically from one generation to the next through family and community "authority." Today an individual's cultural profile is diffracted more than ever before and is the product of many sources: inherited traits, but also constantly evolving personal choices assembled from a mobile and diverse menu of alternative employments, religious and other affiliations, family configurations, recreational interests, even shifting geographic locations. Individuals have multiple, different, partial, and evolving identities. A society of such mutants cannot subsist without a minimal covenant guaranteeing that these evolving identities cohere, or at least are somewhat compatible. This covenant is what is usually referred to as citizenship. Citizenship is a kind of broad ensemble of moral contracts defining the desirable and workable degree of *integration*, a word covering everything from tolerated ethnic enclaves, to negotiated *modus vivendi*, to assimilation to the dominant culture.

In the modern context the notion of citizenship has been characterized by different rules of membership, different intensities of belonging and participation required, and greater or lesser cultural homogeneity. The polity has become involved both in affirming, winning public acceptance for, ensuring, and maintaining an agreed degree of cultural integration, and in ensuring that the corridor of diversity, in the broadest sense of the term, is contained within viable bounds. This is the very complex world that the Charter has entered and tampered with. My argument is that its thrust has contributed dramatically to supporting the state-centricity of the "Big G" regime and the official multiculturalism policy that it introduced in the 1970s, and has been instrumental in considerably hardening the features of this model. In so doing it has considerably slowed down the emergence of the alternative polycentric "small g" regime and the transcultural, cosmopolitan or mixing model of intercultural relations that appears to stem naturally from it.

A Blind Leap of Faith and Two Flawed Assumptions

In his book *La contre-démocratie* Pierre Rosanvallon (2006) suggests that modern democracies like Canada have entered an age of mistrust characterized by greater surveillance of officials, an emphasis on resisting, vetoing, and sabotaging their actions, and a great amount of adjudication and judicialization in place of democratic conversation. The Charter may be regarded both as part of this process and as something that has given it a harder edge in Canada.

In such a world public decision-making has become strained and neurotic. It is based more than ever before on hunches and impressions rather than facts. Governments address a broad array of disparate projects in desultory fashion without much rigour or critical thinking. Top echelons centralize power, and are characterized by narcissistic needs, desire for attention and visibility, action for action's sake, and an unreflective style of decision-making (Juillet and Paquet 2002). The Charter has most certainly added a quantum effect to this process and its impact was all the more insidious given that Canadians in general, as opposed to interest groups that have made careers out of making use of it, have only the vaguest idea what the Charter is, and what it has done for and to them. Moreover, the interpretations of the Charter are quite different in English Canada and French Canada, being generally communitarian in French Canada and anti-communitarian elsewhere (Burelle 2007).

This is not to say that Canadians are not very supportive of the Charter. In their own way they are supportive: more than half of Canadians polled in 2007 thought that it has had a positive effect on Canada in the past and is moving Canadian society in the right direction for the future. Yet, given the fact that different groups read into this Rorschachian document whatever they want to see, it is difficult to take these opinions seriously. The title of the document refers to rights and freedoms, which are obviously good things, so the uninformed citizenry is prone to make a leap of faith. Yet as soon as the conversation becomes more concrete and citizens gain a better appreciation of what the Charter has made possible—for example, two thirds of the Charter decisions by the Supreme Court involve the protection of the rights of those accused of crimes—Canadians are most of the time quite surprised and less enthralled. It is therefore reasonable to say that the positive opinion of Canadians about the Charter is not an informed opinion.

Notwithstanding their ignorance about the Charter, Canadians' views on many issues have been significantly shaped by its diktats. Key judicial decisions have become incontestable reference points, sacred cows celebrated as "progressive" in the media, and they have shaped Canadians' politically correct attitudes. These views have become mental prisons that can be challenged only at one's peril, for the Charter propaganda has come to make court interpretations of the Charter into an infallible echo of the non-negotiable foundational principles on which this country is purported to have been built. So-called "shared Canadian values" and egalitarianism have thereby become icons.

Indeed, reference to "shared Canadian values" has become a staple product of the Charter. This is an echo effect of the folk sociology that used to identify shared values as a way to characterize societies. Yet it is quite difficult to find such shared values in a pluralistic society. One may reasonably say, as Joseph Heath has in the John L. Manion Lecture (2003), that the myth of shared values is based on the false presumption that "social integration is achieved through value consensus" (p. 2), that shared values are what make people cohesive as a group, and that the state exists to promote these values. While most sociologists have by now abandoned the theory of shared values, "shared values theorists" remain an impressive phalanx within the federal bureaucracy. This theory has had an impact on the extraordinary popularity of values in the federal bureaucratic discourse over recent years. One of the main problems with the Charter, as Heath has shown, is that it has been interpreted as a system of values rather than as a set of instrumental principles, such as efficiency, equality, autonomy or non-violence, deemed to be helpful in maintaining the neutrality of the state and other public institutions in respect of different notions of the good.

In a deeply diverse and pluralistic society it is impossible to identify what shared values are because individuals and groups have very different notions of the good life. The best one can hope for, especially in a turbulent world where the means and ends of individuals and groups are continually redefined as the result of evolving circumstances, is agreement on some principles that are likely to preserve the neutrality of the public order.

The confusion between values and principles, and the excesses that this confusion has generated, is most flagrant in the case of the notion of equality, which has come to be interpreted wrongly and most unhelpfully by the courts as meaning that each person or group must be treated identically. The basic principle of equality calls only for the state to be neutral in respect of the different preferences and projects of individuals and groups. It does not entail in any way that uniformity must be enforced (Heath 2003, p. 28).

A sense of the distortion that ensues when principles are transmogrified into values is illustrated by the case of same-sex marriage. As Heath suggests, the courts, instead of declaring that marriage as a sacrament is not a matter in which the state should be involved, has chosen to insist that both homosexual and heterosexual couples should be treated identically, and be allowed to make use of the sacrament. The reasonable way out was obviously for the state to be ordered out of the sacrament business and directed to recognize civil unions as the only legal institution—the very solution that the Quebec political process had elected. This is not what the courts decided.

The fixation on interpreting the Charter as defining shared values has infected jurisprudence with a philosophy of egalitarianism that is quite foreign to the principle of equality. The Charter has allowed interest groups to take advantage of the new instrument to advance their causes by invoking egalitarianism, insisting that the contents of their particular project be assigned not only equal consideration but identical treatment.

Egalitarianism is a basic philosophy that states that "all human beings should be treated with equal consideration unless there are good reasons against it" (Kekes 2003, p. 1). Given the extraordinary variety of human conditions, and the differences among individuals in talents, capacities, and projects, it is difficult to understand why this cautious presumption has come to be interpreted as an imperative for *identical* treatment, and for arrangements that make rights and resources more equal to be considered as a foundational precondition and imperative for progress. Such a philosophy allows one principle, equality, to take precedence over all others, at the expense of all others, and ordains indiscriminate compassion for any person claiming to be at a real or imagined disadvantage, on the basis of an optimistic faith that every human being is by nature equally worthy, and that evil is ascribable to bad political arrangements generating non-uniformity of treatment. As a result it is argued by egalitarians that the search for absolute equality should guide the design of social architecture and political arrangements.

Practical reason points in quite different directions from that sort of ratiocination. It focuses instead on the particularities of persons and circumstances. Imposing an absolute egalitarian credo that trumps all other features and takes precedence over all other considerations is quite a crippling ideology. Yet this egalitarian ideal has become the basis for the framing of many decisions in the courts, where equality rights have become the principle that has been allowed to trump all others. The framing of questions in terms of equality rights has not only allowed the courts to gain the upper hand in their dialogue with the legislatures, but it has also allowed the judiciary to become instrumental in forcing the state to intervene when and where it had chosen not to, or where, it can be argued, it should not be present. This has often been done at great costs to Canadians and has resulted in the courts' superseding the polity in the shaping of social policy in numerous areas.

This has often been done in ways that were neither in keeping with what the majority of Canadians felt was warranted, nor with the required neutrality of the state. This hardening of the egalitarian ideology by the courts as a result of the Charter has largely been a matter of convenience. Playing equality as trump allows the courts to escape from having to delve deeper than before to take the particularities of each different situation into account.

Moreover, the courts have disregarded the dynamics of envy that such an egalitarian narrative unleashes. As de Tocqueville argued, in a plural and deeply diverse society the utopian egalitarian pursuit is not only unreasonable and intolerable, but fuels the uniformity generation machine and brings it to the level of fury. The smaller and the more symbolic the differences between agents or groups become or remain, the more vicious the fights to eliminate them (Laurent and Paquet 1991). When the courts have begun to calibrate what any non-uniformity may do to the "dignity" of different agents and groups, they have come very close to some modern version of how many angels can fit on the head of a pin. Indeed, they have come close to inventing new standards of political correctness that might be the harbingers, as Justice John Sopinka once warned in an address at Concordia University, of some restriction on free speech. There are times when "effrontery" and "indecency" may be called for (Lukes 1997).

Practical reasoning usually escapes from such absolutism and generates reasonable responses *in situ*, even if problems have not been completely theorized (Sunstein 2000). Trade-offs between different principles are arrived at pragmatically. This is how utopian egalitarianism gets tamed in the real world into some form of *equability*, applying a principle that calls for a sustained effort to eliminate unacceptable or especially troublesome inequalities. The courts, on the other hand, have pursued a quixotic quest to explore the limits of equality (Richer 2006).

The basic thrust of the Charter movement, centred on shared values and egalitarianism, may be contestable, but it has been effectively marketed by the Charter party and remains quasi-hegemonic in the public mind to this day. Through its celebration in the media it has also had a major impact on the national discourse. Yet there is another most important and fundamental channel through which the Charter has had an impact: diffuse as it may appear, the Charter has transformed the lay public narratives in Canada through its impact on the Canadian *Zeitgeist*. The Charter has interacted in a symbiotic way with the sociopolitical context, and has contributed significantly to strengthening and hardening certain features of the national public discourse and the narratives in good currency. In some of the national debates about health care, for example, it has led to a passion for uniformity such that envy has become a national virtue. The whole debate about the elimination of the state monopoly on basic health care, and about the possibility of allowing private-sector suppliers to offer services to those able and willing to pay, has generated a vibrant opposition to such a scheme, fundamentally based on the bizarre credo that "if I cannot get such a service, nobody else should be allowed to obtain it."

The Psychosocial Echo Box as Multiplier

Three contextual features may be said to have been catalyzed and reinforced by the impact of the Charter: the fundamentalism of entitlements; the idolatry of rights; and the despotism of political correctness.

The complex dynamics of citizen's claims in the name of real or imaginary entitlements, and of state-centricity as a mechanism to ensure that these entitlements will be honoured, had already created a vicious self-reinforcing cycle in the world of the welfare state. Post-war governments have thrived at the electoral level by inventing a large number of entitlements without paying any attention to the sort of wealth generation necessary to finance them, or even to the sort of reduction in the responsibilities of the citizen that might be triggered by such paternalism. Welfare state governments not only graciously bestowed free public goods and services on citizens, they also persuaded citizens that they were "entitled" to these goods and services. Canadians developed an "entitlement speak," and their sense of responsibility for their own sustenance and survival went to sleep. The Charter, echoing the enthusiasms of its time, dramatically bolstered this sense of entitlement and conveyed to Canadians not only that it would ensure freedom from state intrusion, but also, and most importantly, that it would guarantee entitlements to state benefits. This indoctrination was so successful that the very definition of Canadian citizenship came to be reduced to a bouquet of such entitlements in many public debates, and Canadian identity became confused with medicare benefits and the like.

Interpreted in an egalitarian frame of mind by the courts, the Charter became an invitation for all groups feeling relatively disadvantaged, or having preferences different from the majority, to argue that equality in the Charter was to be interpreted not as equality of opportunity, but as equality of outcome. This inflation of entitlements was considerably bolstered by a crippled epistemology (Hardin 2002) that has permeated the whole sociopolitical system as a result of the influential impact of the Berry–Taylor doctrine, which came into good currency during the 1980s.

This doctrine, named for the prominent scholars John W. Berry and Charles Taylor, stemmed from the same delusional world that brought forth egalitarianism, and was marked by the same sentimentality, indiscriminate compassion, and the deep narcissism of the tribe from which, supposedly, one should not be weaned (Kekes 2003, Chapter 13, and Hill 2000). It developed an approach to deep cultural diversity in a plural society based on two basic propositions: *the multicultural assumption*, which asserts that only those who are secure in their ethnocultural/diverse background will be open to others and tolerant toward others (Berry, Kalin, and Taylor 1977); and *the politics of recognition*, which asserts that such an integration-prone setting can best be achieved through an explicit recognition of the ethnocultural identities of these persons and groups (Taylor 1992). These two propositions clearly reinforce each other and produce a psychosocial dynamics that provides much support for multiculturalism as a strategy. Both have been accepted without much critical thinking as providing the theoretical foundation for the Canadian strategy, and the canonical version has been propagandized and extended by Will Kymlicka, who has added the feature that affirmative action is required to repair not only present but also past cultural prejudices (Kymlicka 1995).

These propositions are contestable. They tend to allow certain cultural features to be dominant and almost exclusive markers, and to suggest that formal and official recognition of these markers as foundational, and therefore their reification in their present state, should be pursued with the active support of the state, to the exclusion of, or at least in preference to, others. The Charter underpinned this shaky theorization. It provided an intellectual scaffolding to support a particular strategy of integration built on a hardening of cultural differences and the granting of crucial importance to the redistribution of symbolic resources—for recognition and redistribution amount to the same thing (Tully 2000)—based on the egalitarian philosophy that all cultures have the same rights.

The fundamentalism of cultural entitlements generated by egalitarianism and the Charter has become immunized from critical evaluation both by the aura of legitimacy bestowed on these entitlements, because they are couched in a language of rights, and by the added protection of political correctness, which allows spurious beliefs and groundless presumptions to escape challenge. The Berry–Taylor problematic has become the new canon, and has received both academic and political accolades.

Egalitarianism and the entitlement mentality have also benefited from one of the major defence mechanisms against critical thinking: the wholesale adoption of the language of rights. This is a potent rhetorical device. Rights have an aura of legitimacy, as if they were the result of virgin birth out of high principles, and therefore are not obvious candidates for any debate. Few remember that they are the results of political haggling and discussion in not always enlightened legislatures. The nimbus around them may be said to have emerged in the late 1940s, when the Universal Declaration of Human Rights, covering a whole range of economic, social, and political claims, was put forward as an ideal to be pursued. This did much to blur rights, preferences, ideals, and the like into an amalgam. In the era of the welfare state, which gave more and more precedence to security over freedom and autonomy, this document became a blueprint of entitlements to be acquired. The rhetorical power of such claims led to a displacement of the language of needs, always contestable, by the language of rights, which, it was claimed, were not contestable.

The notion of *displacement of concepts* (Schön 1963) is most useful to capture the subtle but fundamental transformation in the notion of rights over the past sixty years. Michael Ignatieff labels this discontinuity "rights as politics" and "rights as idolatry" (Ignatieff 2001). The central idea is that human rights have drifted from connoting pragmatic political instruments for protecting human agency against abuse, oppression, and degradation—and therefore being identified with negative freedom—to connoting any aspiration or anything desirable that can be pronounced a right, on the basis that some have felt it necessary, with or without any foundation for the claim, for the individual to develop as fully as he/she can or would like to—so that rights come to be identified with positive freedom. As Ignatieff points out, since legitimate core rights are a "tool kit against oppression" one should not automatically define anything desirable as a right, because that is bound to erode the legitimacy of those core rights. In Canada minority groups have come to define all sorts of things as rights guaranteed by the Charter, from being allowed to bring your homosexual boyfriend to the high school prom, to receiving welfare benefits even though you live with a spouse who can financially afford to support the entire household. This has led to an abuse of the language of rights.

The dynamics triggered by the displacement of concepts evoked above, especially when it is robustly propelled by judicial activism, has entailed not only an inflation of rights, but a dominance of *righteousness.* This sleight of hand has allowed the courts to entertain any complaint about wishes in the clothing of rights. In normal times, in a normal country, such excesses would have been contained by strong voices from civil society or vigilant legislatures. This is not the case in countries where deference and political correctness have become major forces in certain domains, and where "progressivism"—often defined as the ideological lever used whenever what one wants to propose a policy that one cannot persuasively defend on rational grounds—is the new Pole Star. Political correctness has prevented people from denouncing "luxury rights" for fear of being branded non-progressive, and this has led to an orgy of frivolous cases. Indeed, claiming anything as a right has become a conversation-stopper, and thereby also an obstacle to deliberation.

This new despotism of political correctness has left elected officials so intimidated by the Charter and its rhetoric that they have routinely chosen not to challenge the courts, even when the rulings were clearly unreasonable, as in the Singh case, where the court's decision entailed a loss of control on the country's borders. This is the case even though elected legislators have a necessary tool for putting the courts back in their place, in the form of the notwithstanding clause in the Charter itself (section 33). Yet the false aura of the Charter has been such that governments have proved incapable of articulating anything but timid and unpersuasive responses to undesirable court decisions, and have even failed to convince the rights-minded population that invoking the notwithstanding clause would not necessarily curtail their freedom.

Together, the fundamentalism of entitlements, the idolatry of rights, and the despotism of political correctness have had a toxic impact. Not only have they dramatically slowed down the drift from "Big G" government to "small g" governance, but they have, syncretically with the Charter, generated a crippled epistemology that has led to extremism and fanaticism. This, in turn, has prevented the emergence of a less inadequate governance regime, the more so as some sections of the Charter—namely 7 (life, liberty and security of the person), 15 (equality rights), and 27 (multiculturalism) —have come to be used more aggressively by the Charter party.

The Charter as Blockage to Intercultural Interaction

As noted earlier, it is not possible in a relatively short book, still less in one chapter of it, to examine all the ways in which the Charter has affected the process of change in Canadian society. Consequently, I shall focus mainly on one issue, intercultural relations, to illustrate what is meant when one states that the Charter has blocked the emergence of alternative policies. By stating sharply (in section 27) that the whole document has to be interpreted in the light of the Canadian engagement to maintain and enhance a commitment to multiculturalism, the Charter has clearly blocked the way to the exploration of meaningful and superior alternatives to multiculturalism. Yet multiculturalism has generated many problems and is clearly not the *optimum optimorum*. Multiculturalism not only tribalizes society and prevents citizens from forgetting where they come from, it also presumes and insists that it is desirable to maintain and enhance these origins. In the parlance of Jason Hill, we have weaned ourselves from our mothers' breasts, but not from "the name of the tribe, the race, the ethnos, and the *Volk*," and thus Hill speaks of a "prolonged nursing sanctioned by the state" (Hill 2000, pp. 5–6).

I shall try to deal with the question in two stages: first, by underlining the way in which the Charter has stultified societal adjustments in general; and, second, by discussing a most promising alternative to multiculturalism that, because of the Charter, has not been explored as fully as it should have been. This alternative may be called "intermediate cosmopolitanism" (as in Chapter 6), or, more appropriately, *transculturalism*.

The first element of stultification has to do with the fact that the Charter has dramatically shifted the power to define basic principles for governing the country from elected officials to an unelected oligarchy of judges and commissars. This shift is likely both to accentuate the centralization of governing and to take power away from the provinces. The entrenchment of the Charter in the Constitution has dramatically Americanized our governance. While the Supreme Court in the United States has reigned for more than two hundred years as the definer of inalienable rights that neither the federal government nor state governments may infringe, in Canada the supremacy of Parliament was not questioned until the Charter was adopted in 1982. That did not mean that, in practice, freedoms were less valued or secure in Canada than in the United States, but that the final arbiter on these issues remained the Canadian Parliament. Now, however, the unelected and unrepresentative federal judiciary has the upper hand, and it is likely, given its egalitarian mindset, to support a high degree of centralization within the federation.

It must also be appreciated that the either–or *modus operandi* of the judiciary, with its imperial mindset, may be expected to modify the balance between federal and provincial powers. The "peace, order, and good government" clause of section 91 of the British North America Act 1867 (now renamed the Constitution Act 1867) bestowed residual powers on the federal government, but this has effectively come over time to be restricted to *emergency* situations. Section 92 (13) has become *de facto* the principal residuary clause, providing the provincial parliaments with claims to residual authority in normal times. This delicate balance in favour of the provincial parliaments could be tipped by Supreme Court decisions, significantly reducing the capacity of the different provinces to follow different paths and giving greater power to the federal government than is desirable.

A second element of stultification is the crystallization of the notion of cultural identity that has been triggered by the Charter and its circumstances. The human agency of a multitude of Canadians has been severely reduced to the culture each is perceived to belong to, even though this is only one dimension of these human beings. Moreover, the commitment to maintain and enhance multiculturalism (in section 27) has contributed to reifying and congealing the state of communities at a particular stage of their development. This is tragic for the First Nations, which would appear to be caught in a time warp, but it also applies to other cultural communities.

A third element is the degree of formalization and contestability in front of courts that has plagued all adjustments, including intercultural adjustments, in the post-Charter world, and stunted the process of evolutionary integration. When the focus of adjustment is based on litigation much of the subtlety of this process, which is complex and multidimensional, vanishes. Indeed, it may even be conducive to a much greater degree of ideological warfare than is necessary. This has emerged most graphically in the rhetoric used in some extraordinary defences of Canada's multiculturalism policy. A particularly interesting and intemperate piece that deserves some clinical deconstruction is V. S. Wilson's presidential address to the Canadian Political Science Association, which illustrates the sort of dead end that the idolatry of egalitarianism and ethnocentricity leads to (Wilson 1993): complacency, denial, self-congratulation, speculation about others' motives, rants, and deafness in the face of any of the arguments offered by those who have expressed unease about the thrust of Canadian multiculturalism policy.

A fourth blockage is the extraordinarily thin notion of citizenship engineered by the courts as a result of Charter cases, with citizenship being reduced to a bouquet of almost unbounded entitlements. This was clearly established by the courts in the Singh case. Mere presence on Canadian territory appears to suffice for all the privileges of citizenship, except the right to vote, being bestowed on a new entrant. The Lebanese crisis of 2006 also revealed that the mere possession of a Canadian passport was sufficient basis for claims to an unlimited entitlement to protection and repatriation, even when the individual who holds that passport has other citizenships and has no meaningful links with Canadian society such as paying Canadian taxes (Cohen 2007, Chapter 3).

By embedding multiculturalism in the Constitution of the country the Charter has bound Canada to a policy that generates the tribalization, the formalization, and the judicialization of intercultural interaction. Indeed, the seduction of the Berry–Taylor doctrine, as presented by its originators, has wrongly and unduly defined the range of alternatives to multiculturalism to a few possibilities—assimilation, apartheid or marginalization—and has declared them all socially unacceptable. Our point is that not all genuine alternatives need be so.

The symbiosis between the Charter and the Berry–Taylor doctrine feeds a great deal of toxicity. Their joint insistence on maintaining and enhancing the commitment to originary cultural features appears to presume that one's cultural identity is hard-wired and determinant in perpetuity. In fact, agents and groups are always in a process of *becoming* (as John Dewey put it), and therefore in a process of self-creation likely to take the form of new layers of identity, hybridization, and all sorts of dynamic change. This is the very process that both the Charter and the Berry–Taylor doctrine seek to slow down by insisting on building on a foundation of false essentialisms in which citizens are involuntarily encapsulated. In thus reifying intercultural interaction the Charter has blocked the way to experimenting with other approaches to intercultural integration, notably transculturalism, which is intent on bridging intercultural differences, in contrast to multiculturalism, which insists on preserving "inherent" differences.

This alternative to multiculturalism is not a new idea. Before the Charter closed the possibility of moving in this direction it was regarded, not necessarily as a panacea, but at least as a promising alternative built on rapprochement rather than distance. Many have attacked transculturalism as a brand of cosmopolitanism, and as utopian and unrealistic (as discussed in Chapter 6), but there is more to be said about it. As used by the Vice Versa group, which published a magazine with that title between 1983 and 1996 (and rekindled its activities in 2007 at viceversamag.com), transculturalism connotes a dynamic, evolutionary, and continuous process of *becoming* that breaks out of the shackles of originary cultures and celebrates open mixing. It builds on dynamic and continuously evolving identities, and frontally challenges multiculturalism as "a new form of racism" that exorcizes difference by absolutizing it (Visker 1994, p. 89).

Modern societies are neither monolithic nor static. Constitutionalizing divisions among Canadians, or judicializing their social interactions, can only cause degeneration into some form of multitribalism. As an alternative to the multiculturalism policy, which "has now forced the judiciary and the right of law to define culture, identities, thus making identities a political issue and no longer a societal issue, decided and debated in the public space" (Cuccioletta 2001–02, p. 7), transculturalism may be interpreted as suggesting that multiculturalism is only, at best, a preliminary and initial stage in the process of evolution following the modern demographic shuffle. It should not be reified, but rather kept in as fluid a state as possible, for the only thing that multiculturalism achieves is recognition that assimilation, apartheid, and marginalization impose unjust institutional orders on others. It does not in any way spell out what the preferred alternative reasonable terms of integration might be.

These terms of integration are better spelled out by transculturalism. They entail, as Donald Cuccioletta explains (Cuccioletta 2001–02, pp. 8–9):

> [a] new form of humanism based on the idea of relinquishing the strong traditional identities and cultures which in many cases were products of . . . empires. . . . Contrary to multiculturalism, which, most experiences have shown, reinforces boundaries based on past cultural heritages, transculturalism is based on the breaking down of boundaries. In many ways, transculturalism . . . based on a culture of *métissage* [mixing], is in opposition to the singular traditional cultures that have evolved from the nation-state. This process of recognizing oneself in the *other* leads inevitably to a cosmopolitan citizenship. This citizenship, independent of political structures and institutions, develops each individual in the understanding that one's culture is multiple, *métis* [mixed], and that each human experience and existence is due to the contact with the *other* who in reality is like oneself.

The fundamental difference between multiculturalism and transculturalism is that, while the former emphasizes boundaries and essentialist identities, the latter emphasizes the fostering of heterogeneous interaction. The foundations of multiculturalism are the basis for much of the "humiliation industry," generating claims by almost every group demanding a right to be different that such demands have been unduly constrained and that their "dignity" has been impugned. This is the source of many boundary quarrels, but also of denunciations of perceived slights, even when humour is used. The world of multiculturalism is one in which Jonathan Swift would not be welcome. In contrast, transculturalism emphasizes the fuzziness, elusiveness, and evanescence of such cultural boundaries as identifiers. They are as often imaginary as they are real, but they are also always changing and therefore ephemeral.

The "cultural nation" is often offered, in Quebec and elsewhere, as the embodiment of transculturalism, a locus of interaction and mixing, a place where memberships are of necessity "multiple, cumulative, and changing." Yet there is considerable paradoxical content in the epistles written by the apostles of the "cultural nation," who tend to assume, as in the case of Quebec, that some common denominator must exist—not only a common language, but also the active common effort to promote a number of "ideas, civilizational values, and social choices" (Bouchard 1999, p. 25). Consequently, this entails a "boutique transculturalism" and a totalitarian view of identity that is foreign to transculturalism. The "cultural nation," in this sense, remains embedded in pseudo-diversity or surface diversity, of the sort that is echoed when some in East Asia refer to their assimilated brothers in the West as "bananas" (yellow on the outside but white on the inside). This approach remains fundamentally assimilationist, despite its transcultural mask. Too many dimensions must be homogenized for such a society to be called deeply diverse.

There is also a scintilla of deception in such narratives, for the sort of diversity openly and vibrantly proclaimed is in fact bogus. Homogenization at a fundamental level entails nothing less than eradicating genuine pluralism. The congealment and idolatry of elusive but deeply binding cultural markers are not unlike those of the religious markers of yesteryear, and they become extraordinarily dangerous when they are used (by Will Kymlicka for instance) as a rationale for ascribing differentiated rights and citizenship on the basis of past injustices having been suffered. Such differential rights claimed for groups that are said to have been disadvantaged, in the name of the sacred egalitarian norm, raise insoluble problems of interpretation. The Vice Versa group and its magazine helped to expose the deceptive pluralism of the "cultural nation," a strategy that came forth a dollar short and a day late in the debates in Quebec. It pretended up front to allow for mixing, hybridity, and the possibility of an open evolutionary process leading to still undefined new cultural mixtures, but immediately and sharply imposed constraints on this forward-looking process by dramatically limiting these future possibilities and firmly anchoring culture, seen as the foundational dimension of identity, in a truly static and backward-looking sacredness of origins.

Modulating the Charter with the Use of Invisible Institutions

The Charter appears to have locked Canada into a multiculturalist regime that prevents experimenting with promising alternatives. No revolution can be expected to modulate this Charter effect unless it is subtle and comes by surprise. Otherwise change could not occur at all, "for it would be suppressed by the forces that are in favour of the status quo" (Hirschman 1995, p. 136).

One subtle way to put flats and sharps into the Charter score would be through jurisprudence generated by the courts, and especially the Supreme Court, where casuistry is in play. Yet this avenue is rather unlikely to materialize, given the nature of the judicial system in Canada and the guy-wires imposed by the precedents generated over the past twenty-five years. An alternative is the development of a variety of conventions, implicit and explicit, to work around the Charter—what the economist Kenneth Arrow calls "invisible institutions" (Arrow 1974, p. 26). Such soft and informal arrangements, which would not blatantly violate the diktats of the Charter and would remain below the radar screen, would allow pragmatism to trump dogmatism. Moreover, they might even, over time, create an ethos of experimentation and foster evolutionary adjustment.

This subversive and roundabout route may promise only bricolage, baby steps, and local experiments, and such a trial-and-error approach may annoy staunch believers in the sanctity of the formal, the legal, and the clearly explicit. However, things unseen are often part of what governance is all about (Paquet 2005a). As Chester Barnard concluded, some seventy years ago, "among those who cooperate, the things that are seen are moved by the things unseen" (Barnard 1938, p. 284). "Invisible institutions" or conventions are based on trust and "moral creativeness" as fundamental forces in the unfolding of effective coordination. A whole branch of economics dealing with these conventions has emerged in recent years (Batifoulier 2001, Eymard-Duvernay 2006). The core concerns are focused on understanding the whole array of informal agreements among agents that complement the usual standard coordination mechanisms of the market and the state. In game theory these arrangements and agreements have been shown to resolve many situations that otherwise would have resulted in stalemates and dead ends.

My objective in this section is not to explore all such possible contraptions, in all possible directions, but rather to focus on three potential stratagems meant to circumvent the multiculturalism trappings embedded in the Charter. These three avenues call for the use of moral contracts; for the explicit negotiation of reasonable accommodation among cultural groups *in situ*; and for differentiated citizenship to be generalized on the basis, not of past victimization, real or imaginary, but of allowing individuals and groups to choose some stylized packages of obligations that are commensurate with the packages of legitimate entitlements they are seeking.

Moral contracts are not a new thing. From time immemorial they have taken the form of a handshake to seal a deal, the contours of which often remained very fuzzy, because it was contingent on many unpredictable circumstances. The different parties agree to commit to such informal arrangements on the basis of minimal trust, or at least of workable or acceptable levels of distrust. Such moral contracts are not adjudicated or adjudicable by formal tribunals, but are in the nature of moral engagements. They represent a form of social glue, often derived from the sociohistorical (that is, from tradition), based on ligatures that greatly facilitate social intercourse and economize on lawyers' fees. They may be contracts that are internal to an organization, and thus among partners, or external, between insiders and outsiders (Paquet 1991–92). In a sense the development and evolution of moral contracts may be regarded as the equivalent of "jurisprudence," but a kind of jurisprudence that is clearly under the control of the agents and their capacity to imagine workable arrangements, rather than under the sole aegis of exogenously inspired courts. The experimentation that moral contracts allow provides a very subtle means through which social ligatures may be modified in a multiplicity of ways by agreement rather than by litigation.

Examples of the use of such instruments as agents of change have been numerous in recent times (Paquet and Pigeon 2000, Heintzman 2007). They have often built on ligatures such as professionalism and ethics. In fact, the full heuristic power of the moral contract has been illustrated in a most intriguing philosophical paper built on the analogy and congruity between morality and contract. Frank Snare (1977) shows that moral contracts entail reciprocity, so that "if one party does not live up to his side of the bargain, the other is discharged from fulfilling his obligations in return" (p.307). This fundamental point yields important implications that are neither always obvious nor readily acknowledged, but have considerable moral force: "there is no reason why morality should generally operate so as to subsidize flaunted injustice or to tolerate self-declared social parasites" (p. 309). This analysis suggests that a person in contempt of the law, whether it is formal law or an informal moral contract, "could be put out of the protection and aid of the law . . . One consequence of taking seriously the metaphor of morality as contract is that we may begin to see the immoralist as a sort of *moral outlaw* [my emphasis] beyond the pale of the moral contract" (p.303).

Moral contracts are the subject of continuous negotiation, but that does not mean that such negotiation should be allowed to fall prey to blackmail and sabotage, or be stonewalled by unreasonable arguments. David Braybrooke has suggested that there are ways to deal with deliberation when some parties are defending politically absurd positions, by making the issue effectively salient and ensuring that vigilant attention is paid to the issue under discussion so that its non-resolution remains in the public eye (Braybrooke 2000). If these means were to fail, the contractualist view opens the door to a party losing its rights (becoming rightless) as a result of not living up to the commensurate obligation to act reasonably.

This last point is fundamental and has been entirely emasculated by the Charter, which bestows rights without any obligations. This is the very asymmetry that constitutes a considerable blockage to any form of reasonable negotiation. Indeed, the Charter incites unreasonableness. Why *not* claim maximum entitlements, if there is no *quid pro quo*? Why accept *any* reasonable accommodation, when there is no obligation to do so and no cost for being unreasonable?

In this regard it is interesting that one of the last public activities in which Pierre Trudeau, the Father of the Charter, engaged before his death in 2000 was collective work with the InterAction Council of Former Heads of State and Government on the development of a Universal Declaration of Human Responsibilities. A document was proposed on September 1, 1997, with a view to getting it approved on the fiftieth anniversary of the Universal Declaration of Human Rights. The preamble of this document clearly states that "the exclusive insistence on rights can result in conflict, division, and endless dispute, and the neglect of human responsibilities can lead to lawlessness and chaos." Much of the text of the document echoes what had been defined earlier (Chapter 6) as a philosophy of intermediate cosmopolitanism.

It is also interesting to note that Thomas S. Axworthy was an academic adviser to this project and prepared the draft for the InterAction Council (Axworthy, pp. 7–12).

It seems fair to say, then, that, even for Trudeau, one of the main sources of concern about the Charter cases is the perceived lack of balance between the sort of entitlements recognized as legitimate and the sort of obligations considered as commensurate. The major complaint is about the unevenness or unfairness of the bargain, as maximum entitlements and minimal obligations have become the foundation of Canada's institutional order. This in turn has dramatically stalled any process of decentralization, since maximum entitlements entail massive redistribution and massive redistribution entails fundamental centralization, for redistribution cannot proceed without the loot being first brought to the centre.

Any attempt at formally negotiating some fair bargain between entitlements and obligations in the post-Charter world has proved extremely difficult, since the entitlements are already regarded as non-negotiable. The bargain can be struck only through an increase in obligations, a matter that is difficult to sell in general, since it can be argued that additional obligations were not part of the original deal. This is the basic weakness of the judicial approach to "reasonable accommodations" based on the Charter: it provides no basis for demanding that some obligations be accepted if the existing rights are to be enforced.

This is why it is naïve to believe that the fundamental asymmetry built into the Charter is likely to be corrected through the judicial process. It will have to be rebalanced by "auxiliary conditions" negotiated *in situ*, that is, in particular contexts, that would substantially modify the Charter over time through the flats and sharps that such initiatives impose. This is the main lesson to be learned from studies of organizational change (Schön and Rein 1994): local experiments are the way to subvert a constraining framework. For the time being, however, there has been little appreciation of the need to accept incompletely theorized arguments and to experiment locally. The taste is for futile searches for meta-rules that might constrain the work of the courts in interpreting the Charter. This is the meaning of such slogans as "the right to difference and not a difference in rights" (Geadah 2007).

There are two fundamental flaws at the core of the present debate. First, a certain doctrinal attitude mandates the rejection, in general, of any principle of precedence establishing that certain principles are more important than others. This fundamental distaste for placing principles within a hierarchy is a major stumbling block in any negotiation. In the *Zeitgeist* of the post-Charter world everything has to be seen as equally important. This is the mortgage of egalitarianism (Lussato 1989). Second, a cynical pragmatism underpins the refusal to accept anything but "boutique transculturalism," which does not interfere with anything of consequence and remains compatible with imaginary "shared values." This pragmatism underpins the refusal to accept any form of "equal but different" initiative as anything but an effort to obtain special and exclusive gratification. Because there is no principle of precedence, anything different is seen as a sign of special treatment, and there can be no true pluralism. A stalemate ensues. There is no basis on which to choose and, in consequence, there is not much that one is allowed to choose from.

This sanitization of the terrain leaves little space for experimentation. Consequently, instead of "reasonable accommodations" having provided fertile ground for exploring the diverse ways in which local situations could generate mutually agreed arrangements without generating an inflation of demands by extremist groups, the Charter has stultified the process of experimentation. Therefore, except in very special cases where legislatures have had to react in panic to block dangerous precedents—as with sharia law in Ontario—the courts have been asked to adjudicate in the sole light of the rights-based Charter, and have simply become an entitlement-making machine. Moral innovativeness has been neither permitted nor welcome.

This does not mean that we should not guard strongly against both racism and cultural relativism, for both threats are real. The Berry–Taylor doctrine appears not to hold when one looks, for example, at the ghettoization of the Hassidic Jews in Montreal, despite most generous accommodations. And the recurrent resurgence of the "cultural nation" in the political sphere in Quebec can only mean a certain cultural identity politics that may be compatible with pluralism, but not with transculturalism or intermediate cosmopolitanism.

Cultural pluralism, a precursor of multiculturalism, is not necessarily postethnic. It is understood "as risk-averse, favouring narrow, tight, separate communities, a unitary self, and fixity within traditional cultural limits," while, in contrast, transculturalism or intermediate cosmopolitanism is "risk-taking, favouring wide, loose, overlapping communities, multiple selves, and fluidity within universal human limits" (Earle and Cvetkovich 1995, p. 93). Reasonable

DEEP CULTURAL DIVERSITY

accommodations over this cultural range cover a wide variety of quite diverse realities. In no case is ethnocentricity annihilated. Each of us is in some way ethnocentric and denying it is simple word play. We can only hope to transcend our acculturation. Multiculturalists live in islets that are separate and unbridgeable, while for transculturalists separateness evaporates, or at the very least is overcome by — "les hommes passerelles" — bridege makers (Bruckner 1994, p. 62).

The difficulty with the sort of fluidity demanded by transculturalism is that it requires an acceptance of the fact that one is "constantly reweaving and being rewoven," and not simply woven by culture once for all. The temptation for the defenders of the notion of "cultural nation" is to search for meta-rules to define the terms of engagement top down. Transculturalists accept that they have no clear idea of what those terms will be and consider that the best strategy is free experimentation, because we do not know in advance which of our beliefs are going to be changed and which will be retained intact (Rorty 1991, p. 212).

The current search for the Holy Grail by Gérard Bouchard and Charles Taylor, the two intellectuals commissioned by the government of Quebec to illuminate the debate on "reasonable accommodations," is another instance of the search for meta-rules. It is likely to come up with something akin to a sixteenth-century map: elegant, but unlikely to be useful to navigation. Both these eminent scholars are committed communitarians and prisoners of the essentialist identity jail. They are unlikely to question the very bases of the present difficulties: the essentialist notion of identity, and the perceived need for formal recognition of these truly various identities if one is to facilitate and enable integration. They are most likely to simply rehash most of the arguments in favour of the multiculturalist-cum-interculturalist credo. They have no capacity to appreciate the transculturalist option in any way.

It is therefore unlikely that deep cultural diversity will be tackled head on with due regard for William Ross Ashby's law of requisite variety, which states that, for appropriate regulation, the variety in the regulator must be equal to or greater than the variety in the system being regulated. This would entail the deployment of a coordination infrastructure capable of accommodating a very wide and rich range of freely chosen arrangements, which would attempt to keep entitlements and obligations in balance through a nexus of moral contracts, contained and restricted within a certain corridor of what would be regarded as socially acceptable arrangements.

The myth of shared values, the gospel of egalitarianism, and the languages of entitlements, rights, and political correctness have brought forth the multicultural bargain. Transculturalism suggests a rather different perspective: a range of citizenship arrangements as a nexus of moral contracts that would tend to correspond to the sorts of commitments that citizens are willing to make. It would allow for *differentiated citizenship*, an idea that has been banned because it violates the credo of egalitarianism. Yet, if denizens have multiple, partial and evolving identities, should they not be allowed to engage their different "cultural" strands with different degrees of intensity, and in multiple and partial ways? Will Kymlicka and others have rationalized differentiated arrangements in the name of reparation for past victimization and prejudice. Is it not more reasonable to allow members of the community to have a choice among bundles of entitlements-cum-obligations, such that the heavier the obligations, the richer the entitlements?

This approach would, first of all, explode the egalitarian myth that assimilates equality and uniformity, allow citizens to choose the packages that suit them, and mark the end of the present confusion between wanting all the entitlements and being unwilling to shoulder any of the costs or carry any of the responsibilities. One might imagine gold, silver, and bronze citizenships.

Second, this approach would bring to an end the regime of passports of convenience, under which persons who have not resided or paid tax in Canada for years, if ever, can claim entitlement to repatriation from a danger zone as a matter of right, or claim access to the benefits of medicare if and when their family is faced with major illness.

Third, it would lead to a transcultural understanding of citizenship. The dual idea that citizenship requires equal and full membership in the polity, but that it does not mean necessarily exclusive membership in one polity, raises problems. Rainer Bauböck (2001) has suggested that one should not confuse equality with homogeneity, since equal respect is not the same as equal treatment. Sovereignty is already partitioned in federal systems and membership in various vertically integrated polities is common experience. In the same manner the proliferation of denizens with attachment to different separate polities has given rise to dual and multiple citizenships horizontally.

The central question is the simultaneity and the supposed equivalence of the bundle of rights and obligations attached to these different vertically and horizontally separate denizenships. While it has been clear to most observers that there might be a variety of intensities in the nature of the obligations to the different polities willingly accepted by the denizen with numerous affiliations—a higher "thickness" or a greater "thinness" in these relations—it has not been easy to find a way to determine these intensities, and therefore to calibrate the extent of the rights that have to be extended to the denizen so that he/she can be given the means and rights required to fulfill these obligations.

Experiments with differentiated citizenships have been proposed to ensure "citizen plus" status for some groups as a way to provide additional levers for those that have suffered significant disadvantages, and are unlikely to be able to participate equally and fully in the polity, but this would deal only with special cases. The intent in envisaging "recombinant citizenship" is to generalize the process, and to make it less a matter of victimology and more a matter of choice.

Such a generalization of the process would foster recognition of the new realities of multiple and partial identities, and force the denizen to declare some precedence among these loyalties. In particular, it would generate the possibility of allowing choice to prevail in full cognizance of the implications of such choice. For instance, the choice not to pay taxes in Canada might entail not being allowed to benefit from the social services that they finance. It would not allow unlimited or "thick" entitlements on the basis of a chosen status entailing "thin" obligations.

This process of clarification of the *quid pro quo* entailed by the nature of the different types of membership would do much to eliminate flagrant abuses and pathological phenomena, such as the unreasonable claims made by those holding only passports of convenience, while recognizing the freedom of the denizen to opt for "thicker" or "thinner" citizenship. It would also make clear why those whose ambition is to have leadership roles in Canadian society may be expected to opt for a "thicker" version of citizenship that would even eliminate the possibility of holding citizenship of another country.

The operationalization of such arrangements is not intractable, and would do much to eliminate the unfortunate confusion between equality and homogeneity that has plagued post-Charter Canada. It would also have the distinct advantage of providing a language of problem solution for many of the issues emerging in modern plural and deeply diverse societies, where neither simplistic and purist assimilation nor apartheid is acceptable.

Finally, such a strategy might contribute to opening the way to the negotiation of a wider variety of moral contracts, determining the nature of the accommodation that would be acceptable to all the different groups. Instead of hiding the stark realities of integration, which are never painless, and occluding them under the veneer of official egalitarianism, one could entertain the possibility of testing the limits of equality and equability, not in the courts of law, but case by case, in the multilogue between the diverse groups in their particular circumstances. The only major loser in this process would be the Jacobin state.

Conclusion

What is clear is that the vision of the Charter as gospel, of the courts as infallible, and of multiculturalism and "Big G" government as the right way is no longer in good currency. Deep cultural diversity is a fact, but the best way to deal with it remains ill-defined. In most immigrant-receiving countries there is a strong implicit will to build on traditional cultures, but also to accommodate new ones. There is also a taste for accommodation of the different founding groups in multicultural countries, but little taste for counterproductive centrifugal policies that tend to tribalize or retribalize modern societies. There is also a great fear of the ways in which multiculturalist radicalism may influence the law in all sorts of illiberal ways. On the part of the host populations, the greatest source of malaise is the lack of sense of limits, in scope and pace, to the accommodations that may be required by newcomers.

Deep cultural diversity is understood as calling for changes in the ways of belonging (Baumeister 2003). At the core of the transformation is a distinction made by Charles Taylor between "fundamental rights," on the one hand, and "privileges and immunities," on the other (Taylor 1992). Fundamental rights have to be preserved, but privileges and immunities are negotiable, and "can be revoked or restricted for reasons of public policy" (p. 59). These issues raise major problems of interpretation, and are built on essentially contested concepts—what one person might regard as a fundamental right may be regarded by another as a whimsical privilege.

However, multiculturalism is mainly criticized because of its state-centric advocacy of corporate cultural rights. This is indeed the Achilles' heel of multiculturalist policies. The most useful critics have attempted to design various ways of shaking off these constraints. They all have to do with partitioning the problem of citizenship into separate units that can be recombined in more or less innovative ways. One of the most promising avenues has been sketched by Ayelet Shachar (2001) under the general rubric of "transformative accommodation." It is based on a very flexible intercultural dialogue in distinct and yet interdependent domains—very much as law itself has been partitioned into family law, criminal law, and so on—with clearly delineated choices for opting in or out of a group's jurisdiction, thereby preventing the ossification of cultures that one can anticipate when public recognition of differences makes them congeal. Transformative accommodation aims at nothing less than transforming both intergroup and intragroup relations by promoting a sense of cooperation and dialogue.

This is very close to the transcultural strategy propounded by Lamberto Tassinari and the Vice Versa group (Tassinari 1992). Another, more emotionally loaded word for this sort of strategy might be mixing (or *métissage*). It also operates along much the same lines as the intermediate cosmopolitanism discussed in Chapter 6.

In all these cases citizenship is fundamentally relational, the result of continuous interaction. It takes the form of an evolving nexus of moral contracts inventing ways of belonging and of participation. This nexus of relationships constructs a texture of imaginative and creative soft armistices, truces, and bridges, distilled, in a forward-looking way, as arrangements capable of overcoming differences and forging collaborative links. The result of such experimentation aims at going beyond the original ossified identity towards a not yet defined destination, fully understanding that the voyage will reshape the partners.

In this context any person or group transfixed by the need to maintain and defend an existing identity becomes somewhat incapable of recognizing that experimentation means putting one's identity on the line, betting on an evolving macro moral contract of citizenship, and on transformative accommodation. In such a venture the only sure thing is that one will not end up being the same person at the end of the process that one was at the beginning.

The Charter has not helped that process along. In fact, to the extent that it has deterred experimentation and ever so slightly ossified Canadian society, it has been, like tariff barriers, the equivalent of negative railroads.

Conclusion
A Primer on the Governance of Cultures

We must unsettle ourselves and leave home
in order to find home again. —Naoko Saito

The forum where political and social conversations help to forge beliefs, mores, practices, and so on, needs governing as much as the market does, and there is most certainly a role for government in "providing and protecting the forum, and intervening within it" (Tussman 1977, p. vii). Indeed, there is nothing necessarily totalitarian implied in such intervention in the affairs of the mind. Yet extreme prudence is required, because any such intervention in the forum may readily be perceived as manipulative and in the nature of brainwashing, and indeed may easily degenerate into being so.

What is to be done in the face of increasing deep cultural diversity may not be clear, but it cannot be assumed that it is nothing. As has been explained in earlier chapters, there are many dimensions to cultural diversity, and some costs and benefits of all sorts are associated with more or less diversity. It is clearly unsatisfactory to complain about past policies such as multiculturalism and proclaim alternative desirable ideals without following through with some action designed to ensure that workable and socially desirable conditions ensue. Yet any meaningful intervention requires a good understanding of the nature of the problem and the context, a sense of what is meant by optimizing in such a context, and consideration of the sort of regulatory levers that might be legitimate.

The different chapters of this book have probed these issues in a preliminary way. This investigation has revealed the most important mechanisms at work, the major trade-offs that are to be confronted, and the range of instruments likely to be of use. In this conclusion our aim is to pave the way to an operationalization of this endeavour. We start with a certain number of clarifications about the task at hand.

All too often, deep cultural diversity is defined at such a level of generality as to verge on the intractable. Culture is defined in the most vaporous terms and dressed in the most bizarre attires. Indeed, large parts of the debates about culture adopt a sort of sanctimony that prevents any meaningful discussion of its governance. Culture is regarded as sacred and non-negotiable, and granted a sort of immunity from rational discourse, being entirely absorbed instead by emotional narratives. Our intent is to suggest ways in which a rational discourse on cultural matters might proceed, as a first step towards the resolution of the problem of intercultural coordination. In the first instance, we take a more profane and anthropological look at the world of culture to reveal its dynamics. Then we identify the sort of governance likely to fit this complex reality. Finally, we suggest some guideposts for the journey that should lead to transculturalism as a new regime.

The World of Culture

Culture is a form of social capital, an empowering sociality, an enabling resource that helps members of a group to proceed with effective cognition and learning, and to act well in concert. It is unlikely to emerge organically in its optimal form (whatever that may mean) through *laissez-faire*, both because of its degree of publicness and the consequent shirking it entails on the part of many who benefit from it, but may refuse the share the costs to be incurred in building and maintaining it, and because of its diffracted and distributed nature, and the consequent coordination problems that it generates.

Another way to make the fundamental point I am trying to make here is to say that culture is *not* an essence or an organic soul of the group, as is often suggested, but an *assemblage* of more or less complementary component parts, which are self-subsistent, and may be detached and plugged into different assemblages. There is always a temptation to reify and essentialize such assemblages, and to suggest that they have some ontological reality, underpinning some sacred and enduring mind-independent identity (DeLanda 2006). This is particularly toxic in the case of culture, as some temporary versions of it are idealized and declared to be preserved in perpetuity.

DEEP CULTURAL DIVERSITY

Exorcising this essentialist view is a fundamental first step that we have worked towards throughout this book. We think that culture is always evolving, and that a case can be made that some *governing* of these assemblages is required if it is to evolve smoothly and effectively, without maligning groups but without destroying a certain continuity. In such governing some role exists for government, as a provider of varieties of infrastructural capital, but *governance* of cultures cannot be reduced to *government* of cultures. The latter is only a small segment of the former.

The world of culture, like the world of medicine or business or carpentry, is extraordinarily variegated. It is a totality of pieces of equipment (for example, nails) to carry out tasks; these tasks (hammering a nail) are undertaken to achieve some purposes (building a house); and performing such tasks leads one to develop identities (such as being a carpenter). Disclosing such a world means revealing how it is deployed into practices and is organized in styles, that is, the ways that coordinate actions and underpin the manner in which practices are transferred from situation to situation (Spinosa, Flores, and Dreyfus 1997, pp. 17ff).

Equipment, purposes, identities, practices, and styles are components of a sort of *primary culture*, an anthropological ensemble of ways of seeing, ways of doing, and ways of being that have evolved through time as a set of workable and useful social armistices for a group between the geotechnical constraints imposed by the environment, and the values and plans of agents. This primary culture constitutes an instrument for the agents, a decoder of the environment, a filter determining what is to be remembered and what it to be forgotten, and a constraining mindset that selects what is important and what is not, and shapes the agents' actions. It is both enabling and constraining, and is often taken as a somewhat subconscious given. However, one need not presume that culture is necessarily subconscious or fully disclosed, and it cannot be regarded as given except temporarily.

Any culturally inspired act is based on a capacity to perceive differences, to gauge degrees of relevance and quality, but it also requires that diversity be apprehended as a coherent whole and that this whole integrates hierarchies or scales of valuation (Lussato 1989). These capacities to inquire, to differentiate, to integrate, and to provide an evaluative order, all evolve. Environment and equipment change; more knowledge accrues, tasks change, purposes evolve, identities sharpen, practices and styles crystallize differently. Different habituated choices translate into new beliefs, values, and so on, and thus into a new culture (Mesthene 1970). These self-reinforcing mechanisms generate two forms of learning: behavioural learning, which builds on past experience to respond to new situations; and epistemic learning, through which environmental representations are reframed.

This evolution is always unfinished and the culture is always imperfectly adjusted to its context, for three reasons. First, actors have imperfect and incomplete information, and limited rationality. Second, adjustments take time. Third, new circumstances and new agents transform both the environment and the texture of communities, and redefine, more or less slowly, the very nature of the culture.

One must maintain a clear distinction between these variegated primary cultures and *secondary cultures*, which stand in relation to them very much as theology stands in relation to religion (Weinstein 1985). Secondary cultures correspond to "representations" of culture as seen and stylized by opinion-moulders and the like. They are the results of ratiocinations, reconstructions, and reifications of primary cultures by elites, selections of what is perceived as important and significant in them, and of what needs to be done to nudge them in what is seen as the "right" direction. These constructions are shaped by ideology and trigger cultural interventions designed to bring culture into line with some desired or preferred form.

In a world where a large variety of geotechnical circumstances interact with a wide variety of values and plans, Canada's primary cultures are variegated and plural. Primary culture takes a quite different shape in Alberta, for example, than it does in Quebec. To put it maybe a bit too starkly, some would argue that in Alberta the importance of negative freedom is such that the state as monopolist of public coercion is regarded as a potential threat, while in Quebec the priority given to positive freedom calls for a strong state presence as a lever of empowerment. The different assemblages may correspond to greater or lesser degrees of state-centricity.

Culture has "no common unit of account" (Throsby 2001, p. 159). The ensemble of equipment, purposes, identities, practices, and styles underpinning the array of Canadian cultures varies considerably from place to place and from time to time in Canada. The assemblages vary greatly. These ensembles of social armistices may either cohere in some manner, or be made to *appear* coherent by all sorts of ratiocinations. In the first case a kind of family atmosphere may evolve, revealing that relatively similar beliefs, principles, and environments have generated

DEEP CULTURAL DIVERSITY

similar cognitive and relational guideposts. In the second case a secondary culture may be stylized, represented by some observers as the only meaningful order, and used to interpret, assess or even orthopaedically constrain the primary culture. In the first case there is true convergence, but in the second case one representation is used to impose order on the hurly-burly of real-life cultures.

The coinage of cultural citizenship connotes the obsessive search for one such representation that would bind all this ebullience together. It is, like all representations, a sort of stylization that is theatrically inspired—"theory" and "theatre" have the same root in ancient Greek (Nisbet 1976). This is why cultural citizenship generates so much malaise. It suggests that a basic genotype must exist and that this *être de raison* should be regarded as more important than the real thing. In such a scheme the secondary culture takes over, or at least tries to, and ideology looms large.

This fixation on a monoculture for the group is often state-centred and elite-inspired, and underpins ominous cultural policies tainted by a tinge of coercion and brain-washing. When the goddess Reason appears on the scene to impose her dominion, Terror is often not far behind, as citizens were reminded during the French Revolution. Whether any officialized secondary culture can ever avoid smothering primary cultures is a moot question. How could it?

Can there be some infrastructure that could be presented as the *minimum minimorum* relational/cognitive capital on which the effective sociality of a group or country is built? Cultural citizenship would then be regarded as the basic common denominator, shared by all Canadians, for instance. Our view is that this is most unlikely because of the very pluralism of Canada, the variegated nature of the different relational/cognitive capital, and the extraordinary importance of the local milieu in the way it crystallizes. At best, as we suggested earlier, there can be agreement on certain principles of coordination, such as the usefulness of a *lingua franca* if the group is to operate effectively.

What, then, of the idea of a multicultural citizenship that would focus on second-order phenomena, a kind of common toolbox with which the various relational/cognitive capitals might be constructed and loosely cobbled together? This looks like a rather futile effort to fabricate some elusive commonality. Why not go to third-order phenomena, the arsenal of tools used to modify the tool-box? First-order reality is not so easily reducible and is more in the nature of an ecology of cultural arrangements that seems to reek of incommensurability. However, this does not eliminate the need for organizing plurality in order to ensure that the variegated communities of fate cohere somewhat, if only via a steady diet of conflicts that they are capable of resolving (Hirschman 1995, p. 243; Van Gunsteren 1998, p. 112).

Governance: The Central Challenge

Since there is no unique primary culture (unless an artificial one is *fabricated*), and since these diffracted cultures translate into different instruments, different purposes, different identities, different practices, and different styles, the question obviously arises: is a coherent and yet loosely coupled set of governance arrangements possible? The answer is yes, but such a scheme is of necessity complex and cannot be imposed top down.

The danger of some overarching theology being imposed on this effervescent reality is at all times great. The only way to avoid such a mutilation is to recognize explicitly *ex ante* that primary cultures are bottom-up crowd phenomena, and that there is only a need to invent a *modus vivendi* that would allow the different primary cultures to thrive without chaos ensuing, by providing a modicum of relational/cognitive capital that would prevent the country or the broader set of communities from falling apart. This is the challenge of creating some coherence in the face of deep cultural diversity.

Technological change, economic growth, and sociocultural effervescence have generated a genuine dispersive revolution. The need for a heightened capacity for speed, flexibility, and innovation has led not only to the development of new structures and tools, but to a whole new way of thinking. Private, public, and social concerns are no longer drivers of people, but have become "drivers of learning" (Wriston 1992, p. 119). Learning organizations are the new forms of alliances and partnerships, rooted in more horizontal relationships and moral contracts, which are now necessary to succeed. This dispersive revolution has crystallized into new network business organizations, more subsidiarity-focused governments, and increasingly virtual, elective, and malleable communities. The major governance challenge is how to acquire speed, flexibility, and innovativeness in learning while maintaining a modicum of coordination and coherence.

Internetworked technologies have made new linkages possible, but businesses, governments, and communities have concomitantly been confronted with an ever-increasing demand for participation by citizens regarding themselves as partners in the governance process. This has redefined the public space, and founded distributed governance regimes based on a wider variety of more fluid and always evolving communities (Tapscottt and Agnew 1999).

The old trinity of state–nation–territory has also been called into question. Space does not correspond to homogeneous national territories, nor to their topographical sum, but to communities of fate that are often given, cannot be avoided, and have articulated a series of "reciprocal extraterritorialities in which the guiding concept would no longer be the *ius* (right) of the citizen, but the *refugium* (refuge) of the singular" (Agamben 2000, p. 24). The new "lightness and fluidity of the increasingly mobile, slippery, shifty, evasive and fugitive power" (Bauman 2000, p. 14) is not completely aterritorial. It is characterized, however, by new forms of belonging that escape the control and regulation of the nation-state to a much higher degree than before, and by virtual agoras, variegated and overlapping terrains where citizens may land temporarily. The fabric of these new worlds welds together assets, skills, and capabilities into complex temporary communities that are as much territories of the mind as anything that can be represented by a grid map, and it does so on the basis of a bottom-up logic that assigns to higher-order institutions only what cannot be accomplished effectively at the local level.

In earlier times, when the context was placid, it may have been possible for tyrants to govern the cultural game top down by simply imposing some version of secondary culture and ignoring the diverse primary cultures altogether. Such cultural imperialism may even have succeeded in contexts where governments or potentates were regarded as the only legitimate sources of authority, or at least were able to impose their will by force as masters of the game. As the context has become more turbulent and deference to authority has disappeared, one is faced, more and more, with games without any master. Governance in such a context has had to emerge from the bottom up. However, there is no assurance that wise results will ensue unless certain conditions are met: diversity of inputs, independence from coercion, decentralization of decision-making, and some adequate way of aggregating the diverse opinions of the different groups in the crowd. This last requirement explains the popularity of market-based methods in recent years (Surowiecki 2004).

There may be differences of opinion about the necessary conditions for this new philosophy of governing to succeed, or about the basic forces on which one has to rely as a matter of priority. Some have underlined the centrality of dissent (Sunstein 2003), while others have celebrated the powers of self-organization and emergence, and the capacity of these forces to generate bottom-up coordination that works (Johnson 2001). The core message of the literature on emergence has been that there is much more to self-organization than is usually believed, and that much of what is observed in nature is often based on simple local rules and effective feedback. The possibility also exists of system failures, and consequently there is a need to have fail-safe mechanisms in place that kick in when the system is in danger of becoming chaotic (Hubbard and Paquet 2002).

In the short term coordination failures may be eliminated through process redesign—a change in the social technologies to eliminate obstacles to the collaboration of the different stakeholders within the learning cycle, and to develop the relationships, conventions or relational transactions required to define mutually coherent expectations and common guideposts. These conventions differ from sector to sector, but they provide the requisite coherence for a common context of interpretation, and for some "cognitive routinization of relations between firms, their environments, and employees," for instance (Storper 1996, p. 259). Such coherence must, however, remain somewhat loose: the ligatures should not be too strong or too routinized. A certain degree of heterogeneity, and therefore social distance, might foster a higher potentiality of innovation, because the different parties bring to the conversation a more complementary body of knowledge (Granovetter 1973).

In the medium term coordination failures may be eliminated more radically through organizational architecture work—structural repairs, the transformation of the structural capital of networks and regimes, and defining the capabilities of the learning socioeconomy. Coherence and pluralism are crucial in the organizational architecture of a learning concern. This is what makes federal structures so attractive from a learning point of view, since they provide coordination in a world where the centre is more a network than a place (Handy 1995). This is also the reason why federal-type organizational structures have emerged in so many sectors in most continents.

In the longer term coordination failures may have to be dealt with through some reframing of the purposes pursued by the community. Often, the reconciling of technology, structures, and theory may be achieved by tinkering with the plumbing or the architecture of the system, its technology and structures, but just as often the theory must be revisited. The assumptions on which the system and actions within the system are based—assumptions that one may or may not be aware one is making—must be questioned, and the very notion of the nature of the enterprise one is involved in, its philosophy and its broad directions, must be refounded (Schön 1971, Schön and Rein 1994).

The shift in the vision of the state over the past twenty years (Le Grand 2003) provides an interesting example of such a refoundation process. There has been a move from a view of public-sector professionals as knights at work for the benefit of passive citizen-pawns to a view of self-interested public-sector workers as knaves facing citizens requesting to be treated like queens. A new public philosophy and mental toolbox then become necessary to serve as a gyroscope, as motivation, agency, and the whole learning process must be completely transformed when worlds change in this way (Paquet 1996–97). The sort of governance that will succeed in squaring the circle, by finding effective ways to have most of the advantages of a coherent system while also obtaining all the advantages of a decentralized system, entails avoiding two pitfalls. First, it must avoid the illusion of totality and control, because there is no totality, but only assemblages, and most of the time there is no way to impose control. Second, it must avoid the delusion of Candide, because it is naïve to believe that the appropriate retooling, restructuring, and reframing will always emerge organically in the best possible way, and in a timely fashion. Both these forms of naïvety are echo effects of the essentialist notions of totalities, instrumental and organic, merrily imposed on mere social assemblages.

The best one may hope for is a new fluid form of "ecology of governance." Walt Anderson describes it as "many different systems and different kinds of systems interacting with one another, like the multiple organisms in an ecosystem" (Anderson 2001, p. 252). Such arrangements are not necessarily "neat, peaceful, stable or efficient . . . but in a continual process of learning and changing and responding to feedback." Their main objective is to ensure resilience, that is, the capacity of the system to spring back on its feet undamaged.

One example of such a governing arrangement is VISA as "chaord." Dee Hock has described in great detail the saga that led to the design of a governing apparatus for the credit card company VISA (Hock 1995, 1999). The governing apparatus in place is presented as the result of a process through which deliberation about purpose and principles led to the creation of a new organizational structure, which

Hock calls "chaord." "Chaord" (a combination of "chaos" and "order") is defined by Hock as a "self-organizing, adaptive, non-linear, complex system, whether physical, biological or social, the behaviour of which exhibits characteristics of both order and chaos or, loosely translated to business terminology, cooperation and competition" (Hock 1995, p. 4). The design of this new form of non-centralized organization was seen as the only way to ensure durability and resilience in a complex organization that had to adjust constantly to a vast array of turbulent contextual circumstances, but also had to face the immense coordination challenge involved in orchestrating the work of more than 20,000 financial institutions in more than 200 countries and in trying to serve hundreds of millions of users.

This new form of organization had to provide the mix of relational norms and mechanisms likely to underpin the realization of the main purpose of the venture through bottom-up effervescence within the context of some loose framework of guiding principles agreed to by all. Hock has given some examples of these principles, defining the sort of organization used to cope with these challenges in the construction and design of organizations of this sort (Hock 1999, pp. 137–39):

> • the organization must be equitably owned by all participants; no member should have an intrinsic advantage; all advantages should result from ability and initiative;
> • power and function must be distributive to the maximum; no function and no power should be vested with any part that might be reasonably exercised by any lesser part;
> • governance must be distributive; no individual or group of individuals should be able to dominate deliberations or control decisions;
> • to the maximum degree possible, everything should be voluntary;
> • it must be infinitely malleable, yet extremely durable; it should be capable of constant, self-generated modification without sacrificing its essential nature;
> • it must embrace diversity and change; it must attract people comfortable with such an environment, and provide an environment in which they can thrive.

What would this mean for the cultural world? The world of culture is a world of equipment, purposes, identities, practices, and styles. Overemphasizing the identity dimension opens the door to ideological framing and the planning of the cultural field in line with such an ideological frame. The major flaws of any such univocal approach to culture are essentialist holism and reification. Instead of culture being appraised as an ensemble of social technologies, structures, and frames, and recognizing that they play a wide diversity of roles, it comes to be referred to as a totality with a singular mission. This illusion of totality is cleverly hidden behind some lip-service references to subcultures, but it generates a global and reified view of culture. Indeed, once the cultural field is labelled as such there is a great temptation to map it and to plan it, to flatten the cultural world onto a managerial surface.

An alternative is, obviously, to bet on unrestrained competition leading over time to the dissolution of all local cultures into a new homogeneous cultural soup. For reasons we have explored earlier, such a new organically generated essence is unlikely to emerge. Balkanization in enclaves is much more likely.

Uncomfortably located between these two grand hopes is a more modest and more effective approach that would be more in the nature of bricolage. The most one can hope for in the world of culture is the highest and best use of certain basic principles, such as those set out by Hock.

Polycentric Governance, Guiding Principles, and Tipping-Point Leadership

The drift from a monocultural, state-centric, elite-driven "government of culture" to a pluralistic, cosmopolitan, diversity-driven "governance of culture" is less a wish than a conjecture and a fact. Most advanced countries already have a form of polycentric governance of culture. It emerges from an image of governance as a wide array of concurrent games, plagued with multiple authorities and overlapping jurisdictions, and linked into complex networks of interactions. Indeed, the cultural game is structured to avoid anyone being able to become a master of the game, and appropriately so.

Yet this fact is neither fully acknowledged nor fully understood nor fully socially acceptable. Acknowledging it would entail some recognition that culture is a game without a master, a proposition that denies any potentate or cultural czar the capacity, or even the right, to think of deliberately shaping culture. For most citizens, fearing totalitarianism, this would be reassuring, but there is also an equally important fear of change that would eliminate in short order all the reference points that have been in good currency. The idea that the new turbulence, complexity, and diversity might entail that every aspect of primary cultures is now likely to be dispensed with, that there are no limits to the required accommodation, that nothing is sacred and everything has to be renegotiated anew over a very short period, has instilled a strong malaise and a certain amount of fear about there being no master of the game.

This is the basis of the yearning for an intermediate position built neither on totalitarianism nor on *laissez-faire*, but on a better understanding of what polycentric governance means, on a better appreciation of the modest guiding principles likely to be of use in determining what has to be preserved and what can be let go, and on the need to use tipping-point mechanisms likely to eliminate blockages and unfreedoms, but also to ensure that change will proceed at a pace that is regarded as workable.

A systematic deconstruction of culture suggests that the cultural ecosystem is not governable top down, that its main features emerge bottom up and therefore originate in local milieus, and that it is largely self-governed (McGinnis 2000, Rheingold 2002). This does not mean, however, that everything happens in an indistinct governance soup, or that there is not a certain division of labour among the different families of stakeholders.

There is a *prima facie* case for the state's being charged with providing infrastructure, while not intervening in purposes and practices. The role of the public sector in the cultural world is therefore twofold: first and foremost, to provide the public space and the basic equipment for an effective forum; and then to work at eliminating the blockages constituting unfreedoms that emanate from deprivation of political liberties, economic facilities, social opportunities, transparency guarantees, and protective security (Sen 1999). This politics of cognition and social capitalization should not shy away from the task of raising awareness and should accept the duty of enlightening, so as to urge citizens to attend to the necessary agenda. Yet it should be focused on extending the realm of choice, playing the role of facilitator, and helping a robust sociality to emerge, rather than trying to influence choices and shape sociality. This will always be imperfectly done, because government cannot be entirely neutral. Besides informing, exposing, balancing, developing critical senses, chaperoning, and so on, government also often enters the forum as an authoritative voice. This is why government has an important duty to act in a restrained manner, *un devoir de réserve*.

For example, there is nothing contentious in suggesting that the provision of public space or the promotion of democratic literacy constitute a basic facilitation role that appears to fall clearly within the competence of the public sector. However, through bans on certain use of airwaves and the selective granting of permissions to carry on activities, the State may allow vocal minorities to exert a dramatic influence on the contours of official culture and to inflict their views on the citizenry. One might drift into a world of minority preferences at public expense. One can only fathom, with unease, the prospect of such preferences being transmuted into cultural rights and shaping an official culture. Such concerns underpin the sense that there should be limits to the scope of cultural regulation by the state. It is certainly difficult to defend interventions that reek of censorship, or hide massive intergroup redistribution behind the cloak of defending some form of culture.

In matters of the mind the provision of relational/cognitive capital should not in any way limit choices. It should indeed be clear that state actions must ensure that private citizens and groups are enabled to develop their purposes and practices. As for identities and styles, they should be left to the forces emerging in civil society. Any attempt to control them would inevitably lead government to become explicitly manipulative and therefore objectionable. This is why attention must be given to scrutinizing the principles that should guide government in intervening beyond the uncontroversial act of providing opportunities through infrastructure, when it becomes regulator of "time, place, and manner" (Tussman 1977, p. 110).

Many general principles come to mind and must be balanced: efficiency (avoiding waste), legitimacy, transparency, recognition that some competition helps, that greater participation also helps, that price–cost relations must not be obfuscated, and so on (Jacquet et al. 2002, Banner 2002). Identifying these guiding principles and calibrating their valence is probably the most difficult task facing stakeholders. In gauging their guideposts they must recognize the need to mix these principles in a meaningful way. Any governance entirely dedicated to the maximization of one single particular objective is likely to be unduly reductive.

This is where the reliance on self-governance plays its most important balancing role. It is the dynamics of the forum that should inflect the mixture in one direction or another, not the state. The subtle if necessary action of the state should focus on providing relational/ cognitive capital in ways that promote inclusiveness and transparency as much as possible.

The prudence required of the state does not prevent it from intervening lightly but effectively, by removing blockages that may prevent mechanisms of self-correction, self-re-enforcing, self-steering, and self-transformation from playing themselves out. Such blockages prevent agents and groups from taking full advantage of all the available opportunities and facilities. They are often detected by economic, social and political entrepreneurs, and taken advantage of. They may require collective action.

Among the mechanisms to eliminate unfreedoms, one should focus in particular on tipping points, where a small action is likely to have a significant effect (Gladwell 2000, Seifter et al. 2001, Badaracco 2002). In all such cases the state is not entirely neutral. Dealing with bottlenecks is bound to be selective and therefore to have uneven effects on different groups. Yet the requirement for a "light touch" approach at the very least prevents intrusive and destructive interventions of an orthopaedic nature.

Nor should prudence prevent the state from ensuring that the requisite fail-safe mechanisms are in place to avoid irreversible damage being done to the fabric of society. This brings us back to the argument we made at the very beginning of the book in favour of a wise use of the precautionary principle. At a time when there are reasons to believe that the legitimate order is in danger of being irremediably damaged, fail-safe mechanisms have to come into play. This sort of intervention will always be contentious. Libertarians will denounce any use of coercion, and it is not unlikely that even a use of coercion that is regarded as legitimate will generate abuses of authority and undue actions. The use of the former War Measures Act in 1970 is a good example of the sort of excesses likely to occur. Fail-safe mechanisms are temporary measures and their misuse is not much tolerated in democracies, but failing to use them may entail such social costs that one cannot afford not to have them available for such occasions. However, this should not be interpreted as condoning, even indirectly, the use of a "state of exception" in the manner it has been used of late. (The use of a permanent state of emergency, through which entire groups of citizens are disenfranchised, has been appropriately analyzed and denounced by Giorgio Agamben 2003.)

The Journey to Transculturalism

These carefully worded musings cannot, however, provide sufficiently robust directions. One may legitimately ask how the journey from a clearly flawed multiculturalism strategy, built on emphasizing differences inherited from the past, to a more promising neorepublican strategy of transculturalism, emphasizing forward-looking experimentation and *métissage*, might best be carried out. Suffice it to say that it will not be easy, and that my anticipatory guided tour of the prospective journey is likely to sound immensely politically incorrect.

In summary, one may say that Canadians are condemned to a slow evolution from multiculturalism to transculturalism. This may be ascribed, first, to the crab-like diagonal and careful way in which Canadian public discourse proceeds (a cultural trait that has its advantages); second, to the series of mental prisons in which they have been trapped by their politicians over the past forty years; and, third, to some learning challenges that they will have to overcome. The sort of large-scale social experimentation that is called for will not be embraced until those mental prisons have been dismantled and those learning challenges have been met.

More than thirty-five years of cultural programming by the multicultural engine, and the particularly powerful endorsement of this strategy in section 27 of the Charter of Rights and Freedoms in 1982, have made quite an impact on the Canadian way of dealing with deep cultural diversity. Preserving and enhancing inherent differences is the guiding principle in good currency in our multicultural regime. Division and fracture lines are automatically conceded. The road away from this current position will be long and will require nothing less than a revolution in the minds of Canadians. What might be regarded as a plausible route cannot avoid dealing with the following families of concerns.

First, section 27 will have to be modulated. For the time being, the multicultural strategy deeply rooted in the Charter and section 27 is like a time bomb likely to be used at any time to reinforce the intercultural fracture lines in Canada. This is in the hands of the Supreme Court, which has interpreted the Charter in ways that are decidedly not neorepublican. All sorts of rights have been merrily confounded with the basic conditions of citizenry. From the irresponsible Singh decision onwards, the Supreme Court has redefined citizenship. It has of late taken to dabbling in matters of "dignity" and it is entirely predictable that it will find it permissible to widen the ambit of section 27 considerably. Nothing less than a clear statement by Parliament on this matter will do. It might serve to indicate what it will not allow the Supreme Court to do, and become the basis for the use of the notwithstanding clause if and when the justices choose to reinforce the fracture lines nonetheless.

Second, tribalism and ethnie will have to be tamed. It will not be possible to modulate section 27 unless Parliament is willing to use a Citizenship Act to tame tribalism and ethnie, and to open the door to transculturalism. Nothing less can open the door to a reinterpretation of the whole Charter. No one is naïve enough to believe that tribal and ethnic forces will ever be annihilated: they are too powerful for that, and it would be quixotic even to try. However, it is quite clear that the new cultural diversity has prepared the minds of Canadians to play down these dimensions and to require from newcomers that they do also. Instead of enhancing the role of fracture lines, one may wish to play up the bridging power of transculturalism within a bilingual society. Indeed, it corresponds to the current drift of the country.

The fact that governments have chosen to be completely silent in the face of local but significant initiatives to allow tribal, ethnic or religious forces to generate re-enforced fracture lines (as in the case of Afrocentric schools in Toronto) is ground for concern. It has revealed that a certain lack of courage amongst politicians is preventing them from playing their role as fail-safe mechanism. It is particularly troublesome since this initiative might very well represent the thin edge of the wedge and contribute to harden considerably cultural and racist barriers at a time when the reverse would appear to be called for. This unhampered initiative may prove catastrophic if it were to trigger ghettoization initiatives by other cultural groups throughout the country.

Third, egalitarianism will have to be toned down. Earlier chapters have made the case against egalitarianism. The extraordinary ideological power of egalitarianism and of the language of rights will not be easily toned down, especially after some thirty-five years of boosterism almost entirely based on those foundations. It may prove very difficult to persuade Canadians that the sort of identity politics that it has underpinned is not the way. Yet this is not a matter of choice. Several flawed narratives are based on these foundations, and are fuelling *ressentiment* and recrimination. Those who claim to be the defenders of prudence and moderation—and there are many—

will have to accept that no progress can be made until this musket is disarmed. This is part of the conceptual refurbishment that is called for by the transformation of the welfare state into a strategic state.

Fourth, democratic competence will have to be restored. The neorepublican notion of citizenry is rooted in action, participation, and competence, yet public ignorance is alive and well (Hardin 2006). In fact, citizens are woefully uninformed and the cost of being well-informed is so high that it is naïve to expect citizens to incur it. This has important neglected implications. It has led to a derailing of much electoral campaigning towards a focus on black-and-white issues that have a chance to attract the attention of voters and get them to gravitate toward the position of one political party or another. Restoring democratic competence may call for a transformation of parties into more preceptoral and educational entities. Whether they can so transform themselves is questionable, but is there any hope without such a transformation, and is there not a duty upon the intelligentsia to act as clarifiers? For the time being intercultural interaction remains too foggy an issue to lend itself to useful discussion by the uninformed, and both the intelligentsia and the media have failed miserably at their job of clarification.

However, even if these four daunting blockages were all removed, many more challenges would remain. In particular, there are five learning challenges to be overcome.

First, it is necessary to shake off cognitive dissonance. If there is one crucial characteristic of deeply diverse societies, it is that they are by definition transfixed by irreducible variety. If variety could be attenuated or significantly limited, the society would not remain deeply diverse. This entails that the law of requisite variety applies: one cannot imagine ways of regulating such societies that would not have the same degree of variety as the complex reality they want to tame. Much of the essentialism in good currency, whether of the statist, nationalist or other type, is rooted in an effort to deny deep cultural diversity and to assume that it is a much more superficial phenomenon than it really is. This leads to a lack of acknowledgement of Myrdal's cumulative causation mechanism and to some wishful thinking about all the differences melting down over a few generations. Integration is seen as likely to emerge organically, as if by immaculate conception, requiring no intervention and no effort to put in place a governance regime capable of generating dynamic and transculturally oriented *métissage*.

This perspective is flawed in two ways. What we know about the dynamics of intercultural relations promises considerable violence in this so-called interim period, which not only may last for one hundred years or more, but may also allow irreversible balkanization and damage to the country. The Panglossian view that integration will take care of itself may lead to a failure to take action that would promise a less destructive future. Breaking down the barrier of complacency is a necessary condition for intercultural relations to become a serious policy concern and not only a taboo topic. Yet it may not be sufficient, for the forces of dynamic conservatism are at work proactively ensuring that the enormous difficulties of any action on this front are overblown. This generates a great deal of cognitive dissonance. Awakening a society to impending dangers usually requires a major scandal or crisis. The assassination of Theo Van Gogh in the Netherlands became just such a wake-up call. What might be required to get the attention of the citizenry is nothing less than the moral equivalent of war or the sociological equivalent of defeat and the imperative of reconstruction. It is unlikely that the emotions around "reasonable accommodations," as with the Bouchard–Taylor Commission in Quebec, will suffice.

Second, breaking down the high degree of denial and cognitive dissonance may not suffice either. Even when the problem blows up in the forum, there will always be a tendency to search for panaceas, simplistic grand designs, and magnificent schemes based on some sort of magical thinking. As we have tried to show, when deep cultural diversity has hit societies between the eyes and it has become clear that the problem will not go away the first reflex has been to imagine simple contraptions, such as a section in the Charter of Rights and Freedoms, or canonical approaches, such as bills, charters or declarations of rights, or simplistic mechanisms, such as the Berry–Taylor assumption or the efforts to naturalize nationalism as a way to gain unity and order, and to present them as meaningful responses to the challenge of effective governance of deeply diverse societies. Such gimmicks are based on a simplistic evaluation of the situation and a most unrealistic appreciation of the dynamics at work, and, as we have shown, have succeeded only in stultifying and reifying an evolutionary process that calls for exactly the obverse of these stratagems. A more complex, experimental, and risky strategy can succeed only if ways are found to counter the infirmity of imagination, and the risk-aversion of the policy-makers and stakeholders, so that the difficulties and costs of dealing with them are reduced, and are not used up front to oppose

DEEP CULTURAL DIVERSITY

any action. Albert O. Hirschman has referred to this act of collibration (putting a finger on the scales to rebalance costs and benefits) as the use of "the principle of the hiding hand" (Hirschman 1967, Chapter 3). It is essentially a transition mechanism to entice decision-makers to take risks. It can take one of two forms, either showing that costs are likely to be overestimated by the risk-aversion of decision-makers, or providing a stimulus to action by fleshing out more fully the sort of improved situation that might ensue.

Third, a recombinant citizenship and a richness of varied moral contracts are likely to help, but only on condition that the scope of citizenship is dramatically reduced and the ambit of locally defined moral contracts is dramatically expanded. Only neorepublicans appear to have a sufficiently modest notion of citizenship. For them citizenship is the primary office: citizens are producers of governance. This means that citizenship pertains to the public realm, the *polis*, and that it does no require the elimination of differences of standing and power (Van Gunsteren 1998, p. 26). For neorepublicans social rights are not citizen rights (p. 106), and they stand firm against the trend, beginning with T. H. Marshall, in favour of allowing an unbounded extension of the rights attached to citizenship. We have shown the sort of abuses that such extensions have led to. Citizens need to be competent and to have the sort of rights required to carry out their duty of governing in the community of fate. They are not agents of identity groups. They can negotiate various particular arrangements for groups, as long as such compromises or accommodations do not create too many new inequalities or conflicts. Pragmatism is the rule.

Emergent social movements may well generate new dynamics by expressing new needs and desires, produce new actors, make questionable what was not previously questioned, and expand the options discussed within the public sphere (Angus 2001, pp. 55ff). In that sense emergent publics feed the public debate on citizenry. It would be naïve to look for simple consensus, for in conditions of deep cultural diversity the public is always divided, and the range of arrangements, formal or informal, that different fragments will find workable is quite wide. Practically this may translate not so much into uniform and homogeneous arrangements as into a variety of diverse accommodations within a corridor of arrangements regarded as not too politically destabilizing. This accommodates the agency of persons with multiple and limited identities. As long as the different levels of citizenship balance rights and duties, one may be allowed to define the sort of constellation of citizenship arrangements that suits his/ her preferences. Such differentiated citizenships already exist in many countries. The only difference is that most of the time they are not a matter of choice but are imposed for all sorts of reasons. The more reduced the scope of citizenship, as neorepublicans suggest, the more it is rooted in action and practice, and the more the preconditions that are not related to action and practice, the less contentious is the notion of differentiated citizenship.

More importantly, this approach might resolve, in a manner that provides for agency but with some sense of precedence, the thorny question of multiple citizenships. Each person would have the choice of balancing rights and responsibilities *ex ante*, in a manner that may resolve the conundrum generated by the tension between diversity and solidarity. Differentiated citizenship might provide for major and minor attachments, and so resolve the problem of "citizenships of convenience" and the possibility of merrily collecting multiple entitlements, such as pensions, while shirking all responsibilities. This would also free much of the negotiation space for the development of a multitude of different moral contracts suited to local circumstances.

Fourth, we shall have to become accustomed to what Hirschman (1995, p. 243) calls "a steady diet of conflicts." Some have opposed the drift towards "thin" or "lean" citizenship and the deployment of a richness of moral contracts as likely to generate conflicts, yet it is both a utopian dream and a fundamental misconception of democracy to hope for an end to conflict. That would be the end of politics itself, for the suppression of conflict would kill the very dynamics that generates social learning and trust. Canada has a myriad of different terms of integration in place over the land. Reasonable accommodations need not be the same in Toronto, Montreal, and Vancouver, and they need not be arrived at by consensus. Indeed, as long as conflicts can be reframed so that they are "more or less" instead of "either–or," moral contracts will evolve and arrangements will ensure that the regime also evolves. Such conflicts cannot be resolved by fiat. Discussions and debates must lead to agreement on some principles of precedence, some hierarchy among the different principles at play, such as the agreement that meeting basic needs takes precedence over whimsical wishes. While such debates are not always easily resolved, the very process of discussion has a civilizing effect and contributes to expanding the public sphere by including groups previously excluded, and thereby taming the conflicts between conflicting goals.

DEEP CULTURAL DIVERSITY

Unloading the present shackles of multiculturalism policy would do much to establish the foundations for intercultural accommodation. The Charter and the paraphernalia of cultural rights have done much to transform "more or less" conflicts into "either–or" ones, and to create a culture of judicialization and adjudication that not only does not encourage negotiation or accommodation, but underpins a routine tendency to go to the courts in order to obtain full satisfaction of one's wishes by simply labelling them rights. Transculturalism and *métissage* can materialize only as a result of the social learning generated by a steady diet of a multitude of locally resolved conflicts, leading to the emergence of a new mindset.

Finally, in the order of precedence that one may have to work hard to develop one may need to insist on the primacy of agency. The debate about citizenship has to proceed beyond the state (Hoffman 2004). The ultimate principle is the freedom of the citizen, as producer of governance, to embody multiple loyalties and to maintain a maximum amount of choice in these matters. This in turn constitutes a defence of casuistry, for it is only case by case that it can be determined whether the pre-eminence of agency generates external "malefits" that legitimize constraining it. These principles underpin the sort of strategies that have been propounded throughout this book: strategies of maximum choice and requisite variety; as little pressure for uniformity as possible; a modicum of distrust for grand designs, panaceas, and formal rules; and a propensity to allow arrangements to blossom bottom up rather than being imposed top down. The only major complementary concern that would require the same valence and should be allowed to guide intrusive interventions is the need to ensure that fail-safe mechanisms are in place to avoid irreversible damage to the fabric of a society. The combination of agency and fail-safe mechanisms may not be easy to engineer in a world where freedoms are not at a premium, and security deters experimentation, but it appears to be the only promising road to transculturalism.

Conclusion

In all this the core responsibilities of the state remain indispensable: to ensure that the basic relational/cognitive capital is in place, to remove unfreedoms, to ensure that the requisite fail-safe mechanisms are in place, and to live up to its preceptoral role. This is bound to entail the imposition of certain basic constraints and to call for some creative ways of exercising leadership.

For instance, it is not possible to think of the cosmopolitan ethos taking hold and guiding an open evolution without the citizens being able to converse, to engage in dialogue, to communicate one with the other. Consequently the assurance that citizens can communicate in a *lingua franca* may well be a *sine qua non*.

As for the removal of unfreedoms, which stand in the way of the smooth evolution of the configuration of moral contracts likely to bring forth the requisite basic coherence of a society in a process of emerging, the role of the state must remain subsidiary because it may create distortions and do more harm than good by intervening imprudently in cultural affairs. The caveat remains that fail-safe mechanisms must be in place and that the precautionary principle must inspire their use.

When it comes to the preceptoral role of the state, one must be duly modest. It is fair to say that misinformation and deception have been the daily bread of so many politicians and bureaucrats that the citizenry has become cynical and is unlikely to be willing to invest in listening to them. Moreover, to a not insignificant degree the betrayal of the intellectuals and the media, which, with few exceptions, have collaborated in trepanning the citizen, has contributed to the dumbing down of the forum. It is difficult to believe that any renewal can be realistically expected until there is a change of the guard.

The basic argument of this conclusion is that arrangements based on a "chaordic" regime, rooted in a few guiding principles and moral contracts, and enriched by state bricolage, with some help from the intelligentsia, may be our best hope. The role of the state in such a maze of loosely-coupled regimes should be guided by the importance of transparency, participation, competition, and so on; directed to the elimination of blockages and unfreedoms through subtle interventions at tipping points; and conducted always with the consent of, and in collaboration with, other stakeholders.

As to the likelihood of this transition to transculturalism proceeding quickly, one should not be too hopeful. The mental prisons mentioned above may not have walls, but their hold over Canadians' minds is woefully strong, and the learning challenges identified entail nothing less than Herculean efforts, if not Sisyphean ones. Yet the history of the world is strewn with even more unlikely events.

This is where the enlightenment role of the intelligentsia might become most important: providing the requisite vision of what is possible. *Possibilism*, as Hirschman (1971) defines it, is a deliberate investment in the discovery of paths, however narrow, leading to an outcome that appears to be foreclosed on the basis of probabilistic reasoning alone, in a strategy built on the possibility of increasing the number of ways in which change can be visualized (Paquet 1993, p. 280). How can this be done? In the face of full awareness of the awesome proportions of the social conditions required to effect the transition to a more promising regime, what may be necessary is nothing less than the capacity, for those who feel up to the task, to do what Leszek Kolakowski (translated by and quoted in Hirschman 1967, p. 32) says is necessary:

> if society is to generate the energy required to effect changes in
> social and human relations. For this purpose, one exaggerates
> the prospective results into a myth so as to make them take on
> dimensions which correspond a bit more to the immediately
> felt effort . . . [The myth acts like] a Fata Morgana which makes
> beautiful lands arise before the eyes of the members of a caravan
> and thus increases their efforts to the point where, in spite of all
> their sufferings, they reach the next tiny waterhole. Had such
> tempting mirages not appeared, the exhausted caravan would
> inevitably have perished in the sandstorm, bereft of hope.

Acknowledgements

This book is the result of work done, on and off, over roughly the past twenty years, though many of its conclusions have crystallized over the past five. It owes a great deal to the locus of research created by the Centre on Governance of the University of Ottawa, and has benefited from comments by many colleagues and friends who have not always reacted well to my insistent disquisitions on these issues. Jean Burnet, Linda Cardinal, Harry Chartrand, Monica Gattinger, Jean Guiot, Jak Jabes, Rudy Kalin, Jean Laponce, John Meisel, Christian Navarre, Joseph Pestieau, and Jeffrey Roy have all commented in some way on the papers that form the bases of this book, and their trains of thought have left traces upon them, although they should not in any way be held responsible for the outcome.

Special thanks are due to Paul Laurent and Paul Reed, each of whom was a co-author on a separate paper, for allowing me to transform those papers into chapters of this book; and to Robin Higham, who has done more than anyone else to force me to think through these issues ever more carefully over the past few years.

I must also express my gratitude to the Social Sciences and Humanities Research Council of Canada for financial support for many of the years during which this book has been evolving.

Finally, I gratefully acknowledge the assistance of Anne Burgess, Marise Guindon, and Marc Racette.

Although they have been modified substantially a number of times, segments of several chapters have been drawn from previously published papers, as follows.

Chapter 2: Laurent, Paul, and Paquet, Gilles. (1991). "Intercultural Relations: A Myrdal–Tocqueville–Girard Interpretative Scheme." *International Political Science Review* 12:3.

Chapters 3 and 8: Paquet, Gilles. (1994). "Political Philosophy of Multiculturalism," in John W. Berry et al. *Ethnicity and Culture in Canada*. Toronto: University of Toronto Press.

Chapter 4: Paquet, Gilles. (1989). "Multiculturalism as National Policy." *Journal of Cultural Economics* 13:1.

Chapter 5: Paquet, Gilles, and Paul Reed. (2003). "Are There Limits to Diversity?" *Optimum Online* 33:1. online at optimumonline.ca.

Chapter 7: Paquet, Gilles. (2006). "Moral Contract as Enabling Mechanism." *Optimum Online* 36:3. online at optimumonline.ca.

Chapter 8: Paquet, Gilles. (2004). "Governance and Emergent Transversal Citizenship, Pluralism and Governance: Toward a New Nexus of Moral Contracts," in Pierre Boyer, Linda Cardinal, and David Headon, ed. *From Subjects to Citizens: One Hundred Years of Citizenship in Citizenship in Australia and Canada*. Ottawa: University of Ottawa Press.

Conclusion: Paquet, Gilles. (2005). "Governance of Culture: Words of Caution," in Caroline Andrew et al., ed. *Accounting for Culture: Examining the Building Blocks of Cultural Citizenship*. Ottawa: University of Ottawa Press.

DEEP CULTURAL DIVERSITY

Bibliography

Ackerman, Bruce A. (1984). *Reconstructing American Law*. Cambridge, MA: Harvard University Press.

Agamben, Giorgio. (2000). *Means Without Ends: Notes on Politics*. Minneapolis: University of Minnesota Press.

Agamben, Giorgio. (2003). *État d'exception*. Paris: Éditions du Seuil. [trans. as (2005). *State of Exception*. Chicago: University of Chicago Press.]

Akerlof, George A. (1976). "The Economics of Caste and of the Rat Race, and Other Woeful Tales." *Quarterly Journal of Economics* 90.

Anderson, Walt T. (2001). *All Connected Now*. Cambridge, MA: Westview Press.

Angus, Ian H. (2001). *Emergent Publics: An Essay on Social Movements and Democracy*. Winnipeg: Arbeiter Ring Publishing.

Ansoff, H. I. (1960). "A Quasi-Analytic Method for Long-Range Planning," in C. West Churchman and Michel Verhulst, ed. *Management Sciences: Models and Techniques*. London: Pergamon Press.

Appiah, Kwame Anthony. (2005). *The Ethics of Identity*. Princeton, NJ: Princeton University Press.

Appiah, Kwame Anthony. (2006). *Cosmopolitanism: Ethics in a World of Strangers*. New York: W. W. Norton.

Arnal, Marc (1986). "Canadian Values and Canadian Citizenship: Challenges for the Future," in R. R. Gadacz, ed. *Challenging the Concept of Citizenship*. Edmonton: CSC Consulting Services.

Aron, Raymond. (1974). "Is Multinational Citizenship Possible?" *Social Research* 41.

Arrow, Kenneth J. (1974). *The Limits of Organization*. New York: W. W. Norton.

Australian Citizenship Council. (2000). *Australian Citizenship for a New Century*. Canberra: Australian Citizenship Council.

Axworthy, Thomas S. (2005, Summer). "The Responsibility Crisis in Canada." *Canadian Parliamentary Review*.

Badaracco, Joseph L. (2002). *Leading Quietly*. Boston, MA: Harvard Business School Press.

Banfield, Edward C. (1958). *The Moral Basis of a Backward Society*. New York: Free Press.

Banner, Gerhard. (2002, November 6). "La gouvernance communautaire au coeur du processus de décentralisation." *Problèmes économiques* 2783.

Banting, Keith G. (1999). "Social Citizenship and the Multicultural Welfare State," in A.C. Cairns et al., ed. *Citizenship, Diversity and Pluralism: Canadian and Comparative Perspectives*. Montreal: McGill–Queen's University Press.

Banting, Keith G. (2007). "Canada as Counter Narrative." *Optimum Online* 37:3. online at optimumonline.ca.

Banting, Keith G., and Will Kymlicka, ed. (2006). *Multiculturalism and the Welfare State*. Oxford: Oxford University Press.

Banting, Keith G., et al. (2007). *The Art of the State*, Vol. 3, *Belonging?* Montreal: IRPP.

Barbalet, J. M. (1988). *Citizenship*. Minneapolis: University of Minnesota Press.

Barnard, Chester I. (1938). *The Functions of the Executive*. Cambridge, MA: Harvard University Press.

Barry, Brian (2001). *Culture and Equality: An Egalitarian Critique of Multiculturalism*. Cambridge, MA: Harvard University Press.

Bastarache, Michel. (1988). "Dualité et multiculturalisme." *Revue de l'association canadienne d'éducation de langue* 16.

Batifoulier, Philippe, ed. (2001). *Théorie des conventions*. Paris: Economica.

Bauböck, Rainer. (2001). "Recombinant Citizenship," in Martin Kohli and Alison E. Woodward, ed. *Inclusions and Exclusions in European Societies*. London: Routledge.

Bauman, Zygmunt. (2000). *Liquid Modernity*. Cambridge: Polity Press.

Bauman, Zygmunt. (2001). *Community*. Cambridge: Polity.

Baumeister, Andrea. (2003). "Ways of Belonging." *Ethnicities* 3:3.

Becker, Gary. (1957). *The Economics of Discrimination.* Chicago: University of Chicago Press.

Berger, Lawrence A. (1989). "Economics and Hermeneutics." *Economics and Philosophy* 5.

Bergson, Henri. (1932). *Les deux sources de la morale et de la religion.* 3rd ed. Paris: Alcan.

Berry, John W. (1977). "Multiculturalism and Intergroup Attitudes," in S. V. C. Dubois, ed. *Conference on Multiculturalism in Education.* Toronto: Ontario Association for Curriculum Development.

Berry, John W. (1991, May). "Sociopsychological Costs and Benefits of Multiculturalism." mimeo.

Berry, John W., Rudolf Kalin, and Donald M. Taylor. (1977). *Multiculturalism and Ethnic Attitudes in Canada.* Ottawa: Supply and Services Canada.

Bibby, Reginald W. (1990). *Mosaic Madness.* Toronto: Stoddart.

Bissonnette, Lise. (1988, July 30). "Vice Versa Targets Transcultural Society." *Globe and Mail* [Toronto].

Boisvert, Raymond D. (2005). "Diversity as Fraternity Lite." *Journal of Speculative Philosophy* 19:2.

Bolduc, Denis, and Pierre Fortin. (1990). "Les francophones sont-ils plus xénophobes que les anglophones au Québec?: Une analyse quantitative exploratoire." *Canadian Ethnic Studies* 22.

Bouchard, Gérard. (1990). "Les rapports entre l'individu, la société et l'État dans un contexte pluriethnique: à la recherche d'un modèle." *L'Action Nationale* 80:8.

Bouchard, Gérard. (1999). *La nation québécoise au futur et au passé.* Montreal: VLB.

Bourdieu, Pierre. (1972). *Esquisse d'une théorie de la pratique.* Geneva: Droz.

Braudel, Fernand. (1979). *Civilisation matérielle, économie et capitalisme, XVe – XVIIIe siècle.* Paris: Armand Colin.

Braybrooke, David. (2000). "How is Democratic Deliberation to Deal with the Politically Absurd?" mimeo.

Breton, Raymond. (1984). "The Production and Allocation of Symbolic Resources: An Analysis of the Linguistic and Ethnocultural Fields in Canada." *Canadian Review of Sociology and Anthropology* 21:2.

Breton, Raymond. (1986). "Multiculturalism and Canadian Nation-Building," in Alan Cairns and Cynthia Williams, ed. *The Politics of Gender, Ethnicity and Language in Canada*. Toronto: University of Toronto Press.

Breton, Raymond. (2003). "Societal Governance and Increasing Ethnic Diversity." *Optimum Online* 33:1. online at optimumonline. ca.

Breton, Raymond, et al. (1990). *Ethnic Identity and Equality*. Toronto: University of Toronto Press.

Brock, Gillian. (2002). "Cosmopolitan Democracy and Justice: Held versus Kymlicka." *Studies in East European Thought* 54.

Brotz, Howard. (1980). "Multiculturalism in Canada: A Muddle." *Canadian Public Policy* 6.

Bruckner, Pascal. (1994). *Le vertige de Babel: cosmopolitisme ou mondialisme*. Paris: Arlea.

Buchanan, Allen. (1991). "Toward a Theory of Secession." *Ethics* 101:2.

Buchignani, Norman. (1982). "Canadian Ethnic Research and Multiculturalism." *Journal of Canadian Studies* 17.

Burelle, André. (2007). "Deux lectures opposées de la Charte canadienne." *Options politiques* 28:7.

Burnet, Jean. (1976, April). "Ethnicity: Canadian Experience and Policy." *Sociological Focus*.

Caccia, Fulvio. (1984). "L'ethnicité comme post-modernité." *Vice Versa* 2:1.

Cairns, Alan. C., et al., ed. (1999). *Citizenship, Diversity and Pluralism: Canadian and Comparative Perspectives*. Montreal: McGill–Queen's University Press.

Caldwell, Gary. (2001). *La culture publique commune*. Quebec City: Nota Bene.

Cameron, David R. (1974). *Nationalism, Self-Determination, and the Quebec Question*. Toronto: Macmillan.

Cameron, David R. (1990). "Lord Durham Then and Now." *Journal of Canadian Studies* 25.

Canada, Government of. (1991). *Shaping Canada's Future Together: Proposals*. Ottawa: Supply and Services Canada.

Canadian Centre for Management Development. (1999). *A Strong Foundation: Report of the Task Force on Public Service Values and Ethics*. Ottawa: Canadian Centre for Management Development.

Canadian House of Commons Standing Committee on Multiculturalism. (1987). *Multiculturalism: Building the Canadian Mosaic.* Ottawa: Supply and Services Canada.

Cardozo, L. A. (1988, January 19). "In Defence of the Federal Government's Multiculturalism Policy." *Ottawa Citizen.*

Carter, Stephen L. (1998). *The Dissent of the Governed: A Meditation on Law, Religion, and Loyalty.* Cambridge, MA: Harvard University Press.

Cohen, Andrew. (2007). *The Unfinished Canadian.* Toronto: McClelland & Stewart.

Colas, Dominique, Claude Emeri, and Jacques Zylberberg, ed. (1991). *Citoyenneté et nationalité.* Paris: Presses Universitaires de France.

Coleman, James S. (1988). "Social Capital in the Creation of Human Capital." *American Journal of Sociology* 94, Supplement.

Collingbridge, D. (1982). *Critical Decision-Making.* London: Frances Pinter.

Coppieters, F. (1984). *Les structures politiques des communautés et des régions en Belgique.* Brussels: Institut d'information et de documentation.

Corbo, C. (1991, September 21). "Contre le multiculturalisme, pour l'intégration." *Le Devoir* [Montreal].

Cuccioletta, Donald (2001–02). "Multiculturalism or Transculturalism: Towards a Cosmopolitran Citizenship." *London Journal of Canadian Studies* 17.

Dahrendorf, Ralf. (1974). "Citizenship and Beyond: The Social Dynamics of an Idea." *Social Research* 41.

Dahrendorf, Ralf. (1988). *The Modern Social Conflict.* London and New York: Weidenfeld & Nicolson.

Denton, Trevor. (1966). "The Structure of French Canadian Acculturation, 1759–1800." *Anthropologica.*

DeFaveri, Ivan. (1986). "Jaenen on Multiculturalism," in Kach, Nick, ed. *Multiculturalism: Perspectives and Reactions.* Occasional Paper 86–1 of the Department of Educational Foundations. Edmonton: University of Alberta.

De Landa, Manuel. (2006). *A New Philosophy of Society.* New York: Continuum.

de Tocqueville, Alexis. (1961). *De la démocratie en Amérique* [1840]. 2 vols. Paris: Gallimard.

Dimock, Marshall. (1990, January–February). "The Restorative Qualities of Citizenship." *Public Administration Review* 50.

Donaldson, Thomas, and Thomas W. Dunfee. (1994). "Towards a Unified Conception of Business Ethics: Integrative Social Contracts Theory." *Academy of Management Review* 19:2.

Donaldson, Thomas, and Thomas W. Dunfee. (1995). "Integrative Social Contracts Theory: A Communitarian Conception of Economic Ethics." *Economics and Philosophy* 11:1.

Douglas, Mary. (1986). *How Institutions Think*. Syracuse, NY: Syracuse University Press.

Drummond, Lee (1981–82). "Analyse sémiotique de l'ethnicité au Québec." *Questions de culture* 2.

Dumont, Fernand. (1990, November–December). "Pourquoi le nationalisme?" *Relations*.

Dumont, Louis. (1983). *Essais sur l'individualisme*. Paris: Éditions du Seuil.

Dumouchel, Paul, and Jean-Pierre Dupuy (1979). *L'enfer des choses*. Paris: Éditions du Seuil.

Dupuy, Jean-Pierre. (1982). *Ordres et désordres*. Paris: Éditions du Seuil.

Dupuy, Jean-Pierre. (1985). "Libres propos sur l'égalité, la science et le racisme." *Le Débat* 37.

Dwivedi, O. P., ed. (1989). *Canada 2000: Race Relations and Public Policy*. Guelph, ON: Department of Political Studies, University of Guelph.

Earle, Timothy C., and George T. Cvetkovich. (1995). *Social Trust*. Westport, CT: Praeger.

Eckstein, Harry (1984). "Civic Inclusion and its Discontents." *Daedalus* 113.

Economic Council of Canada. (1991). *New Faces in the Crowd*. Ottawa: Supply and Services Canada.

Edwards, John, and Lori Doucette. (1987). "Ethnic Salience, Identity, and Symbolic Ethnicity." *Canadian Ethnic Studies* 19:1.

Eymard-Duvernay, François. (2006). *L'économie des conventions: Méthodes et résultats*. 2 vols. Paris: La Découverte.

Fish, Stanley. (1999). *The Trouble with Principle*. Cambridge, MA: Harvard University Press.

Foster, George M. (1972). "The Anatomy of Envy: A Study of Symbolic Behavior." *Current Anthropology* 13:2.

Francis, Diane. (2002). *Immigration: The Economic Case.* Toronto: Key Porter.

Frankfurt, Harry G. (1988). *The Importance of What We Care About.* Cambridge: Cambridge University Press.

Friedenberg, Edgar Z. (1975). *The Disposal of Liberty and Other Industrial Wastes.* New York; Doubleday.

Friedmann, John. (1979). *The Good Society.* Cambridge, MA: MIT Press.

Friedmann, John, and George Abonyi. (1976). "Social Learning: A Model for Policy Research." *Environment and Planning* A.8.

Fritzsche, David J. (1997). *Business Ethics: A Global and Managerial Perspective.* New York: McGraw–Hill.

Gagnon-Tremblay, Monique. (1990). *Au Québec, pour bâtir ensemble.* Quebec City: Gouvernement du Québec.

Gallie, W. P. (1964). *Philosophy and the Historical Understanding.* London: Chatto & Windus.

Gans, Herbert. (1979). "Symbolic Ethnicity." *Ethnic and Racial Studies* 2.

Gauchet, Marcel. (1998). *La religion dans la démocratie.* Paris: Gallimard.

Gauchet, Marcel. (2000). "Quand les droits de l'homme deviennent une politique." *Le Débat* 110.

Geadah, Yolande. (2007). *Accommodements raisonnables.* Montreal: VLB.

Geertz, Clifford. (1986). "The Uses of Diversity." *Michigan Quarterly Review* 25:1.

Giliomee, Hermann. (1987). "Apartheid, Verligtheid, and Liberalism," in Jeffrey Butler, Richard Elphick, and David Welsh, ed. *Democratic Liberalism in South Africa: Its History and Prospect.* Cape Town: David Philip.

Girard, René. (1972). *La violence et le sacré.* Paris: Grasset.

Girard, René. (1978). *Des choses cachées depuis le début du monde.* Paris: Grasset.

Girard, René. (1982). *Le bouc émissaire.* Paris: Grasset.

Gladwell, Malcolm. (2000). *The Tipping Point.* Boston, MA: Little, Brown.

Glazer, Nathan. (1983). *Ethnic Dilemmas 1964–1982.* Cambridge, MA: Harvard University Press.

Gluckman, Max. (1967). *The Judicial Process Among the Barotse of Northern Rhodesia*. 2nd ed. Manchester: Manchester University Press.

Goldberg, V. P. (1980). "Relational Exchange: Economics and Complex Contracts." *American Behavioral Scientist* 23.

Goodhart, David. (2004, February). "Too Diverse?" *Prospect*.

Granovetter, Mark. (1973). "The Strength of Weak Ties." *American Journal of Sociology* 78:6.

Gray, Barbara. (1989). *Collaborating: Finding Common Ground for Multiparty Problems*. San Francisco: Jossey–Bass.

Gray, John. (2002). *Straw Dogs*. London: Granta Books.

Grimond, John. (1991, June 29). "For Want of Glue: A Survey of Canada." *The Economist*.

Gutmann, Amy. (2003). *Identity in Democracy*. Princeton, NJ: Princeton University Press.

Hampden-Turner, Charles, and Fons Trompenaars. (1993). *The Seven Cultures of Capitalism*. London and New York: HarperCollins.

Handy, Charles. (1992). "Balancing Corporate Power: A New Federalist Paper." *Harvard Business Review* 70:6.

Handy, Charles. (1995). *Beyond Certainty*. London: Hutchinson

Hardin, Herschel. (1974). *A Nation Unaware*. Vancouver: J. J. Douglas.

Hardin, Russell. (2002). "The Crippled Epistemology of Extremism," in Albert Breton et al., ed. *Political Extremism and Rationality*. Cambridge: Cambridge University Press.

Hardin, Russell. (2006). "Ignorant Democracy." *Critical Review* 18:1–3.

Harney, Robert F. (1988). "'So Great a Heritage as Ours': Immigration and the Survival of the Canadian Polity." *Daedalus* 117.

Harvey, Julien. (1990a, November). "Vouloir l'identité québécoise." *Relations* 565.

Harvey, Julien. (1990b, November). "Identité québécoise et nationalisme." *Relations* 565.

Hasenclever, Andreas, Peter Mayer, and Volker Rittberger. (1997). *Theories of International Regimes*. Cambridge and New York: Cambridge University Press.

Heath, Joseph. (2001). *The Efficient Society: Why Canada is as Close to Utopia as It Gets*. Toronto: Viking Penguin.

Heath, Joseph. (2003). *The Myth of Shared Values in Canada*. Ottawa: Canadian Centre for Management Developoment.

Heintzman, Ralph. (2007). "Toward a New Moral Contract: Reclaiming Trust in the Public Service." *Optimum Online* 37:3. online at optimumonline.ca.

Held, David, et al. (1999). *Global Transformations*. Cambridge: Polity Press.

Hilgartner, Stephen, and Charles L. Bosk. (1988). "The Rise and Fall of Social Problems: A Public Arenas Model." *American Journal of Sociology* 94.

Hill, Jason D. (2000). *Becoming a Cosmopolitan: What It Means to Be a Human Being in the New Millennium*. Lanham, MD, and Oxford: Rowman & Littlefield.

Hirsch, Fred. (1976). *Social Limits to Growth*. Cambridge, MA: Harvard University Press.

Hirschman, Albert O. (1967). *Development Projects Observed*. Washington, DC: Brookings Institution.

Hirschman, Albert O. (1971). *A Bias for Hope*. New Haven, CT: Yale University Press.

Hirschman, Albert O. (1995). *A Propensity to Self-Subversion*. Cambridge: Harvard University Press.

Hock, Dee. (1995). "The Chaordic Organization: Out of Control and into Order." *World Business Academy Perspectives* 9:1.

Hock, Dee. (1999). *Birth of the Chaordic Age*. San Francisco: Berrett–Koehler.

Hoffman, John (2004). *Citizenship Beyond the State*. London: Sage.

Howard-Hassmann, Rhoda E. (1999). "'Canadian' as an Ethnic Category: Implications for Multiculturalism and National Unity." *Canadian Public Policy* 24:4.

Hubbard, Ruth, and Gilles Paquet. (2002). "Ecologies of Governance and Institutional *Métissage*." *Optimum Online* 32:4. online at optimumonline.ca.

Hubbard, Ruth, and Gilles Paquet. (2007). *Gomery's Blinders and Canadian Federalism*. Ottawa: University of Ottawa Press.

Ignatieff, Michael (1984). *The Needs of Strangers*. New York: Viking.

Ignatieff, Michael. (1989). "Citizenship and Moral Narcissism." *Political Quarterly* 60.

Ignatieff, Michael. (1993). *Blood and Belonging*. New York: Viking.

Ignatieff, Michael. (1999). *Warrior's Hour: Ethnic War and the Modern Conscience*. London: Vintage.

Ignatieff, Michael. (2000). *The Rights Revolution.* Toronto: Anansi.

Ignatieff, Michael. (2001). *Human Rights as Politics and Idolatry.* Princeton, NJ: Princeton University Press.

Jacquet, Pierre, et al. (2002). "De quelques principes pour une gouvernance hybride." *Problèmes économiques* 2755 and 2767.

Jaenen, Cornelius J. (1986). "Multiculturalism: An Historian's Perspectives," in Kach, Nick, ed. *Multiculturalism: Perspectives and Reactions.* Occasional Paper 86–1 of the Department of Educational Foundations. Edmonton: University of Alberta.

Janis, Irving L. (1982). *Groupthink: Psychological Studies of Policy Decisions and Fiascos.* 2nd ed. Boston, MA: Houghton Mifflin.

Janoski, Thomas. (1998). *Citizenship and Civil Society: A Framework of Rights and Obbligations in Liberal, Traditional and Social Democratic Regimes.* Cambridge and New York: Cambridge University Press.

Janowitz, Morris. (1980). "Observations on the Sociology of Citizenship: Obligations and Rights." *Social Forces* 59.

Jenson, Jane, and Martin Papillon. (1999). *The Changing Boundaries of Citizenship: A Review and a Research Agenda.* Ottawa: Canadian Policy Research Networks.

Jenson, Jane, and Martin Papillon. (2000). *Citizenship and the Recognition of Cultural Diversity: The Canadian Experience.* Ottawa: Canadian Policy Research Networks.

Johnson, Steven. (2001). *Emergence: The Connected Lives of Ants, Brains, Cities, and Software.* New York: Scribner.

Joppke, Christian. (2004). "The Retreat of Multiculturalism in the Liberal States: Theory and Policy." *British Journal of Sociology* 55:2.

Juillet, Luc, and Gilles Paquet. (2002). "The Neurotic State," in G. B. Doern, ed. *How Ottawa Spends 2002–03: The Security Aftermath and National Priorities.* Don Mills, ON: Oxford University Press.

Kahneman, Daniel, and Amos Tversky. (1979). "Prospect Theory: An Analysis of Decision Under Risk." *Econometrica* 47.

Kallen, Evelyn. (1982a). "Multiculturalism: Ideology, Policy, and Reality." *Journal of Canadian Studies* 17:1.

Kallen, Evelyn. (1982b). *Ethnicity and Human Rights in Canada.* Toronto: Gage.

Kaplan, William. (1991). *About Canadian Citizenship.* mimeo.

Kapuscinski, Ryszard. (2005). "Encountering the Other: The Challenge of the 21st Century." *New Perspectives Quarterly* 22:4.

Keane, John. (1998). *Civil Society.* Cambridge: Polity Press.

Kearney, Richard. (1979, April). "Terrorisme et sacrifice: Le cas de l'Irlande du Nord." *Esprit.*

Kekes, John. (1993). *The Morality of Pluralism.* Princeton, NJ: Princeton University Press.

Kekes, John. (2003). *The Illusions of Egalitarianism.* Ithaca, NY: Cornell University Press.

Kelly, George A. (1979). "Who Needs a Theory of Citizenship?" *Daedalus* 108.

Kolm, Serge-Christophe. (1985). *Le contrat social libéral.* Paris: Presses Universitaires de France.

Krasner, Stephen D., ed. (1983). *International Regimes.* Ithaca, NY: Cornell University Press.

Kymlicka, Will. (1989). *Liberalism, Community and Culture.* Oxford: Oxford University Press.

Kymlicka, Will. (1995). *Multicultural Citizenship.* Oxford: Oxford University Press.

Kymlicka, Will. (2001). *Politics in the Vernacular.* Oxford: Oxford University Press.

Lafrance, Guy, ed. (1989). *Ethics and Basic Rights.* Ottawa: University of Ottawa Press.

Langlais, Jacques, Pierre Laplante, and Joseph Lévy. (1990). *Le Québec de demain et les communautés culturelles.* Montreal: Éditions du Méridien.

Laurendeau, André. (1962). *La crise de la conscription 1942.* Montreal: Éditions du Jour.

Laurent, Paul, and Paquet, Gilles. (1991). "Intercultural Relations: A Myrdal–Tocqueville–Girard Interpretative Scheme." *International Political Science Review* 12:3.

Le Grand, Julian. (2003). *Motivation, Agency and Public Policy.* Oxford: Oxford University Press.

Leishman, Rory. (2006). *Against Judicial Activism: The Decline of Freedom and Democracy in Canada.* Montreal: McGill–Queen's University Press.

Leslie, P. M. (1986). "L'aspect politique et collectif." *Cahiers de droit* 27.

Light, Ivan H. (1972). *Ethnic Enterprise in America.* Berkeley: University of California.

Light, Ivan H. (1984, April). "Immigrant and Ethnic Enterprise in North America." *Ethnic and Racial Studies* 7:2.

Lind, Michael. (2000, October). "National Good." *Prospect* 56.

Lowi, Theodore J. (1975). "Toward a Politics of Economics: The State of Permanent Receivership," in Leon N. Lindberg et al., ed. *Stress and Contradiction in Modern Capitalism*. Lexington, MA: D. C. Heath.

Lukes, Steven. (1997). "Humiliation and the Politics of Identity." *Social Research* 64.

Lupul, Manoly R. (1982). "The Political Implementation of Multiculturalism." *Journal of Canadian Studies* 17:1.

Lussato, Bruno. (1989). *Le défi culturel*. Paris: Nathan.

Margalit, Avishai. (1996). *The Decent Society*. Cambridge, MA: Harvard University Press.

Markell, Patchen P. (2000). "The Recognition of Politics." *Constellation* 7:4.

Marshall, Alfred. (1907, March). "The Social Possibilities of Economic Chivalry." *Economic Journal*.

Marshall, T. H. (1964). *Class, Citizenship and Social Development*. Chicago: University of Chicago Press.

McGinnis, Michael D., ed. (2000). *Polycentric Games and Institutions*. Ann Arbor: University of Michigan Press.

McNeill, W. H. (1986). *Polyethnicity and National Unity in World History*. Toronto: University of Toronto Press.

Meghji, A. (1990, May 15). "Keeping 'Ethnics' at the Periphery." *Toronto Star*.

Melonio, Françoise. (1986). "Introduction à la Seconde Démocratie." Alexis de Tocqueville. *Oeuvres*. Paris: Laffont.

Mercer, Colin. (2002). *Towards Cultural Citizenship: Tools for Cultural Policy and Development*. Stockholm: Bank of Sweden Tercentenary Foundation.

Mesthene, Emmanuel G. (1970). *Technological Change: Its Impact on Man and Society*. New York: Mentor.

Mintzberg, Henry, and Jan Jorgensen. (1987). "Emergent Strategy for Public Policy." *Canadian Public Administration* 30.

Morissette, D. (1991). *Multiculturalisme versus interculturalisme: une autre facette du débat sur la sécurité culturelle du Québec*. Montreal: Bureau des relations fédérales–provinciales.

Mukherjee, Bharati. (1985). *Darkness*. Harmondsworth: Penguin.

Myrdal, Gunnar. (1944). *An American Dilemma*. New York: Harper.

Myrdal, Gunnar. (1957). *Economic Theory and Underdeveloped Regions*. London: Duckworth.

Nash, Manning. (1989). *The Cauldron of Ethnicity in the Modern World*. Chicago: University of Chicago Press.

Nielsen, R. (1991). "How We Got Where We Are." *The Idler* 32.

Nisbet, Robert. (1976). *Sociology as an Art Form*. New York: Oxford University Press.

O'Donnell, Guillermo. (1998). "Horizontal Accountability in New Democracies." *Journal of Democracy* 9:3.

Oldfield, Adrian. (1990). "Citizenship: An Unnatural Practice?" *Political Quarterly* 61.

Oliver, Dawn. (1991). "Active Citizenship in the 1990s." *Parliamentary Affairs* 44.

O'Neill, Onora (2002). *A Question of Trust: The BBC Reith Lectures 2002*. Cambridge: Cambridge University Press.

Oriol, Michel. (1979). "Identité produite, identitée instituée, identitée exprimée: confusions des théories de l'identité nationale et culturelle." *Cahiers internationaux de sociologie* 66.

Orsini, Christine. (1986). *La pensée de René Girard*. Paris: Retz.

Ostrom, Elinor. (1990). *Governing the Commons*. Cambridge: Cambridge University Press.

Palmer, D. L. (1991). "Contact Effects and Changing Levels of Prejudice in Canada." mimeo.

Paquet, Gilles. (1986). "Entrepreneurship canadien-français: mythes et réalités." *Transactions of the Royal Society of Canada* Fourth Series, 24.

Paquet, Gilles. (1988). "Pour une socio-économie franco-ontarienne." Paper presented at conference, Les Voies de L'Avenir Franco-Ontarien.

Paquet, Gilles. (1989a.) "Pour une notion renouvelée de citoyenneté." *Transactions of the Royal Society of Canada* Fifth Series, 4.

Paquet, Gilles. (1989b). "Multiculturalism as National Policy." *Journal of Cultural Economics* 13.

Paquet, Gilles. (1991–92). "Betting on Moral Contracts." *Optimum* 22:3.

Paquet, Gilles. (1993). "Sciences transversales et savoirs d'expérience: the art of trespassing." *Revue générale de droit* 24:2.

Paquet, Gilles. (1994a). "Citoyenneté dans une société de l'information: une réalité transversale et paradoxale." *Transactions of the Royal Society of Canada* Sixth Series, 5.

Paquet, Gilles. (1994b). "Political Philosophy of Multiculturalism," in J. Berry and J. Laponce, ed. *Ethnicity and Culture in Canada.* Toronto: University of Toronto Press.

Paquet, Gilles. (1996–97). "The Strategic State." 3 parts. *Ciencia Ergo Sum.* 3:3, 4:1, and 4:2.

Paquet, Gilles. (1998). "Canada as a Disconcerted Learning Economy: A Governance Challenge." *Transactions of the Royal Society of Canada* Sixth Series, 8.

Paquet, Gilles. (1999a) *Governance Through Social Learning.* Ottawa: University of Ottawa Press.

Paquet, Gilles. (1999b). "Innovations in Governance in Canada." *Optimum* 29:2/3.

Paquet, Gilles. (2000a). "Gouvernance distribuée, socialité et engagement civique." *Gouvernance* 1:1.

Paquet, Gilles. (2000b). "E-gouvernance, gouvernementalité et État commutateur." *Relations Industrielles/Industrial Relations* 55:4.

Paquet, Gilles. (2001a). "Le droit à l'épreuve de la gouvernance." *Gouvernance* 2:1/2.

Paquet, Gilles. (2001b). "La gouvernance en tant que conditions auxiliaires." in Linda Cardinal and Caroline Andrew, ed. *Gouvernance et démocratie.* Ottawa: Presses de l'Université d'Ottawa.

Paquet, Gilles. (2002) "Pepin–Roberts Redux: socialité, régionalité et gouvernance," in J. P. Wallot, ed. *La Commission Pépin–Roberts: quelques vingt ans après.* Ottawa: Presses de l'Université d'Ottawa.

Paquet, Gilles. (2004). *Pathologies de gouvernance.* Montreal: Liber.

Paquet, Gilles. (2005a). *Gouvernance: une invitation à la subversion.* Montreal: Liber.

Paquet, Gilles. (2005b). *The New Geo-Governance: A Baroque Approach.* Ottawa: University of Ottawa Press.

Paquet, Gilles. (2005c). "Gomery as Glasnost." *Literary Review of Canada* 13:7.

Paquet, Gilles. (2006a.) "Une déprimante culture de l'adjudication." *Options politiques* 27:5.

Paquet, Gilles. (2006b). "Moral Contract as Enabling Mechanism." *Optimum Online* 36:3. online at optimumonline.ca.

Paquet, Gilles, and Lise Pigeon (2000). "In Search of a New Covenant," in Evert Lindquist, ed. *Government Restructuring and the Future of Career Public Service in Canada.* Toronto: Institute of Public Administration of Canada.

Paquet, Gilles, and Paul Reed. (2003). "Are There Limits to Diversity?" *Optimum Online* 33:1. online at optimumonline.ca.

Paquet, Gilles, and Jean-Pierre Wallot. (1987). "Nouvelle-France, Québec, Canada: A World of Limited Identities," in Nicholas Canny and Anthony Pagden, ed. *Colonial Identity in the Atlantic World*. Princeton, NJ: Princeton University Press.

Parry, Geraint. (1989). "Democracy and Amateurism: The Informed Citizen." *Government and Opposition* 24:4.

Passaris, Constantine E. (1985, May). "Multicultural Connections: Government and Business Should Draw Upon the Rich Racial and Cultural Diversity of Present-Day Canada to Build Worldwide Trade Relations." *Policy Options* 6:4.

Perlmutter, H. V. (1965). *Towards a Theory and Practice of Social Architecture*. London: Tavistock.

Peter, Karl A. (1978). "Multicultural Politics, Money and the Conduct of Canadian Ethnic Studies." *Canadian Ethnic Studies Association Bulletin* 5.

Pogge, Thomas W. (2002). "Cosmopolitanism: A Defence." *Critical Review of International Social and Political Philosophy* 5:3.

Popper, Karl. (1942). *The Open Society and its Enemies*. 2 vols. London: Routledge & Kegan Paul.

Porter, J. N. (1979). "On Multiculturalism as a Limit of Canadian Life," in Hédi Bouraoui, ed. *The Canadian Alternative: Cultural Pluralism and Canadian Unity*. Downsview, ON: ECW Press.

Putnam, Robert D (2007). "*E Pluribus Unum*: Diversity and Community in the 21st Century." *Scandinavian Political Studies* 30:2.

Ravetz, J. R. (1986). "Usable Knowledge, Usable Ignorance: Incomplete Science with Policy Implications," in W. C. Clark and R. E. Munn, ed. *Sustainable Development of the Biosphere*. Cambridge: Cambridge University Press.

Reszler, André. (1990). *Le pluralisme*. Geneva: Georg.

Rheingold, Howard. (2002). *Smart Mobs: The Next Social Revolution*. Cambridge: Perseus.

Richer, K. (2006). *Policy-Making and the Relationship between Parliament and the Supreme Court of Canada in the Post-Charter Era*. Kingston, ON: Queen's University.

Roberts, L. W., and R. A. Clifton (1982). "Exploring the Ideology of Canadian Multiculturalism." *Journal of Canadian Studies* 17:1.

Robin, Régine. (1989). "La langue entre l'idéologie et l'utopie." *Vice Versa* 27.

Rorty, Richard. (1986). "On Ethnocentrism: A Reply to Clifford Geertz." *Michigan Quarterly Review* 25:3.

Rorty, Richard. (1991). *Objectivity, Relativism, and Truth*. Cambridge: Cambridge University Press.

Rosanvallon, Pierre. (2006). *La contre-démocratie: La politique à l'âge de la défiance*. Paris: Éditions du Seuil.

Rosenau, James N. (2003). *Distant Proximities: Dynamics beyond Globalization*. Princeton, NJ: Princeton University Press.

Ross, Malcolm, ed. (1954). *Our Sense of Identity*. Toronto: Ryerson Press.

Saint-Onge, Hubert. (1996, March–April). "Tacit Knowledge: The Key to the Strategic Alignment of Intellectual Capital." *Strategy and Leadership*.

Scheler, Max. (1958). *L'homme du ressentiment*. Paris: Presses Universitaires de France.

Schön, Donald A. (1963). *Displacement of Concepts*. London: Tavistock.

Schön, Donald A. (1971). *Beyond the Stable State*. New York: W. W. Norton.

Schön, Donald A. (1983). *The Reflective Practitioner*. New York: Basic Books.

Schön, Donald A., and Martin Rein. (1994). *Frame Analysis*. New York: Basic Books.

Schumacher, E. F. (1977). *A Guide for the Perplexed*. New York: Harper & Row.

Seifter, Harvey, et al. (2001). *Leadership Ensemble: Lessons in Collaborative Management from the World's Only Conductorless Orchestra*. New York: Henry Holt.

Sen, Amartya. (1987). *On Ethics and Economics*. Oxford: Blackwell.

Sen, Amartya. (1999). *Development as Freedom*. New York: Knopf

Shachar, Ayelet. (2001). *Multicultural Jurisdictions: Cultural Differences and Women's Rights*. Cambridge: Cambridge University Press.

Sheridan, W. (1987). *Le multiculturalisme canadien: questions et tendances*. Ottawa: Bulletin d'actualité, Bibliothèque du Parlement.

Smith, R. M. (1988). "The American Creed and American Identity: The Limits of Liberal Citizenship in the United States." *Western Political Quarterly* 41.

Snare, Frank (1977). "Dissolving the Moral Contract." *Philosophy* 52.

Spicer, Keith. (1988, July 13). "The Best and Worst of Multiculturalism." *Ottawa Citizen.*

Spinosa, Charles, Fernando Flores, and Hubert L. Dreyfus (1997). *Disclosing New Worlds.* Cambridge, MA: MIT Press.

Stasiulis, D. K. (1980). "The Political Structuring of Ethnic Community Action: A Reformulation." *Canadian Ethnic Studies* 12:3.

Stasiulis, D. K. (1988). "The Symbolic Mosaic Reaffirmed: Multiculturalism Policy," in K. A. Graham, ed., *How Ottawa Spends.* Ottawa: Carleton University Press.

Steinberg, Jonathan. (1976). *Why Switzerland?* Cambridge: Cambridge University Press.

Storper, Michael. (1996). "Institutions of the Knowledge-Based Economy," in *Employment and Growth in the Knowledge-Based Economy.* Paris: Organization for Economic Cooperation and Development.

Sugunasiri, Suwanda. (1990, October 29). "'Minority Ethnics' Build Walls of Seclusion." *Toronto Star.*

Sunstein, Cass R. (2000). "Practical Reason and Incompletely Theorized Arguments," in E. Ullmann-Margalit, ed. *Reasoning Practically.* Oxford: Oxford University Press.

Sunstein, Cass R. (2003). *Why Societies Need Dissent.* Cambridge, MA: Harvard University Press.

Sunstein, Cass R. (2005). *Laws of Fear.* Cambridge: Cambridge University Press.

Sunstein, Cass R. (2006). *Infotopia: How Many Minds Produce Knowledge.* Oxford: Oxford University Press.

Surowiecki, James. (2004). *The Wisdom of Crowds.* New York: Doubleday.

Taguieff, Pierre-André. (1987). *La force du préjugé: Essai sur le racisme et ses doubles.* Paris: La Découverte.

Tapscott, Don, and David Agnew. (1999, December). "Governance in the Digital Economy." *Finance and Development.*

Tassinari, Lamberto. (1989). "La ville continue: Montréal et l'expérience transculturelle de Vice Versa." *Revue internationale d'action communautaire* 21:61.

Tassinari, Lamberto. (1992). "Ethnicité, inaccomplissement et transculture," in Caroline Andrew et al., ed. *L'ethnicité a l'heure de la mondialisation.* Ottawa: ACFAS/Outaouais.

Taylor, Charles. (1985). "Alternative Futures," in A. Cairns and C. Williams, ed. *Constitionalism, Citizenship and Society in Canada.* Toronto: University of Toronto Press.

Taylor, Charles. (1992). *Multiculturalism and the Politics of Recognition.* Princeton, NJ: Princeton University Press.

Taylor, Charles. (2004). *Modern Social Imaginaries.* Durham, NC: Duke University Press.

Thacher, David, and Martin Rein. (2004). "Managing Value Conflict in Public Policy." *Governance* 17:4.

Thomas, D. (1990). *Immigrant Integration and the Canadian Identity.* Ottawa: Employment and Immigration Canada.

Throsby, David. (2001). *Economics and Culture.* Cambridge: Cambridge University Press.

Tully, James. (2000). "Struggles over Recognition and Distribution." *Constellations* 7:4.

Tussman, Joseph. (1977). *Government and the Mind.* New York: Oxford University Press.

Tussman, Joseph. (1989). *The Burden of Office: Agamemnon and Other Losers.* Vancouver: Talonbooks.

Tversky, Amos, and Daniel Kahneman. (1981, January 30). "The Framing of Decisions and the Psychology of Choice." *Science* 211.

Valaskakis, Kimon. (1990). *Canada in the Nineties: Meltdown or Renaissance?* Ottawa: World Media Institute.

Van Gunsteren, Herman. (1998). *A Theory of Citizenship: Organizing Plurality in Contemporary Democracies.* Boulder, CO: Westview Press.

Van Schendel, Nicolas. (1989). "Nationalité, langue et transculture." *Vice Versa* 27.

Vickers, Geoffrey. (1965). *The Art of Judgment: A Study of Policy-Making.* London: Methuen.

Vipond, Robert C. (1996). "Citizenship and the Charter of Rights: The Two Sides of Pierre Trudeau." *International Journal of Canadian Studies* 14.

Visker, Rudi. (1994). "Transcultural Vibrations." *Ethical Perspectives* 1–2.

Walzer, Michael. (1983). *Spheres of Justice.* Oxford: Martin Robertson.

Watzlawick, Paul, ed. (1988). *L'invention de la réalité.* Paris: Éditions du Seuil.

Weinberg, A.M. (1972). "Science and Trans-Science." *Minerva* 10.

Weinstein, M. A. (1985). *Culture Critique: Fernand Dumont and New Quebec Sociology*. Montreal: New World Perspectives.

Wihtol de Wenden, Catherine. (1989). "Citoyenneté, nationalité, et immigration." *Revue internationale d'action communautaire* 21:61.

Wilson, Robin. "Republicanism, Multiculturalism and Cosmopolitanism." Talk given at the Humanist Summer School on Freethinking and Diversity, 26 August 2006. <nireland.humanists.net/docs/article29.doc>, (12 November 2007).

Wilson, V. S. (1993). "The Tapestry Vision of Canadian Multiculturalism." *Canadian Journal of Political Science* 26:4.

Wriston, Walter B. (1992). *The Twilight of Sovereignty*. New York: Scribner.

INDEX

A

B

C

Canadian Citizenship Act, 115–16, 125, 174
Canadian Constitution, 43, 144
"Canadian mosaic," 49, 57
Canadian Multiculturalism Council, 58
Canadian Political Science Association, 144
"chaord," 167–68
Charlottetown Accord, 87, 120
citizenship
    asymmetric, 109
    Australian Citizenship Council, 118–19
    as belonging, 71
    Canadian Citizenship Act, 115–16, 125, 174
    Canadian *vs.* Australian, 116–24
    Charter of Rights and Freedoms, 144
    civic republican view of, 71–72
    as civil rights, 109
    of civil society, 104
    common, 13
    communitarianism and liberalism, 112
    as a "community under law," 113
    in contemporary liberal democracies, 113
    of convenience, 72
    cosmopolitan, 146
    as covenant, 103, 133
    covenant, as loose, 72, 109
    covenant, ligatures defining, 108
    cultural, 163
    cultural diversity and, 113
    debates on, 71, 74–75, 109, 120, 122, 179
    deep cultural diversity, 84, 127
    definition, 106
    definition by Canadian officials, 73
    "different but equal," 114
    differentiated, 73, 111, 155, 178
    dual relationship, 105
    duties, 111
    egalitarianism, 114
    as entitlements and rights, 122, 139
    equivalent and equipotent, 103
    as federal gratification, 121

misconception of, 176

modernity and, 29

parliamentary, 119

participation in, 108

political, 113

transcendence of politics, 104

Western style, 129

Denton, Trevor, 34, 189

"different but equal," 36–37, 63, 79, 94, 114

diversity

accommodation of, 95, 98, 101

among native-born citizens, 101

anomie-generating pressures, 95

anxiety, major source of, 101

bedrock of modern culture, 13

betting on, 21

betting on, as moral act, 13

bogus, 147

ceiling on, 67

celebration of, 68

challenge of increasing, 109

of civil society, 122

cohabitation of identity groups, 98

as a coherent whole, 161

in common society, 2

complex relationships, 68

composite citizenship, 122

concensus, as end of, 21

conditions for, 13

constraint of, 123

constraint on social development, 21

coping with, 1

corridor of, 133

cult of, 17

cultural, 21–22, 25–27, 32, 35, 38, 58, 113, 130, 159, 174

cultural imprints, 99

debates in Canada, 73

deep, 5, 105

deep, taming, 82

deep cultural, 8, 23, 39, 77, 83–84, 95, 127, 130, 139, 153, 156, 159–60,

E

I

minority rights, 5, 7, 17–19, 34, 115, 141

moral contracts, 16, 44, 48–49, 70, 72, 74, 93–101, 104, 106–9, 113–19, 121–24, 126, 133, 149–50, 154, 156–57, 164, 177–78, 180

Mukherjee, Bharati, 61–63, 196

multicultural

    assumption, 6, 78, 139

    heritage, 41, 77

    strategy, 7–8, 22, 85, 173

multiculturalism

    according to Bissonnette, 49

    according to Boisvert, 4

    according to Fish, 107

    "Big G" government, 156

    bilingual framework, 58

    Canadian, 5–8, 29, 41, 57–58, 142

    Canadian Constitution, 43, 144

    Canadian culture, 90

    "Canadian mosaic," 49, 57

    Canadian Multiculturalism Council, 58

    celebration of, 47

    Charter of Rights and Freedoms, 44, 48, 58, 77, 87, 142–45, 179

    Citizenship Act, 125

    as a "containment policy," 43

    cosmopolitanism vs., 82–83

    cultural jealousies, 64

    cultural pluralism, 152

    culture, 47, 145–46

    diversity of native-born citizens, 101

    egalitarianism, 61, 78, 80, 127, 154

    equality, 54

    ethnic Canadians, 45

    ethnocultural groups, 63

    French-Canadian community, 39

    French Canadian nationalism vs., 6, 49

    House of Commons Standing Committee on Multiculturalism, 58

    language of rights, 5

    Multiculturalism Act, 58

    national policy, 7, 29, 39, 43, 45–46, 48–49, 53–54, 57, 59–62, 64–65, 77, 114, 125, 133, 145

    polyethnicity, 124

Q

R

U

United Kingdom, 47, 84–86
United States, 2–3, 41, 61–62, 79, 86, 121, 143
Universal Declaration of Human Rights, 140, 150

V

violence
    competition for same objects, 31
    envy-reducing arrangements, 35–37
    intercultural tensions, 8, 26, 176
    passion for distinction, 31
    position on social ladder, 31
    prospect of, 34
    reducing mechanisms, 33–34
    renunciation of, 33
    resentment and envy, 32–34, 36, 110
    sacrificial, 32
    scapegoat, 32
    in segregated society, 2
    stratagem for containing, 33
    unreasonable expectations, 114
    vicious circle of, 32

COLOPHON

Printed and bound in April 2008
by L'IMPRIMERIE GAUVIN, Gatineau, Quebec,
for THE UNIVERSITY OF OTTAWA PRESS

Typeset in 10 pt. Adobe Caslon
on 13 pt. leading
Copy editor: Patrick Heenan
Proofreader: Alex Anderson
Index: Clive Pyne
Cover: Cathy Maclean
Typeset and Diagrams: Kevin Matthews

Printed on Rolland Opaque Natural 60 lb paper